Diversity, Equity, & Inclusion

by Dr. Shirley Davis

for
dummies
A Wiley Brand

Diversity, Equity, & Inclusion For Dummies®

Contents at a Glance

Table of Contents

PART 3: IMPLEMENTING AND OPERATIONALIZING DEI ACROSS THE ORGANIZATION131

Introduction

Welcome to *Diversity, Equity, and Inclusion For Dummies*. As I write this, the timing for this book couldn't be more perfect given the predictions about the workplace of the future. I can't tell you what an honor is to write the first-ever book of this type in this series. I'm Dr. Shirley Davis, and I've spent over 30 years in Human Resources and as a Chief Diversity and Inclusion Officer, a corporate executive, and now a global workforce consultant. I believe that all my experiences (both professional and personal) have prepared me to contribute this body of work.

Since the 2010s, the global workforce, marketplace, and communities have undergone significant demographic shifts, making workplaces more diverse than ever before. And research reveals that this trend will continue. Diversity, equity, and inclusion have taken a front seat for organizations seeking to capitalize on new talent — more women, greater ethnicity, five generations, and different abilities, backgrounds, experiences, thinking styles, beliefs, and ways of working — and build world-class cultures. They recognize that in order to attract, engage, and retain top talent and new customers, clients, and members, they must have strong leaders who can work effectively across differences, and they must foster a work environment where *all* talent enjoys a sense of belonging and inclusion and has an equal opportunity to succeed.

Most organizations aren't there yet, though, and most leaders still aren't comfortable or knowledgeable about diversity, equity, and inclusion. Transforming a rigid, hierarchical, and homogeneous culture to a world-class one can take years. The same goes for developing inclusive, first-rate leaders. But you can get there with intentionality and a commitment of time, effort, and resources. And trust me; this new generation of top talent is demanding it.

So leaders at all levels (from the boardroom to the C-suite to the mid-level supervisor) have a unique opportunity right now to embrace these new realities. You can begin by first developing the skills, competencies, and behaviors needed to lead effectively across differences. Then you can start implementing the proven strategies that position your organization to be an employer of choice and a great place to work and do business.

About This Book

Diversity, equity, and inclusion (DEI) work can't be a nice thing to do or a check-the-box exercise that provides a temporary fix until the cameras go away and the noise is quieted. True and sustainable culture transformation requires bold, innovative, and courageous leadership, long-term commitment, and accountability.

Diversity, Equity, and Inclusion For Dummies is the one-stop resource guide you need to get a comprehensive understanding of what this work is all about, how it contributes to the organization's success, what your role is as a leader, and how to implement DEI in every area of your organization. In this book, I explain everything from the common terminology to the continued evolution of DEI to how the demographics continue to change, plus strategies for tasks like the following:

>> Sourcing and recruiting diverse talent and growing the skills to lead a diverse workforce

>> Assessing your organization's current culture and cultivating and sustaining one of inclusion, equity, and belonging

>> Making the business case for DEI and addressing the obstacles to DEI

>> Aligning DEI with your strategic priorities and creating a DEI strategic plan

>> Measuring the success of your DEI efforts

>> Launching DEI councils and employee resource groups

In this book, I share from my 30-plus years of experiences, proven strategies, and results achieved as a human resources veteran and a former chief diversity, equity, and inclusion officer for several large global organizations. I also share from a personal perspective as someone who personally experienced being marginalized, oppressed, discriminated against, overlooked, and undervalued in my rise to the C-suite. And what I've come to realize is that my stories are still the reality for so many workers today who report that they're experiencing these same things in their workplaces and from their leaders.

I also understand the value of building a diverse team and capitalizing on the different perspectives, experiences, and talents of that team (to which I dedicate Chapter 11). So I modeled this mindset and sought out three other DEI thought leaders, researchers, and educators to contribute to this body of work so that it offers even broader and more comprehensive tips, strategies, and proven practices.

One person, whom I've known and worked with in DEI and implicit bias for ten years, brings a unique perspective as a young, white, gay, male educator and consultant who grew up all over the world as the child of a military family. Another contributor identifies as an African American, cisgender, heterosexual, Christian. She holds a PhD and is a college professor and practitioner of leadership development, DEI, and HR, and she came highly recommended through my network. And so did my third contributor, a 70-year-old, white, Jewish, LGBTQ woman from the Bronx in New York. And because of this diverse team of contributors, the final product is much better.

This book contains answers to the many questions that leaders ask and the plethora of concerns and misnomers that exist, and it demystifies DEI to make it practical, understandable, and implementable. It speaks directly to middle managers and leaders at the top who may not have the title of chief diversity and inclusion officer but do have the responsibility to lead diverse teams; recruit, hire, and develop diverse talent; serve diverse customers; and foster a welcoming, inclusive, and high-performing workplace culture. In other words, all leaders at all levels can benefit from this book.

What this book isn't: It isn't meant to represent the views, experiences, and practices of all DEI thought leaders around the world. That's the point of this book and the beauty of this work. Everyone brings different lenses, models, frames of reference, and unique experiences that inform their decisions. This book is also not designed to be a prescription for implementing the strategies and tips in the same way. Every organization is at (and in) a different place, working at a different pace, and has varying degrees of resources, complexities, and levels of commitment. Therefore, this book isn't a one-size-fits-all reference guide. Use to find information, ideas, and guidance for where you are and to help you get to where you want to go on your DEI journey. This book is only one source; I refer to many others throughout the book that can supplement your development.

I also want to quickly point out a few things that may help you better navigate and use this book:

>> Whenever I introduce a new important term in a chapter, I place it in *italics* and follow with a quick definition or explanation.

>> Keywords and action steps in lists appear in **bold.**

>> Sidebars (look for the gray shaded boxes) feature content that is interesting and informative but not essential to your understanding of a topic. If you're wanting to get in and out quickly, you can safely skip them.

Foolish Assumptions

I know what they say about making assumptions, but for the sake of this book I did make a few of them so that I could best serve your needs. I assumed the following:

>> You're working at an organization in a manager or leader role.

>> You recognize that the world of work is changing demographically, and you want to better understand it.

>> You have little or no knowledge and experience in leading DEI initiatives and want to pick up the fundamentals.

>> You may have reservations and discomfort about DEI. You may even wonder why it's getting so much focus.

>> You want to develop into a more effective and inclusive leader.

Icons Used in This Book

Throughout this book, you find icons that help you pick up what I'm laying down. Here's a rundown of what they mean:

TIP

This icon alerts you to helpful hints. Tips can help you save time and avoid frustration before, during, and after your transition out of the military.

REMEMBER

This icon reminds you of important information you should read carefully.

WARNING

This icon flags actions and ideas that may cause you problems. Often, warnings accompany common mistakes or misconceptions people have about the transition process.

Beyond the Book

This book contains lots of ideas, strategies, checklists, tools, resources, references, best practices, and other sources that give you more than enough to work with. But there's more! It includes an online Cheat Sheet that provides guidance and tips for spotting and dealing with common DEI barriers, a list of questions to test your cultural competence, and ways to help employee resource groups (ERGs) success so that they can, in turn, help aid your DEI efforts. To access this handy Cheat Sheet, go to dummies.com and type **Diversity, Equity, and Inclusion For Dummies Cheat Sheet** in the search box.

Additionally, if you, your team, or members of your organization need DEI training, coaching, a keynote speaker, or consulting on any of the processes I share in this book, or want to obtain a certificate in DEI, you can access information on my website at www.drshirleydavis.com. You can also access a number of free resources as well.

Where to Go from Here

I hope reading this book make you more informed and inspired to become an inclusive leader. I hope that it answers questions you have, clears up any confusion about DEI, and gives you a greater appreciation for the complexity and necessity of this work.

This book isn't linear, so how to move forward depends on you and where you are. But Chapters 1 and 2 will get you off to a great start; they set the foundation for really understanding DEI. Feel free to use the Table of Contents to skip around and use the book to meet you right where you are. One day you may need to know how to establish a DEI Council. If so, go to Chapter 14. Another day you may need to know how your organization goes about hiring a more diverse talent. Head over to Chapter 9. And when you want to know how to articulate the business case for DEI refer to Chapter 4.

You're not expected to become a DEI expert. There are those of us who hold that title. Nor do you have to hold a DEI title in order for you to do great DEI work in your organization. I do hope you sharpen your skills and apply what you read here so you can help those experts help you. Take the time to internalize the information. Be honest with yourself, but also cut yourself some slack. Realize that DEI is a learning process and a journey, and you won't get it right overnight. Make a commitment to change some behaviors and attitudes along the way that you know could be wreaking havoc on an employee's experience. Strive to be that leader that everyone wants to do their best work for because they feel valued, respected, and included.

1

Getting Started with Diversity, Equity, and Inclusion

Examine how diversity, equity, and inclusion have evolved from a nice-to-do and compliance-driven activity to being a key driver for achieving a competitive advantage. Explore common terminology and the multiple dimensions of DEI.

Uncover the changing workforce demographics and their effects in the workplace.

Recognize the skills and competencies that every leader should have in order to lead the new generation of talent.

Describe the business case for DEI and the many benefits it offers in the workplace.

Identify the benefits and logistics of hiring a chief diversity, equity, and inclusion officer.

Chapter **1**

Understanding the Fundamentals of Diversity, Equity, and Inclusion

I f you chose to pick up this book, chances are you realize that the workforce is changing, and if you want to remain relevant, competitive, and successful, you and your organization must change too. By now, you've seen or heard how the demographic shifts have already reshaped the workplace, and you recognize that as a leader you must embrace and value diversity more readily, adopt new ways of thinking and working with people who are different from you, and assess your own attitudes and behaviors that can impede workers' experiences. Likewise, organizations recognize that they must foster the kind of work environment that attracts top talent and creates a safe, respectful, and inclusive culture where all talent can succeed and where people want to stay.

This is not a passing fad. The work of diversity, equity, and inclusion (DEI) has been evolving over the past 40 years and continues to expand today in terminology, practices, strategies, and its effects. As such, no one can tout that they know everything there is to know about DEI. I have been in this work for more than 30 years, and I'm still learning new things today. What I can surmise from my experience is that every leader is at a different stage and phase of this work. I've met people who have been on the journey as long as I have and still feel ill-equipped. They've had stops and starts along the way but need to go deeper. I've met some who just recently started their journey (as a result of the George Floyd murder), and they ask the question, "Why didn't I see this before?" referring to the history of inequities, social injustice, and the many aspects of diversity. I've met people who have been advocating and practicing this work for decades and still believe there is a long way to go. And yes, I still meet people who don't see the value of DEI work and believe that it's a distraction in the workplace, and that they have no role to play in implementing it. And this is part of the journey as well. We all see the world differently based on our own upbringing, experiences, beliefs, and values. What's interesting is that I also work with organizations and clients whom I find at these exact phases and stages too.

Re-Shifting the Focus to Diversity, Equity, and Inclusion Work

I write this book at a time when the world is facing some of the most unprecedented and disruptive events in modern history. Throughout 2020 and 2021, life as the world knew it changed dramatically because of the COVID-19 global pandemic. In early 2020, in a matter of weeks and with little time to prepare, schools were forced to shut down, sending millions of kids home to learn entirely virtually. Businesses were required to close offices and send employees home to work; many companies went out of business permanently, leaving millions of people without a paycheck. All public modes of transportation, such as air travel, transit railway systems, taxis, and rideshares, experienced record-low ridership. And the list goes on. Daily life had been upended in ways that were unexpected and unlike anything people had ever experienced.

You may ask "What does this global pandemic have to do with diversity, equity, and inclusion?"

A lot. Contrary to earlier assertions that COVID-19 was the great equalizer, it turned out to be the great revealer. It exposed and exacerbated longstanding and widespread disparities and inequities in healthcare, education, employment, and socioeconomics. Here are just a few examples:

>> When the world had to shelter in place and work from home, those most affected with job loss were essential workers (Black and brown people, and women) whose jobs couldn't be performed remotely (for example, workers in restaurants and hotels, bus drivers, cleaning personnel, warehouse and manufacturing workers, and so on). And a lack of resources, such as Internet/Wi-Fi or a computer, had an adverse effect on others' ability to work from home or for their children to learn virtually.

>> Caregiving responsibilities brought on by school and childcare closures and an increased need to care for sick and elderly family members fell mostly to women. Additionally, women were far more likely than men to be furloughed or terminated altogether.

>> Black and brown people were also some of the demographics hardest hit by the pandemic, with higher death rates due to disparities in access to health-care and treatment.

>> Poverty levels rose significantly during the pandemic, exposing food shortages around the world. Nearly 1 billion people in the world went hungry in 2020, according to the UN report on the *State of Food Security and Nutrition in the World*.

While the global pandemic was devastating millions, another major event of 2020 that I believe will go down in the history books as a tipping point and defining moment in DEI work was the murder of George Floyd. The world watched this unarmed Black man in Minneapolis, Minnesota, being murdered at the hands (or in this case, the knee) of a white police officer on May 25, 2020. With much of the world under stay-at-home orders and able to watch the news coverage replay it over and over for weeks, the event sent shockwaves and launched protests reaching all seven continents.

For me and my DEI colleagues who have been in this work for a long time, we felt the sense of urgency like never before. It was as if we had been thrust to the front lines overnight. For years, we had been hoping for senior-level officers to place a greater focus/priority on DEI work because we observed too many companies becoming complacent; reverting to old ways and habits of being exclusionary and oppressive; and showing a blatant disregard for diversity, equity, and inclusion. We saw how divided and polarized the world was becoming, and our hearts were breaking while wondering whether the years of implementing DEI strategies were all in vain.

But nothing could've prepared us for *how* this re-shifting would happen. George Floyd's murder, along with those of several other unarmed Black people that occurred just a few months earlier (such as Ahmaud Arbery and Breonna Taylor in February and March, respectively), received international news coverage. It changed our collective focus and raised the national consciousness to the racial inequalities, biases, and prejudices that have existed throughout history. Immediately following the murder of George Floyd, my firm and many others in DEI consulting were inundated with requests to consult with CEOs, presidents, and public relations and communications directors on crafting both public-facing and internal statements of commitment (and recommitment) to fighting injustices and inequities and creating cultures of inclusion and belonging.

My team and I conducted well over 100 listening sessions, focus groups, and staff town hall meetings within a ten-month period and administered countless inclusion and engagement surveys, DEI audits, and training programs on a range of topics such as DEI fundamentals, implicit bias, how to have courageous and impactful conversations, recruiting and building a diverse pipeline, building cultural competence, and cultivating cultures of inclusion and belonging. And for many of us, the demand hasn't slowed down.

And I anticipate that it won't, given the current and impending challenges we face. Leaders around the globe are grappling with the mental toll, the psychological trauma, and the stresses and fatigue felt by workers at all levels. And these effects from the COVID-19 pandemic, the exposed injustices and disparities, and the uncertainty of the economic recovery will be felt for years to come. Additionally, this book is timely and relevant (and, I would add, overdue) with the expected demographic shifts over the next decade, the complexities of working in a global marketplace, the continued advancements in technology that are redefining the way people work, the new kinds of skills that will be needed, and the ongoing war for top talent.

REMEMBER

Re-shifting focus to diversity, equity, and inclusion work in times like these not only makes good business sense but also is necessary for creating a new and better world — one that recognizes humanity, celebrates diversity, and makes equity and inclusivity the reality. Diversity, equity, and inclusion should be a priority in every organization and a required responsibility of every leader.

Understanding the History of Diversity and Inclusion in the Workplace

Diversity, equity, and inclusion work isn't new. Human and civil rights movements and laws date back centuries, but understanding the historical context and the many ways that it has evolved over the years is important. This section brings to light the historical societal events that have greatly influenced the diversity, equity, and inclusion shift in the workplace and other institutions.

The Magna Carta (1215), the English Bill of Rights (1689), the French Declaration on the Rights of Man and Citizen (1789), and the U.S. Constitution and Bill of Rights (1791) are the foundations of a long history of the fights for human and civil rights. When they were originally translated into policy, they excluded women, people of color, and members of certain social, religious, economic, and political groups. The Universal Declaration of Human Rights (UDHR) was adopted by the 56 members of the United Nations in 1948, establishing human rights standards and norms.

Since then, more historical events have significantly influenced civil and human rights across the world. In turn, they've brought about awareness to the importance of diversity and inclusion practices in the workplace and beyond:

>> **1960 — Sharpeville Massacre (South Africa):** In Sharpeville, South Africa, police fired on a group of Black people participating in an anti-apartheid demonstration without provocation.

>> **1963 — March on Washington (United States):** Dr. Martin Luther King Jr. delivered his world-famous "I Have a Dream" speech at the March on Washington. In the speech, Dr. King called for civil and economic rights and an end to segregationist policies and racist acts.

>> **1964 — United States Civil Rights Act (United States):** This landmark policy put into law the prohibition of discrimination based on race, color, religion, sex, or national origin. It also banned racial segregation in schools, employment, and public entities and unequal voter registration requirements. This act has been amended to include those with disabilities and the LGBTQ community.

>> **1965 — Executive Order 11246 (United States):** This order signed by U.S. President Lyndon B. Johnson became a key milestone in a series of federal actions aimed at ending racial, religious, and ethnic discrimination. Also known as Affirmative Action, it protects the rights of workers employed by federal contractors to remain free from discrimination on the basis of their race, color, religion, sex, sexual orientation, gender identity, or national origin and opens doors of opportunity through its affirmative action provisions.

>> **1965 — United States Voting Rights Act (United States):** This law prohibits racial discrimination in voting, as well as acts that prohibit a person's ability to vote.

>> **1965 — United Kingdom Race Relations Act (United Kingdom):** This act was the first kind of legislation in the United Kingdom to ban discrimination on the basis of color, race, and ethnic and national origin.

- **1969 — Stonewall Riots (United States):** In response to a police raid at the Stonewall Inn (a gay club in New York City), members of the LGBTQ+ community held a number of violent protests.

- **1976 — Soweto Uprisings (South Africa):** Black schoolchildren held protests in response to the government's announcement that schooling would take place in Afrikaans, the language based on that of South Africa's European Dutch settlers.

- **1987 — publication of *Workforce 2000* (United States):** Among this book's predictions was that the future U.S. labor force would include more women and underrepresented groups. Many experts used it as the impetus for creating and making a business case for diversity training.

- **1994 — Don't Ask, Don't Tell (United States):** This U.S. military policy prohibited gay, lesbian, and bisexual people from openly serving in the military. In 2011, this policy was dismantled.

- **2006 — Civil Union Act (South Africa):** This South African law established legal civil unions for same-sex marriage and civil unions for unmarried opposite-sex and same-sex couples.

- **2013 — Marriage Act (United Kingdom):** Established legal same sex marriage in England and Wales.

- **2015 — Equal Marriage Act (United States):** The U.S. Supreme Court legalized same-sex marriage in 50 states and required that all states recognize out-of-state same sex marriage licenses.

- **2020 — Crown Act (United States):** This law prohibits discrimination against hairstyles and textures in the state of California.

- **2020 — George Floyd murder (United States):** George Floyd, a Black man, was murdered by a white police officer who held his knee on George Floyd's neck for more than nine minutes, cutting off his ability to breathe. This event triggered massive outrage, outcries, and international protests for social justice reform and for greater equity and inclusion.

The laws (from various countries across the globe) have evolved in a sequential process from basic human and civil rights to matters of compliance and then the moral and social imperative. As this book explores, organizations' policies and practices related to DEI matters tend to follow a similar evolutionary process. This similarity leads to a universal experience for diversity, equity, and inclusion programs: They're normally initiated with awareness and affinity programs, followed by the establishment of the business case for diversity practices. Keep in mind the local, regional, and national laws vary depending on your location.

REMEMBER

Also consider that these social movements, those of the 1960s especially, strived more for racial and gender equality, but not within the specifics of diversity, equity, and inclusion. Therefore, examining these terms (as I do in the following section) and how they've evolved into workplace standards and benchmarks is important.

Defining Diversity, Equity, and Inclusion

Considering the social and political climate since 2011, diversity, equity, and inclusion are now terms that are part of the vocabulary of business, educational, and political systems. But the conversation surrounding DEI has become quite muddled because people often use the terms interchangeably without specifying each term's own unique identity. Like most, you may ask these common questions: "Are these terms one and the same?" "How different and similar are they?" "What do I really need to know and do about DEI?"

I address these questions and concerns throughout this chapter and the book. But in the following sections, I discuss and define the relationship between diversity, equity, and inclusion.

Diversity

Simply put, *diversity* is the collection of unique attributes, traits, and characteristics that make up individuals. They include values, beliefs, experiences, backgrounds, preferences, behaviors, race, gender, abilities, socioeconomic status, physical appearance, age, and so on. Some of these traits are visible, and many others are invisible.

For decades, I've been defining diversity as being comparable to an iceberg (see Figure 1-1). Scientists say that 90 percent of what makes up an iceberg is invisible or below the waterline, and only 10 percent is above it. Think about diversity. People can only see about 10 percent of visible traits that make you diverse. The rest is invisible (beneath the surface). Sometimes you can see the diversity, and sometimes you can't.

REMEMBER

Diversity also has different meanings within various cultural contexts. For example, the U.S. perspective of diversity suggests all the various ways you can see or describe people. But in some European countries, diversity leans more toward gender differences. In Middle Eastern countries, diversity often speaks to religious beliefs.

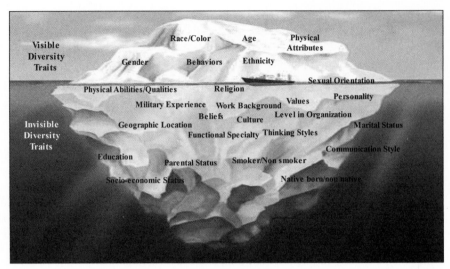

FIGURE 1-1:
Just like an iceberg, most diversity traits are below the surface.

Courtesy of Dr. Shirley Davis

Generational differences are also a key component of diversity. Much like people born within the same time frame share so many coming-of-age experiences (such as music), generations tend to understand and view diversity similarly as well. For example, Generation X (born between 1965 and 1981) and baby boomers (born between 1946 and 1964) lean toward describing diversity in terms of race, gender, and ethnic background. On the other hand, millennials (born between 1981 and 1996) think of diversity beyond demographics to the manner in which people think, learn, and have various experiences. I talk more about generational diversity in Chapter 2.

Multiple dimensions of diversity

In 1990, well-respected diversity pioneers Marilyn Loden and Judy Rosener developed a framework for thinking about the different dimensions of diversity within individuals and institutions. Depicted as concentric circles, their diversity wheel has been used in many different ways to encourage thinking about values, beliefs, and dimensions of identity for people and organizations. It defines the various dimensions of diversity, dividing them into four layers:

>> **Dimension 1 — Personality:** Openness, conscientiousness, extraversion, agreeableness, neuroticism

>> **Dimension 2 — Internal/Primary Dimensions:** Age, gender, sexual orientation, physical ability, ethnicity, race

>> **Dimension 3 — External Dimensions:** Geographic location, income, personal habits, recreational habits, religion, educational background, work experience, appearance, parental status, marital status

>> **Dimension 4 — Organizational Dimensions:** Functional level, work content field, division/department/unit/group, seniority, work location, union affiliation, management status

At the core of these concentric circles is *personality* — the innately unique aspect that gives each person their own particular style. This core aspect permeates all other layers. Moving out from that center are the internal factors, the primary dimensions of diversity. These aspects are the ones you have little or no control over. The next level, secondary dimensions, is made up of external, personal, and societal influences. The fourth dimension encompasses organizational influences such as the type of work you do, your level in the organization, seniority, and so on.

REMEMBER

I hope what you take away from this framework is that it represents who we are from our core dimensions and those that cannot be changed, to those dimensions that we develop over time. This leads to our assumptions, drives our own behaviors, and ultimately impacts others. So, the better we understand ourselves and others, the more effective our interactions and decisions will be.

Equity

Although "equity" and "equality" sound similar, they aren't the same; consider them related, like cousins but not siblings.

Equity practices cast a very broad net. For example, the U.S.-based Government Alliance on Race and Equity stresses that "equity is about fairness, while equality is about sameness." In other words, *equality* is concerned with treating everyone the same, while *equity* offers the opportunity for assistance so that everyone has a just and fair chance to be successful. Figure 1-2 illustrates this concept.

REMEMBER

A democracy assumes that every member of that society has the ability and right to be successful. But the reality of society brings economic, social, and political differences into play along with privilege and exclusion, and these factors can lead to unequal or unattainable access to achieve success. That's why equity practices are crucial.

Although the terms *equity* and *equality* may sound similar, implementing one versus the other can lead to dramatically different outcomes for marginalized or underrepresented people. Here's how I define them. *Equality* is defined as each person or group of people being given the same resources or opportunities. On the other hand, *equity* recognizes that each person has different circumstances and allocates each the exact resources and opportunities they need to reach an equal outcome.

FIGURE 1-2:
Equality versus
equity.

EQUALITY   EQUITY

In Figure 1-2, you see three people who have unequal access to a system — in this case, the tree that provides fruit. With equal support from evenly distributed resources, their access to the fruit is still unequal. The equitable solution, however, customizes the resources that each person needs to access the fruit, leading to positive outcomes for both people.

REMEMBER

The tree appears to be a naturally occurring system, but social systems aren't naturally inequitable. They've been intentionally designed to reward specific demographics for so long that the system's outcomes may appear unintentional but are actually rooted discriminatory practices and beliefs. In order to restore the historical injustices of society (which I discuss later in the chapter) equity is essential for those marginalized individuals to gain access to opportunities once denied.

Employing equity practices involves bridging gaps between minority and majority groups in organizations. Keep in mind that equity looks different in each organization; however, it occurs when there is a level playing field that enables all talent to enjoy the same opportunities to thrive. Equity practices consider what's important to a specific workforce. For example, one equity practice may focus on professional development (mentorship programs, scholarships, bonus distribution) and another on providing opportunities for promotion and growth (succession pipelines).

Equity is the process, and equality is the outcome. In other words, equity is essential to achieving true equality.

Inclusion

I describe *inclusion* as the degree to which an employee perceives that they're a valued member of the work group and encouraged to fully participate in the organization. At the base level, diversity efforts are concerned with representation of various groups; however, don't confuse that with creating an inclusive environment.

You can have diversity and not have inclusion. Diversity just is. Diversity is the human aspect, and everyone is diverse. But inclusion is the environment and the atmosphere people experience and work in. And that's where the work continues. Recruiting and hiring top diverse talent isn't enough; you must create an inclusive work environment where those people feel valued, respected, and treated fairly and have equal opportunity to succeed.

Think about DEI as a continuum with inclusion as the final phase toward sustainability and business outcomes. In the workplace, diversity without inclusion fails to attract and retain diverse talent and doesn't encourage diverse employees to bring their full selves to work, thereby failing to motivate their participation and do their best work.

In short, diversity is easier to measure because humans in all varieties merely exist; however, inclusion is a practice. Diversity can and has been legislated in various policies throughout various locations and organizations. Inclusion often results from a commitment to practicing this type of behavior.

Diversity, equity, and inclusion

The definitions in the preceding sections show that the relationship among diversity, equity, and inclusion is complex and nuanced.

Simply summarized, diversity is the "who," equity is the "how," and inclusion is the "what."

A diverse organization isn't automatically an inclusive one, and an inclusive organization isn't automatically an equitable one.

Recognizing diversity, equity, and inclusion as separate and complex, though related, concepts is an important step for leaders to achieve a diverse, equitable, and inclusive workplace culture. Leaders need to understand that diversifying a workforce doesn't automatically result in new hires' feeling welcome, which suggests that inclusion should be a goal that organizations assign resources to. And their focus on equity needs to be based on the knowledge that not all employees or potential employees have access to the same resources and that they should structure strategies and resources accordingly.

REMEMBER

When all employees are valued and invited to participate fully, they're empowered to bring their best work to the table. Leaders who have an understanding and awareness of the complexities and various elements of diversity, equity, and inclusion are better equipped to recognize and address the gaps that exist within their organizations.

Breaking Down Other Key DEI-Related Terms

In this section, I cover some key terms essential to DEI work. I say "key terms" because I could turn this entire chapter into a glossary, but for the sake of your role as a leader/manager, I just detail the common vocabulary to give you a working knowledge of DEI.

Note: Since 2015, I've been selected as one of more than 100 DEI global experts on the revised editions of the Global Diversity, Equity, and Inclusion Benchmarks (GDEIB), and we all weighed in and adopted many of the definitions I share in the following sections. I talk more about the GDEIB in Chapter 6, where I outline how to assess your organization's current culture.

Ability and disabilities

Equal and fair opportunities should be made to all employees regardless of ability. However, disability diversity isn't often widely discussed within the DEI conversation. Employers have indicated the anticipated (not actual) costs of adapting the workplace for a differently abled individual as the main barrier to hiring differently abled (disabled) people. Researchers have found that this assumption is really a result of unconscious bias. I discuss unconscious bias later in the chapter, but first I want to give you a clear understanding of the definition of disability.

The World Health Organization (WHO) defines *disability* as an umbrella term that covers impairments, limitations, and restrictions on participation. It distinguishes an *impairment* as "a problem in body function or structure," a *limitation* as a "difficulty encountered by an individual in executing a task or action," and *participation restriction* as "a problem experienced by an individual in involvement in life situations." *Ability* refers to one who has the "skills to complete a task, or activity," so disability can affect how well a person can do any task related to their job.

So the term *disability* is more complex than simply physical health. Today, WHO estimates that over 1 billion people (15 percent of the world's population) lives with a disability, and this number continues to rise. Almost everyone will temporarily or permanently experience disability at some point in their life.

REMEMBER

In the United States, the Americans with Disabilities Act (ADA) prevents companies from discriminating against people with disabilities in employment decisions. But hiring is only the first step; businesses also need to create a work environment that makes reasonable accommodations for people with disabilities so they can perform the essential functions of the job.

All countries who are a part of the United Nations have also adopted laws and acts to protect people with disabilities as their contributions toward the achievement of the Sustainable Development Goals (SDGs) and the pledge of the 2030 Agenda for Sustainable Development to "leave no one behind."

Belonging

Belonging is a fundamental human need — the desire to feel a sense of security, safety, and acceptance as a member of certain groups. Belonging is what allows employees to feel like they can be their authentic selves without fear of punishment or without having to cover up and be someone they're not. Workers report that when they feel belonging, they can be more productive.

TIP

If this definition sounds a lot like the ones I introduce for diversity and inclusion earlier in the chapter, keep in mind one of the mantras that DEI professionals use to distinguish the three:

> Diversity is having a seat at the table; inclusion is having a voice; and belonging is having that voice be heard.

BIPOC

The term *BIPOC* gained a lot of traction and visibility over social media following national protests for social justice and equity in 2020-2021. The term describes any group of people native to a specific region — people who lived in a given region before colonists or settlers arrived. It's used to acknowledge that not all people of color face equal levels of injustice.

BIPOC stands for Black and Indigenous People of Color and is pronounced "by-poc." Here's a breakdown:

>> *Black* can refer to dark-skinned peoples of Africa, Oceania, and Australia or their descendants — without regard for the lightness or darkness of skin tone — who were enslaved by white people.

>> *Indigenous* refers to ethnic groups native to the Americas who were killed en masse by white people.

>> *People of color* is an umbrella term for nonwhite people, especially as they face racism and discrimination in a white-dominant culture.

Implicit bias

Bias is a tendency or inclination that results in judgment without question. Often, biases are unreasoned and based on inaccurate and incomplete information. Everyone has bias. It's part of the human makeup; you need bias to protect you from danger. Biologically, people are hard-wired to prefer people who look like them, sound like them, and share their interests. But when left unchecked, biases can have a negative impact in every interaction.

Implicit bias (also referred to as *unconscious bias*) is an unconscious opinion, positive or negative, that you have about a group or person. Implicit biases are the attitudes or stereotypes that are taught and developed early in life, and they strengthen over time, affecting your understanding, actions, and decisions without your knowing it.

With the vast amount of diversity that makes up the global workforce — including more women, people of color, LGBTQ people, veterans, introverts and extroverts, immigrants, people with different abilities/thinking styles/personalities, and people from five generations, to name a few — the level of complexity and potential conflicts that can arise from unconscious bias is sure to increase. Leaders make decisions in the workplace every day, from sourcing to promotions to creating business strategy and beyond. Whether they recognize it or not, implicit bias enters into every one of these decisions.

TIP

To find out more about implicit bias, as well as other types of biases and how you can deal with them, head to Chapter 15.

Intersectionality

Intersectionality refers to complex ways in which people hold many marginal group affiliations at the same time. These identities can combine, overlap, or intersect in a person or group, resulting in multiple, interdependent systems of discrimination or oppression (for example a Black woman, a poor indigenous person, or a gay person with a disability). Thus, the intersectional experience of one person or group is greater than the sum of the individual forms of discrimination or disadvantage.

Isms and phobias

WARNING

In simplest terms, *isms* are forms of oppression and discrimination.

Following are some of the most common isms:

>> **Ableism:** Discrimination or prejudice against people with disabilities

>> **Ageism:** Prejudice or discrimination on the grounds of a person's age

>> **Classism:** Prejudice against or in favor of people belonging to a particular social class

>> **Heterosexism:** Discrimination or prejudice against non-heterosexual people based on the belief that heterosexuality is the only normal and natural expression of sexuality

>> **Racism:** Prejudice, discrimination, or antagonism directed against a person or people on the basis of their membership in a particular racial or ethnic group, typically one that's underrepresented or marginalized

>> **Sexism:** Prejudice, stereotyping, or discrimination, typically against women, on the basis of sex

A *phobia* is an unreasonable or excessive fear or hatred of something or someone. While there are many phobias, several are specific to diversity, equity, and inclusion. Examples include:

>> **Homophobia:** Dislike, fear, or hatred of or discomfort with people who are attracted to members of the same sex

>> **Transphobia:** Dislike or discrimination against trans people or gender nonconforming people because of their gender identity

>> **Xenophobia:** Dislike of people from other countries or anyone deemed "foreign" because of their immigrant or visitor status

>> **Islamophobia:** Dislike or hatred against anyone practicing or perceived to be a practitioner of Islam because of their religious affiliation

COMBATING FEELINGS OF LOSS AND FEAR AROUND DEI

Loss and fear are often at the core of people's feelings around DEI practices. It's the fear that those who benefit from majority-favoring practices and white privilege will lose out on success. But these fears are unfounded. Actually, one workplace leader I know stated that "fear of the unknown could be standing in the way of the success of DEI practices." One thing to note is that diverse employees recognize that their white counterparts aren't responsible for the years of inequity experienced by people of color and other underrepresented categories of people, but these white counterparts can be allies to help dismantle those inequitable systems. However, everyone has to recognize that everyone has to participate in the conversation about DEI (that means including white men).

All people experience fear; it impacts everyone, and therefore everyone needs to be engaged in the DEI conversation. Women, people of color, disabled people, and the LGBTQIA+ community fear mistreatment, prejudice, and continued marginalization. White men, especially, fear living and working in a society where they're no longer the majority. Millennials fear not being respected because of their age. This aspect of humanity can serve as a connection point to help level the playing field in the workplace.

REMEMBER

Belief in these many isms and phobias influence our biases in our everyday life, including the workplace. Recognizing and understanding these beliefs is an important step in our DEI journey so that we become aware of what not to do and what to do more effectively.

LGBTQIA+

(Adapted from Human Rights Campaign's and Catalyst's Glossary of Terms)

An initialism for the community of people who identify as lesbian, gay, bisexual, transgender, queer or questioning, and any other sexual or gender minority. People often refer to the *I* as "intersex" and the *A* as asexual. Some of my colleagues also use the *IA* to refer to inclusion allies.

REMEMBER

The plus symbol (+) at the end of the initialism is significant because it's a symbol of all things on the gender and sexuality spectrum that have yet to be described or defined. As conversations around sex and gender spectrums continue to evolve, new terms will emerge and become prevalent in this space.

Originally, the first four letters of the LGBTQIA+ initialism were commonly used to group various sexual and gender minorities. Although it was first considered an evolution toward inclusion, these four letters proved to be limiting to individuals who didn't identify as lesbian, gay, bisexual, or transgender.

You can refer to the Human Rights Campaign (HRC; hrc.org) to remain up to date on terms and resources related to LGBTQ issues.

Other LGBTQ terms include the following:

>> **Sex:** Biological classification of male or female based on reproductive organs and functions.

>> **Lesbian:** Women and nonbinary people who are attracted to women may use this term to describe themselves.

>> **Gay:** Men, women, and nonbinary who are attracted to people of the same gender may use this term to describe themselves.

>> **Bisexual:** A person who is attracted to more than one sex, gender, or gender identity may use this term to describe themselves. These attractions don't necessarily occur simultaneously, in the same way, or to the same degree.

>> **Transgender:** People who feel that the gender assigned to them based on their biological sex is a false or incomplete definition of themselves. Being transgender doesn't imply any specific sexual orientation. Therefore, transgender people may identify as straight, gay, lesbian, bisexual, and so on.

>> **Queer:** This term is often used as a catch-all adjective to describe many people, including those who don't identify as exclusively straight and/or folks who have nonbinary or gender-expansive identities. This term was previously used as a slur but has been reclaimed by many parts of the LGBTQ movement.

Microaggressions

Microaggressions are subtle verbal and nonverbal slights, insults, indignities, and denigrating messages directed toward a person due to their group membership, often automatically and unconsciously. Microaggressions can be seen as innocent, harmless comments, but they actually reinforce stereotypes and are a form of discrimination.

For example, if you ask the Asian member of your team to complete a task that requires extensive math because you know they'll be great at it, you probably just made the statement without thinking. You don't know the Asian member of your team; you just assumed they'd be great at math based on a stereotype. That's the challenge with microaggressions — they often operate outside of the level of consciousness.

Throughout my career as a woman and a person of color, I've experienced many microaggressions at the hands of supervisors, senior leaders, and other authority figures who were from the dominant group of power and privilege in the organization. I've been complimented for "sounding white and speaking proper," been told how articulate I am, and been used as a photo op for the company's annual report or marketing brochure and as a token for meeting diversity goals. I've been present at the table but had my voice be invisible, been designated as the one to go get lunch for all male colleagues — the list goes on. These microaggressions left me feeling used, undervalued, emotionally exhausted, resentful, and hurt.

Similar to implicit bias, microaggressions are an unfortunate outcome of the human experience. Check out the discussion of microaggressions in Chapter 7 to help to raise your consciousness about these matters and how to mitigate them.

Neurodiversity

The concept of neurodiversity is newer in the DEI space but not the medical and social science fields. *Neurodiversity* is a term that was introduced in 1998 by an autistic sociologist named Judy Singer. It comes from a number of brain studies that reveal that people who think, learn, and process information differently than others have brains that are wired that way. Advocates seek to set the record straight that people who are neurodiverse are not suffering from a disease or dysfunction. Rather, the idea is that people should expand their understanding of what's "normal" in terms of brain function — that many things that have been considered problems are actually just differences.

Neurodiversity is important for the workplace because often those who are considered neurodiverse fall under the disability umbrella; however, John Elder Robison, a neuroscience scholar in residence at the College of William & Mary in Williamsburg, Virginia stated that "neurodiversity is the idea that neurological differences like autism and ADHD are the result of normal, natural variation within the human genome." Neurodiverse people's brains function outside the average brain and have the ability to hyper-focus, which is beneficial in certain job categories and industries.

Prejudice and stereotypes

A *stereotype* is a widely held but fixed and oversimplified image or idea of a particular type of person, thing, or group. *Prejudice* is an attitude or feeling of unfair dislike based mostly on opinions and stereotypes rather than facts and evidence because of some characteristic such as race, age, religion, and so on.

Stereotypes are any commonly known public belief about a certain social group or a type of individual. They can be positive (for example, most people assume that all millennials are tech-savvy). Prejudices, on the other hand, are almost always negative and aren't based on reason or experience. They often are supported by a belief that certain people or groups have less worth or fewer abilities. Prejudiced behavior is often influenced by bias.

Stereotypes are often believed and perpetuated out of humans' need to believe a generalized assumption about a group they don't normally interact with. Stereotyping and prejudiced behavior (that is, discrimination) often go hand in hand because prejudices are often based on believing stereotypes. *Discrimination*, then, is negative, destructive, and exclusionary behavior toward an individual or groups of people based on identity groups (such as race, gender, sex, ethnicity, or social class). Prejudice and stereotypes are perpetuated through discrimination at the individual, institutional, and structural level, and discrimination is put into practice through personal behaviors, practices, cultures, laws, and policies.

Think for a moment about your own experiences with stereotypes. What stereotypes were you taught growing up? What messages did you receive about your group? What messages did you receive about people who are different from you?

Privilege and power

Privilege is advantages, rewards, or benefits given to those in the dominant group solely because of their membership in that group. It operates on personal, interpersonal, cultural, and institutional levels and gives these advantages at the expense of members of target groups. In the United States, privilege is granted to people who have membership in one or more of these social identity groups:

- White people
- Able-bodied people
- Heterosexuals
- Males
- Christians
- Middle- or owning-class people
- Middle-aged people
- English-speaking people

WARNING

Privilege is characteristically invisible to people who have it. People in dominant groups often believe that they've earned the privileges they enjoy or that everyone could have access to these privileges if only they worked to earn them. In fact, privileges are unearned, and they're granted to people in the dominant groups regardless of whether they want those privileges, and regardless of their stated intent.

Power refers to the capacity to exercise control over others, deciding what's best for them and who will or won't have access to resources.

Associated with power are the following terms often used to define social groups that society has afforded more or less power (more/less access):

>> **Marginalized/oppressed/disadvantaged:** Social groups with less power, access, or privilege; social groups that have been disenfranchised, made to be invisible, dehumanized, marginalized, and/or exploited

>> **Dominant/privileged/advantaged:** Social groups with more power, access, and privilege; social groups who have the ability navigate the world without consequence because of unearned advantages at the expense of folks who are marginalized

REMEMBER

Having a leadership role means you're the steward of other people's experiences. As a leader, take a good look at what privilege means for and benefits you. Examining your privilege can be hard, but good leaders have to welcome that discomfort.

Getting Started: Reflection Activity

I open this chapter discussing the reality that all of us are on the DEI journey at different stages and phases. Now that you've read through this chapter, reflect on three things. First, which phase/stage of your DEI journey do you believe you are in? Choose one of the stages described here or. if it's not accurately depicted, describe it yourself under number 5.

1. You've been on the DEI journey more than 30 years and still feel ill-equipped to work effectively across differences.

2. You just recently started your journey within the last 24 months and find yourself asking the question, "Why didn't I see this before?" referring to the history of inequities, social injustice, and the many aspects of diversity.

3. You've been advocating and practicing this work for decades and still believe we have a long way to go in achieving equity and inclusion.

4. You don't see the value of DEI work and believe that it's a distraction in the workplace and that you have no role to play in implementing it.

5. _____

Second, based on the answer you just selected, identify one to two actions you can take to advance on your DEI journey.

Third, think about where your organization is currently on its DEI journey. How would you rate them and why?

You did it! You got through the first chapter. I know that it's a lot to take in and a lot to comprehend, but now you have a good foundation in which to build your knowledge. I hope you're ready to take a journey toward a deeper understanding of the comprehensive and complex nature of DEI work. The rest of this book explores the changing workforce demographics and how they're redefining the workplace, the work, and how work gets done. As a leader, you discover what skills and competencies you need in order to recruit, engage, and retain the new generation of talent. A lot of DEI work still needs to be done, and leaders have a significant role to play in supporting, implementing, and leading DEI initiatives across their organization.

becoming progressively global

» **Examining a more diverse workforce**

» **Looking at how the workplace is becoming more flexible and embracing remote work**

» **Navigating a growing digital workplace**

» **Recognizing how needed skill sets are changing**

Chapter **2**

Exploring Key Demographic Trends that Are Redefining the Workplace

G lobalization, labor shortages, digitization, major demographic shifts, and the global pandemic that began in 2020 have redefined the workforce, workplace, and marketplace. Into the 2030s, workers will continue to experience a new normal in the way they work and live as workforce predictions come true.

In this chapter, I outline the key demographic shifts that have occurred in the workforce and that are predicted to occur in the next 10 to 20 years. I also detail how technological advances continue to impact the way we work and the jobs and skills that will be needed.

REMEMBER

You may have felt or heard that adapting to trends is a disruption you'd rather avoid. However, consider that adapting to demographic changes along the diversity spectrum is an addition to you and your organization, not a disruption. These shifts (sometimes seismic) in demographics impact the workplace. Look at these trends and changes as opportunity for growth, expansion, and even fine-tuning operations. Use them to upskill and reskill as a people leader and manager, because this will be a key driver of employee satisfaction, engagement, and retention in the decades to come. How you anticipate and/or respond determines the type of impact you'll have.

WORKFORCE PREDICTIONS: 2030 AND BEYOND

The workforce predictions for 2030 and beyond are quite informative. Over the years, I've studied workforce trends published by global consulting firms such as PricewaterhouseCoopers (PwC); Accenture; Mercer; McKinsey & Company; EY (formerly Ernst & Young); KPMG; Josh Bersin, and others. They've all conducted extensive research on the future of work and how it will impact workers and leaders. The research findings provide insight into how dramatically different things will be and what new skills, habits, and behaviors people need to adopt in order to remain relevant, competitive, and sustainable. A few notable predictions include the following:

- Our world is rapidly growing older. According to the United Nations Department of Economic and Social Affairs, people aged 65 or older is projected to reach 1.5 billion by 2050.

- Artificial intelligence may replace jobs humans once held and create jobs that didn't exist before.

- Employers may recruit global, contract-based workers instead of employing full-time workers. Traditional offices and corporate headquarters may go by the wayside.

- Traditional retirement will peter out as workers continue working as long they can.

- Workers will demand more comprehensive benefits and "best place to work" environments, which may lead to job hopping.

- You know how a smartwatch can track your steps and health activity? Imagine sensors that employers can use monitor employees, not just at work but all the time

- Driverless cars may make commuting faster.

Increasingly Global

Globalization occurs when a business operates in a country outside its original location. Globalization allows for business growth because it provides a platform for companies to offer products in many locales, regions, and countries. Labor costs and the price of manufacturing vary all over the globe, and countries often offer economic incentives such as tax breaks and land grants to win international business. Expanding to another country presents an opportunity to employ labor from that particular location, which means an opportunity for cultural additions and diversity education.

As companies expand their global footprints, their global workforces expand as well. But this process isn't as simple as it may sound. Essentially, successful global expansion hinges on the following:

>> **Knowledge management:** What does the company know about the countries it wants to expand to or the country where it employs workers? How is the company utilizing that information?

>> **Skillfulness and acumen:** How is the organization using its data analytics to develop and execute strategy for the production stream, operations, and people management?

>> **Agility:** How quickly and appropriately is the company responding to market changes across the globe? And is your workforce mobile (can employees work from anywhere and move quickly)?

Capturing and then strategically utilizing appropriate data is an important factor in effective global expansion. This data should reveal information about the organization and its market. Also, optimizing your data infrastructure is something to consider when expanding globally. What are your current and future IT needs, and how will a transition to the cloud impact those needs while allowing you to grow?

Another important factor is having in-country talent and a knowledge base that ensures your organization's ability to enter or exit a market as business needs change. Establishing partnerships and alliances in the people management and talent development space allows you to meet human resource needs such as hiring, payroll, and performance management.

REMEMBER

Many of today's employees want the ability to live anywhere and work anywhere.

So how do you then attract the best talent from anywhere in the world to work anywhere in the world? Following are three important considerations for hiring globally:

>> **Establish a legal presence in the locale through a foreign subsidiary.**

>> **Hire an independent contractor from overseas.** This approach may be a more viable option until you're ready for a direct hire.

>> **Manage compliance.** Adhering to local and national laws of operations is essential, and to do so, you need talent onboard to manage this area.

If you're interested in recruiting talent to work globally, here are a few tips:

>> Provide the employee with a "best place to work" experience, beginning with the recruitment and onboarding processes.

>> Provide a diverse work community.

>> Establish excellent corporate social responsibility practices.

>> Offer comprehensive and competitive benefits and services.

>> Allow for flexibility in how and when workers work and get paid.

Increasingly Diverse

With increased globalization comes an increasingly diverse workforce. Five generations are currently in the workplace (seniors, baby boomers, Generation X, millennials, and Generation Z), with millennials and Gen Zers making up approximately 50 percent of the workforce. Add gender, race, ability, LGBTQ identity, diversity of thought, and many other attributes, and you're looking at an intricate mosaic of individuals.

In this section, I break down in more detail some examples of how diverse groups will change and what specific challenges organizations will need to address. This is not an exhaustive list, but the implications for these groups can be applied to all diverse groups.

Generational diversity

The biggest demographic shift impacting the diverse workforce is generational diversity. Because people are living longer and healthier lives, they're also working much longer, past the average retirement age of 65. In fact, the United Kingdom recently removed its mandatory retirement age of 65. In the United States, millennials make up 50 percent of the workforce, and that number is expected to reach 75 percent by 2030.

Although people are living and working longer, baby boomers are just now retiring from the traditional full-time workplace. In addition, Gen Xers are looking toward retiring the 40- to 60-hour workweek for more much more flexibility in how and when they work. That makes sense, because Gen Xers are now the in-between generation caring for aging parents and raising children.

With that said, considering how the generational shift will impact your workplace is important. For instance, do you have succession plans and promotion plans in place?

REMEMBER

An organization's competitive advantage often boils down to its human capital — in other words, the people who possess the knowledge, skills, and experience needed in the company. So think of the diversity landscape as a garden of talent that needs to be cultivated. Cultivation takes foresight, planning, execution, and a desired outcome for the growing talent harvest. Think about what your executable plans for growing your talent are.

You can also utilize the following tips toward the shifting aging workforce:

>> Make the most of workers' skillsets through efficient and productive work design.

>> Maintain skilled leaders and managers who can effectively lead across generations.

>> Deal with conflict by managing it fairly, communicatively, and equitably.

>> Foster an inclusive environment that demonstrates value for all ages and the dimensions of diversity.

The huge demographic shift of the aging workforce has the potential to disrupt the productive flow of the workplace. But it also provides an opportunity for lesson-learning and adapting so that the workplace can flourish by gleaning from the top talent aging toward retirement and cultivating the talent in the middle and beginning of the career path.

Gender diversity

Gender diversity is often the first aspect of change within the diversity, equity, and inclusion space. Companies tend to begin their DEI work by increasing the gender diversity within management and leadership roles. According to a 2020 McKinsey & Company study, companies whose leadership was gender and culturally diverse financially outperformed their peers. The study found that companies with more women in its executive ranks were 25 percent more likely to have above-average profitability than companies with less females in its executive ranks.

The broken rung

McKinsey & Company's *Women in the Workplace 2020 Report* found that although women are outpacing men in terms of earning degrees, the disparity in pay and leadership positions in organizations still remains. In fact, the progress toward pay equity is slow. To this point, the United States acknowledges an Equal Pay Day every year to bring light and action toward pay equity for women of all racial and ethnic backgrounds.

Women are still underrepresented in leading corporations, on boards, and in senior executive roles. For example, in 2021, only 41 Fortune 500 corporations were led by women, 2 of whom were Black women. This number is significant because only three Black women have ever led a Fortune 500 company.

This underrepresentation may stem from many causes, but one of the biggest challenges is what Leanin.org called the *broken rung*. A sweeping 2021 study looking at 329 companies employing 13 million people found that the biggest obstacle most women face with being promoted is that first step up from entry-level roles to manager. For example, the study showed that for every 100 men promoted to a management position, 86 women are promoted. At the beginning of 2020, women held only 32 percent of manager positions, while men held 88 percent. So women are significantly left out of entry-level management positions that would put them in the succession pipeline for significant promotion along a leadership track.

COVID-19 and working women

The impact of the COVID-19 pandemic may erase the gains toward equity and parity for women in the workplace. The challenges of the pandemic have pushed women employees to either downshift their careers or leave the workforce altogether. The pandemic has had the worst impact on mothers, women senior executives, and Black women for a variety of reasons, including the following:

>> Lack of flexibility

>> Feeling they need to be constantly "on call"

>> Caregiving burdens due to COVID-19

>> Feelings of being negatively judged because of caregiving during the pandemic

>> Discomfort in sharing challenges with team members or managers

>> Feeling unable to bring their whole selves to work

The pandemic effect on women in the workplace has been so overwhelmingly negative because work performance goals didn't adjust to accommodate the pandemic changes but rather increased to meet market needs (more on this in the later section "Increasingly Digital and Hyperconnected"). The work performance goals and needs were met, but there was little consideration for the added stress and trauma of the pandemic (and other social justice concerns that took place in 2020). Some companies provided supportive services like changes to the performance review process, homeschooling support resources, mental health counseling, and stipends to offset working from home costs, the majority of these measures came from less than 50 percent of employers. So room for growth definitely exists to tangibly support employees in a major crisis such as a pandemic.

REMEMBER

The bottom line is companies can't afford to lose women in the workforce and, in particular, in leadership roles. When COVID-19 hit in 2020, nearly 80 percent of those who exited the workforce were women, and now more needs to be done to engage and retain them. The industries most impacted by COVID-19 were hospitality, retail, travel, and other service-related jobs, most of which are filled with women employees. When women can work and thrive, families and communities thrive.

What are some ways that your company worked to engage and retain women during the global pandemic? What could you have done differently?

Racial and ethnic diversity

Racial minorities are the primary demographic engine of future growth in the United States, countering an aging, and soon-to-be declining white population. The 2020 census data projected that the nation will become "minority white" in 2045. During that year, whites will comprise 49.7 percent of the population in contrast to 24.6 percent for Hispanics, 13.1 percent for blacks, 7.9 percent for Asians, and 3.8 percent for multiracial populations. Among the minority populations, the greatest growth is projected for multiracial populations, Asians and Hispanics with 2018–2060 growth rates of 176, 93, and 86 percent, respectively. The projected growth rate for blacks is 34 percent. The new census projections also indicate that, for youth under 18 (the post-millennial population), minorities will outnumber whites in 2020.

Racial diversity is growing in many nations. According to a recent survey conducted by Pew Research Center, approximately 69 percent of people surveyed across 27 nations said their respective nations have grown more diverse over the last 20 years. Close to half of survey respondents say that they favor a more racially diverse nation. Even though racial diversity is still growing in some nations, other nations, such as Trinidad and Tobago, already have a very diverse population. Groups in this country include East Indians, Afro-Trinidadians, and mixed races. Belize is another country with racial diversity, with its population made up of Mestizos, Kriols, Mayans, East Indians, and other races.

Guyana is also racially diverse. Races that reside in this nation include East Indians, blacks, mixed races, and Chinese.

Other racially diverse countries throughout the world include:

>> Brazil

>> Canada

>> Colombia

>> Panama

>> Suriname

>> United States

In the United States, the most diverse states are California, Texas, Florida, Hawaii, New Jersey, and New York.

While many companies increasingly understand the value of recruiting and retaining diverse talent, many companies fail to recognize the benefits of having a more racially and ethnically diverse workforce. Factors such as prejudice and stereotypes toward certain racial or ethnic groups, whether conscious or unconscious, are still too common. A number of global studies continue to tout the benefits that a more ethnically diverse workforce brings including better returns on sales, more innovative products and services, and the ability to meet the needs of more diverse customers and clients.

Increasingly More Flexible and Working More Virtually

What a difference a year makes when disruption comes and shakes up policies, practices, and beliefs. One of the many effects of the global COVID-19 pandemic for businesses and schools alike was the immense shift to working and learning more virtually. In many cases, it meant working from home because normal gathering networking places had to shut down too. Homes became de facto schools and workplaces. All over the world, people had to pivot; for employers, that meant they had to be more flexible and learn to work very differently to survive and maintain business operations.

A new way of thinking about work

The COVID-19 pandemic changed daily life in a matter of days and weeks. Normal events such as concerts, festivals, graduations, and weddings were cancelled. Travel came to a screeching halt, and places of worship even went virtual.

As dark and disruptive as the global pandemic was, it yielded some very positive outcomes and proven successes for the concept of working virtually and remotely. For years, I had been trying to convince old-school types of leaders that flexible work arrangements were an important practice and benefit that the new generation of talent (across genders, generations, and ethnicities) would expect or even demand as a condition of employment. The constant objections I got were "I need to see them here, butts in seats, so that I know that they're working" and "I don't think people will be as productive if they work remotely." My responses have become a workplace mantra and a common tweet during my training sessions: "Visibility doesn't equal value" and "Many people quit a long time ago; they just didn't leave. Just because you see them in the seat doesn't mean that they're invested, committed, or engaged." In fact, employee engagement surveys conducted by Gallup reveal that less than 40 percent of workers worldwide are "highly engaged."

TIP

Look for ways to say yes to requests for working more flexibly versus finding ways to say no. I've found that workers perform better when allowed more autonomy, because they don't want to lose this benefit.

In 2020, a PwC study showed a 52 percent increase in productivity following the shift to remote work as a result of the COVID-19 pandemic. Workers not only were more productive but also wanted to maintain the ability to work remotely full-time or at least a few days a week when things began to return to normal.

Many companies are now figuring out that working remotely is the future of work — pandemic or not. Some have gone as far as to allow 30 to 50 percent of their workforces to work remotely forever. Others have revised their work-from-home policies to allow for a hybrid workweek such as three days in the office and two from home. A data report by McKinsey & Company suggests that 20 to 25 percent of the workplace in advanced economies across the globe could easily work from home for three or more days a week — that is, if the work doesn't require being in close proximity to clients and/or colleagues. Employers have come to recognize that remote/virtual working has produced a considerable cost savings for physically based operations.

REMEMBER

Remote working isn't a one size fits all solution. Working from home does have some drawbacks. Employees tend to work longer hours when working virtually, and they tend to experience greater levels of isolation, loneliness, and extra interruptions/distractions (from family members, pets, noises in the neighborhood, and weak Internet connections). Leaders have the added responsibility of figuring out how to lead a remote team and how to maintain a sense of belonging, team comradery, and connection.

The impact diversity, equity, and inclusion

The COVID-19 pandemic and the increased amount of virtual work that came with it pushed DEI efforts to the forefront. Offering more remote work increased job opportunities for people across all geographic locations. In other words, workers could basically live anywhere to get work done. The ten most expensive cities in the United States tend to be hubs for many sought-after industries, yet the cost of living in those areas greatly limits affordability. Remote work eliminates this economic barrier and also widens the applicant pool. Think about the number of companies that started hiring again following the pandemic and the economic recovery. So many of them no longer required that you live in the same location where the job was posted.

TIP

A LinkedIn story reports some additional DEI benefits resulting from the shift to remote work:

>> No geographic barriers means no relocation costs and no location bias.

>> Remote work can promote greater psychological safety for LGBTQ employees.

>> Employees with disabilities have no commute and greater access to support.

Although the flexibility of remote work fosters greater inclusivity and diversity, you still need to employ special techniques to keep workers engaged. The Society for Human Resource Management notes six ways to keep remote workers engaged.

Consider which of the following you currently demonstrate effectively and consistently:

>> **Be empathetic:** Create a sense of belonging by showing you care about colleagues and managers.

>> **Encourage participation:** Create a communication plan to engage all team members individually and directly, but also learn your team's communication style to cultivate productive participation during team meetings.

>> **Create structured team building:** Develop games and activities that let you to get to know one another.

>> **Utilize employee resource groups (ERGs):** ERGs can be a source for data collection and ides for inclusive activities.

>> **Be intentional about talent development:** Schedule one-on-one meetings (outside the performance review process schedule) to discuss and plan team members' goals, interests, and career development areas.

REMEMBER

Measure and evaluate inclusion efforts: Consistently interact and engage with remote workers to see how the inclusion practices are progressing. This practice is constant and evolutionary. You fix what isn't working and continue to improve on what is working to keep workers engaged.

Increasingly Digital

Because people are more and more active on their digital devices, they tend to remain connected to those devices more often. A surge in digital platforms and ecommerce has led to exponential growth in digitization across a number of industries. It will definitely influence how people work, as I explain in the following sections.

Considering the COVID-19 pandemic's effects on digitalization

The COVID-19 pandemic was a major contributor to the surge in digitization. The slowdown/shutdown of major economies forced people inside and onto their devices for ordering food and household items, staying connected with family and friends, and even attending events. The pandemic crisis accelerated the rate of digital interactions between consumers and customer service, leading to a shift in product offerings. Across the globe, digital or digitally enhanced product offerings increased ahead of the normal curve thanks to the pandemic-boosted demand for goods and services. And this trend won't subside as companies look to capitalize off it.

The shift in this demographic trend isn't just focused on one locale or region. Between 2018 and 2020, double-digit increases in digital offerings impacted the globe:

>> **Global digital acceleration**: 38 percent

>> **Asia-Pacific:** 24 percent

>> **Europe:** 26 percent

>> **North America:** 40 percent

This uptick suggests that companies have focused on how they deliver their products through digital platforms as opposed to increasing overall product development. It also implies that digitally based products have increased and will continue to abound in the marketplace.

These industries most impacted by this digital offering trend experienced double-digit growth in digitization:

>> Healthcare (think about the rise in telehealth/web-based video conference doctor appointments)

>> Pharmaceutical

>> Financial services (think about how more banks widened their digital platforms for service and about the increase in nontraditional banking such as CashApp, Venmo, Chime, and cryptocurrency)

>> Professional services

>> Hospitality and restaurant industries

Consumer goods manufacturing and the automotive industry also saw consistent (but smaller-scale) growth.

Core internal operations such as back-office procedures, production, and research also experienced an increase in digitization and supply chain. Companies also noted that their responses to COVID-19-related changes were 20 to 25 percent faster than expected. And companies moved remarkably quickly to transition to remote working, averaging 11 days to make the shift. Digital connections clearly made this speedy transition possible.

Examining automation's and artificial intelligence's impact on talent and DEI

Automation and artificial intelligence (AI) are replacing human tasks. This move changes the skills people need to succeed in the workplace. PwC's Future of Work report indicates the following:

>> 37 percent of workers are concerned that automation puts their jobs at risk

>> 74 percent of workers are ready to learn new skills or retrain

>> 60 percent of workers think long-term employment won't be an option for the future

>> 73 percent of workers think technology can't replace the human brain

The automation and AI impact on DEI may make its greatest influence on the first step to working: the screening and selection process. Here are some areas where automation and AI can assist with DEI:

>> Using data tools' algorithms to screen employee information to help managers create diverse interview panels that reduce implicit bias

>> Using AI and data science to match high-potential applicants with job roles regardless of demographic information (such as race, gender, sexual orientation, name, ability, and age)

>> Writing unbiased job postings with gender-neutral language

>> Offering fairer salaries by analyzing market data to recommend more equitable pay ranges

WARNING

AI has the ability to help humans make bias–free decisions only if the systems are built without unconscious bias. A key aspect of AI is that its systems are built on data and learn from data that a human with their own perspective programs in. If programmers build their own implicit biases into the systems, the systems become flawed. For example, many countries already have AI technology that tracks people's movement and has facial recognition. But research indicates that facial recognition technology has the most errors with correctly recognizing Black and brown faces. When authorities use these systems, these errors can have negative effects on citizens.

DEI practices within AI are crucial. A study by AI Now found that only 15 percent of AI researchers at Facebook and 10 percent at Google were women. It also revealed that less than 5 percent of the staff at Facebook, Google, and Microsoft were Black, when the Black workforce in the U.S. is approximately 12 percent of the overall labor force. This lack of diverse engineers and researchers may result in the continuation of AI bias on a large scale. For example, in 2015 only 18 percent of computer science majors in U.S. universities were women, down from 37 percent in 1984. This decrease indicates a pipeline problem with education, hiring, and promotion within the field. Companies must ensure they build diversity, equity, and inclusion — not bias — into the root of AI systems.

Increasingly Underskilled

A major trend shifting the workplace demographic is the growing skilled worker shortage. *Skilled workers* include electricians, plumbers, HVAC technicians, construction managers and workers, carpenters, and so on. Closing this skill gap with technology, more specifically automation and artificial intelligence, is on the horizon, which means workers skilled in the technology that creates and produces these solutions are needed as well.

Accenture's Future of Work research group found that countries that don't invest in technological skill building may lose $11.5 trillion of economic growth. For example, up to 90 percent of human labor time may be replaced by automation and artificial intelligence (though actual numbers vary by industry and type of work). If they don't address the skills gap and shortage, the following players face these potential economic losses by 2030:

>> **China:** 1.7 percent loss of annual growth

>> **Mexico and South Africa:** 1.8 percent loss of annual growth

>> **United States:** $975 billion

>> **Germany:** $264 billion

So how does this information impact the nature of your own business operations, product offerings, and consumer base? Better yet, what can you do differently in your business to address these potential skill shortages? What type of work can you augment with intelligent technology and what work can artificial intelligence complete?

REMEMBER

Creativity, social and emotional intelligence, critical thinking, and complex reasoning are noted skills that are increasingly vital in every workplace role. These skills are also essential to fostering and maintaining a diverse, equitable, and inclusive workplace. The need to focus on building these skills along with technological skills is leading workplaces to require workers with a variety of skills and to make the worthwhile investment in broadening those skills.

Following are three tips for helping underskilled workers to build essential skills:

>> Expand experiential learning opportunities through technical simulation training, on the job training, and apprenticeships. Add AI and virtual reality to immersive learning experiences.

>> Build individuals and institutions. Focus on the professional development workers as individuals that have broad skills bases. Incentivize achievements at the individual and team/department levels.

>> Empower learners and those in more vulnerable categories, such as older workers and lower-skill roles. Create career pathways and professional development/learning plans. Support workers through grant programs and tuition reimbursement for lifelong learning. Provide training in modular and creative ways that fit the individual learner's lifestyle.

WHAT'S NEXT FOR JOBS, 2031–2036 EDITION

Jobs experiencing the greatest growth potential:

- Home health aide
- Nursing assistant
- Construction worker
- Physical therapy aide
- Medical technologist
- Truck driver
- Operations research analyst
- Financial advisor
- Health services administrator
- Registered nurse
- Web developer
- Physical therapist
- Teacher

(continued)

(continued)

Jobs that are predicted to disappear due to AI:

- Driver
- Farmer
- Printer and publisher
- Cashier
- Travel agent
- Manufacturing worker
- Dispatcher
- Food service worker and bartender
- Bank teller
- Military pilot and soldier
- Fast food worker
- Telemarketer
- Accountants and tax preparer
- Stock trader
- Construction worker

Chapter **3**

Cultivating Skills and Competencies for Leading Today's Workers

All too often, large and medium-sized organizations reward their most successful individual contributors by promoting them into leadership roles. Unfortunately, the skills needed to lead projects and other initiatives aren't the same skills needed to be people leaders. In fact, being able to lead a successful team — where everyone feels valued, respected, and included — is one of the most difficult challenges leaders face in today's global and diverse workforce.

In addition to being a subject matter expert in a particular role, division, or department, an effective leader also empowers, inspires, and develops a diverse team that performs at its best both personally and together. After all, leading a team of people would be the easiest thing in the world if everyone on your team was just like you. Without giving it a moment's thought, you'd know exactly what your people needed from you to stay motivated; you'd know how to coach them and how to ensure they were most successful. But the truth is that even those team members who look and think like you bring with them vastly different personality traits, life experiences, and personal preferences. And those who also differ from you by race, gender, sexual orientation, gender identity, physical ability, religion, and a host of other identities are likely to see the workplace in very different ways. The people on your team are different from one another, and they all need different things from the person who leads them.

Assessing Your DEI Leadership Effectiveness

One of the (many) reasons leaders are reluctant to discuss diversity, equity, and inclusion in the workplace is that people associate DEI and morality. Any skill deficit that may be mentioned is treated as an attack on a person's character, as though all a leader needs to lead DEI effectively is a good heart.

I'm going to take for granted that reading this book is evidence you want to do the right thing by all the people you lead and that you hold no conscious animosity against people because of their identities. But this basic state on its own doesn't mean you possess the skills necessary to effectively lead a diverse group of people toward common business goals.

Demonstrating emotional intelligence

Emotional intelligence, sometimes called EQ or *emotional quotient,* is the ability to recognize, regulate, and convey your own emotions and to conduct interpersonal relationships with awareness and empathy of another's emotional state. According to Daniel Goleman, an American psychologist who helped popularize the term, emotional intelligence has five components:

>> **Self-awareness:** Paying attention to your own emotions; knowing your triggers; noting your strengths and weaknesses; possessing humility

>> **Self-regulation:** Remaining calm in emotionally fraught situations; controlling your own behavior despite your emotional state; admitting your mistakes and taking accountability

>> **Motivation:** Knowing why your work is important to you; affirming your values and acting in alignment with them; remaining optimistic, especially when doing so is difficult

>> **Empathy:** Recognizing emotions in others; avoiding judgment; feeling "with" others when appropriate; conveying your understanding of another's emotions and responding appropriately

>> **Social skills:** Practicing vulnerability; praising others without reservation; resolving conflicts fairly and equitably

The following sections dive into each of these components in a bit more detail.

Self-awareness

Leaders who are *self-aware* not only understand how they're feeling at any given moment but also understand how emotions work. As I discuss in Chapter 15, your emotions are generated in a part of your brain that's fundamentally outside your control. Therefore, you can't dictate to yourself what to feel at any given moment. If a colleague receives an award you thought you should've won, you may feel envious. Telling yourself to be magnanimous instead won't make your jealousy go away; in fact, your attempt to control your reaction may have the opposite effect. If your beloved pet dies the night before an important presentation, you'll likely be heartbroken, and masking your grief likely won't be possible. You just have to find a way to get through it. A self-aware leader recognizes their emotions for what they are and accepts them with humility.

In addition, leaders who are self-aware know themselves well enough to know what's likely to trigger negative emotions like anger, fear, or sadness. Though controlling how you feel isn't possible, controlling your response or the environments you're in, or at least preparing for situations in advance, is possible.

Following are some questions to ponder for being more self-aware:

>> Do you have difficulty naming your emotions?

>> Do you have a trusted person or people with whom you can openly discuss how you feel?

>> What are triggers, pet peeves, or situations that may cause an emotional reaction for you?

Self-regulation

Although they can't decide what to feel (see the preceding section), a self-aware leader is often able to separate how they feel from how they behave. You may not be able to feel as generous or noble as you may want to when a colleague beats you out for an award, for example. Admitting that you're jealous and somewhat ashamed of your own jealousy is important, but it's just a first step. The next step is realizing that you don't need to act on your jealousy and that even though angrily storming out of the room may feel good in the short term, doing so will likely have negative long-term effects (mostly to your own reputation).

Behaving based on your emotions only (when the time and place doesn't warrant the reaction) isn't authenticity; it's immaturity. As I discuss in the following section, *authenticity* is better defined as behaving in alignment with your values. The ability to identify and name your emotions (self-awareness) is not only helpful but also necessary if you hope to regulate those emotions so you can behave in in a way that reflects well on you.

REMEMBER

No one is perfect. When you get it wrong (and you will), being fully accountable for your own behavior is important. Feeling defensive and shifting the blame onto other people or situations is natural, but those actions erode trust among those who look to you for leadership.

Here are some questions to consider for self-regulation:

>> Are you able to separate how you feel from how you want to behave when emotions run high?

>> Do you have difficulty remaining calm when you're annoyed or frustrated?

>> Can you manage the impulse to shift the blame for your words and actions onto others?

Motivation (core values)

If authenticity is behaving in alignment with your values, then the obvious first step is to know exactly what your own core values are. What's important to you? What kind of leader do you want to be? Does your organization have stated core values? If so, you agreed to exhibit those in your professional and personal life the day you accepted employment with the company. Additionally, as a leader, part of your job is to model those same values for your team.

TIP

Actions speak louder than words, and walking the talk always supersedes talking the talk. The values you talk about and the behaviors you demonstrate should match.

Following are examples of core value statements:

> Honesty, quality, faith, commitment, and authenticity are my core values. With these I approach all of life's challenges, and they drive my behaviors and my decisions. I believe that you have to be true to who you are, continually strive to become a better version of yourself, and put your very best forward when you commit to something. And to the extent that you can't deliver, be honest and take responsibility.
>
> —Shirley Davis, PhD

> Respect and integrity are really core for me. But my strongest core value is kindness. And not the mopey kind of kindness, which is all about protecting people from hurt feelings. To me, kindness is about much more than being nice. It's acting with others' best interests at heart, even if that means telling them something they need to hear, even if they don't want to. And, of course, it also means not being cruel or overly harsh on purpose. I try to treat others with kindness every day, and I look for that in my leaders and teams.
>
> —Eric Peterson, MSOD

Here are some questions to think about regarding motivation and your core values:

>> Can you articulate why you do the work you do and why it's important?

>> Can you exhibit your organization's stated core values without hesitation? If not, which of these are the biggest challenges for you?

>> How do you contribute to your team's success and its ability to work together effectively?

>> What career goals do you have for the next two years? Five years?

>> What excites you most about your role?

Empathy

When an acquaintance experiences a loss, you're likely to feel sympathy for that person. In this sense, *sympathy* means you have a cognitive understanding of why they're in pain — that it makes sense to you. However, if a close friend or loved one experiences a deep loss, or a great frustration or success, you're much more likely to not only comprehend their emotions but also feel those emotions yourself. This experience of feeling *with* is called *empathy,* and it goes well beyond a cognitive understanding.

For a work team to feel these kinds of emotional bonds is rare (and not always advisable). Nonetheless, great leaders can, when appropriate, make a proactive choice to treat their direct reports with empathy by putting themselves in their reports' shoes.

Choosing empathy in a work setting can feel alien or unprofessional to many who have been taught that emotions have no place in the day-to-day activities of a workplace. But this belief flies in the face of human nature. Humans react emotionally to everything, and a leader who can understand why their direct reports feel as they do can better make decisions that work for those employees. And no, you're not expected to be your team's therapist, parent figure, or best friend. All the same, treating those you work with as human beings, not cogs in a machine, is helpful.

Some questions to ponder for demonstrating empathy include these:

>> Can you usually predict how the people on your team will react to change, a new task, or increased demands on their time?

>> Are you able to put yourself in each team member's shoes?

>> Can you communicate your understanding of team members' emotional states?

Social skills

If you recall the best leader you've ever worked for, they likely possessed all the traits that I discuss in the preceding sections. But above all, they almost certainly were "the kind of person you can talk to." The kind of openness that great leaders possess (and the trust it inspires) can seem hard to pin down, but it has some root causes that you can learn and practice if they don't come naturally to you.

>> **Vulnerability:** Vulnerability isn't as scary as it sounds. A vulnerable leader is simply a person who isn't trying to fool anyone into believing they're perfect. This leader knows their strengths and their weaknesses and isn't afraid to discuss either when appropriate. In that way, being vulnerable is a whole lot easier than being invulnerable and untouchable. As you coach your team through development activities that are meant to capitalize on their strengths and develop their weaknesses, relating to that journey with a few well-chosen stories of your own can go a long way.

>> **Willingness to praise:** A leader with finely tuned social skills doesn't hesitate to praise their team members, both individually and collectively. Yes, giving constructive feedback is important, but praise is equally or even more important. Frequent and sincere praise makes the constructive feedback easier to absorb and act on, and it helps all team members feel that they belong and are valued.

>> **Ability to mediate conflicts fairly:** Social skills enable a leader to mitigate conflicts on the team in a fair and equitable way. When team members are in conflict, you may not be able to find a solution that pleases everyone, but you can make that decision in such a way that all parties feel heard, valued, and respected.

Here are some questions to consider for honing your social skills:

>> Are you able to be vulnerable with your leaders, peers, and direct reports?

>> Do you frequently and sincerely praise your team for a job well done?

>> Can you resolve conflicts on your team in a way that doesn't threaten their sense of value or belonging?

Exhibiting authenticity and transparency

As defined in the earlier section "Self-regulation," authenticity isn't simply "being yourself" every moment of every day. It includes an element of being true to yourself, but let me be very clear: An authentic leader is true to their *best* self. This approach means behaving in alignment with your values.

Applying your core values to lead authentically

Figure 3-1 shows a checklist of values. Spend a moment perusing this list and check the ones that motivate you the most. Draw a circle around your organization's stated core values, if they exist. If a value has little or no meaning to you, cross it out (for instance, if "humility" is a value that resonates for you, then "boldness" may have less value).

Pare that list down to the five values that you believe should guide most of your decisions at work. They may be a mixture of values that are very meaningful to you and those that are essential to success in your role or industry right now. (And don't hesitate to come back to this list when life changes — you become a parent, get a promotion, and so on — to see whether your values have shifted somewhat.)

☐ Abundance	☐ Daring	☐ Intelligence	☐ Preparedness
☐ Acceptance	☐ Decisiveness	☐ Intuition	☐ Proactivity
☐ Accountability	☐ Dedication	☐ Joy	☐ Professionalism
☐ Achievement	☐ Dependability	☐ Kindness	☐ Punctuality
☐ Advancement	☐ Diversity	☐ Knowledge	☐ Recognition
☐ Adventure	☐ Empathy	☐ Leadership	☐ Relationships
☐ Advocacy	☐ Encouragement	☐ Learning	☐ Reliability
☐ Ambition	☐ Enthusiasm	☐ Love	☐ Resilience
☐ Appreciation	☐ Ethics	☐ Loyalty	☐ Resourcefulness
☐ Attractiveness	☐ Excellence	☐ Making a Difference	☐ Respect
☐ Autonomy	☐ Fairness	☐ Mindfulness	☐ Responsibility
☐ Balance	☐ Family	☐ Motivation	☐ Security
☐ Being the Best	☐ Friendships	☐ Optimism	☐ Self-Control
☐ Boldness	☐ Flexibility	☐ Open-Mindedness	☐ Selflessness
☐ Brilliance	☐ Freedom	☐ Passion	☐ Simplicity
☐ Calm	☐ Fun	☐ Performance	☐ Stability
☐ Caring	☐ Generosity	☐ Personal Development	☐ Success
☐ Charity	☐ Grace	☐ Professionalism	☐ Teamwork
☐ Cheerfulness	☐ Gratitude	☐ Quality	☐ Thoughtfulness
☐ Cleverness	☐ Growth	☐ Recognition	☐ Traditionalism
☐ Community	☐ Happiness	☐ Risk Taking	☐ Trustworthiness
☐ Commitment	☐ Health	☐ Security	☐ Understanding
☐ Compassion	☐ Honesty	☐ Service	☐ Usefulness
☐ Cooperation	☐ Humility	☐ Spirituality	☐ Versatility
☐ Collaboration	☐ Humor	☐ Stability	☐ Vision
☐ Consistency	☐ Inclusiveness	☐ Peace	☐ Warmth
☐ Creativity	☐ Independence	☐ Perfection	☐ Wealth
☐ Credibility	☐ Innovation	☐ Popularity	☐ Well-Being
☐ Curiosity	☐ Inspiration	☐ Power	☐ Wisdom

FIGURE 3-1:
What values
motivate you
the most?

Now take stock of those five values. What does behaving in alignment with these five values look like? For instance, if one of your top five values is "family," you may commit to the following:

I'll create boundaries related to work/life integration so I can both thrive at work and fulfill my chosen role within my family.

I'll manage my team in a way that allows members to create the same boundaries, if (and when) they choose to do, recognizing that their ambitions at work and at home may differ from mine significantly.

I'll respect those on my team whose cultures and/or family structures are different from my own and will allow them to define family on their own terms.

Or, if one of your top five values is "growth," you may commit to this:

> When hiring new team members, I won't be satisfied with those who can fulfill the job description as written today but will actively seek those who show a willingness and aptitude for developing new skills.

> When assigning people to important tasks, I won't simply fall back on my go-to people but will look for those who are ready for a challenge.

> I'll ask my strongest performers to mentor others on my team, preparing them for management responsibilities while developing everyone's skills.

> I'll assess all employees based on potential as well as proven ability.

REMEMBER

Research has shown that women and people of color must often prove competence before they're promoted, while white men are often promoted based on their potential (more about this topic in Chapter 15). Therefore, focusing on one's values and determining what authenticity looks like for you can ensure that you treat everyone on your team equitably.

Being clear about transparency

Just as authenticity isn't doing what you feel whenever you feel it, neither is transparency saying everything that pops into your mind as it occurs to you. Rather, *transparency* is a proactive commitment to being appropriately honest, open, and vulnerable with your team members.

WARNING

Sharing everything you know about any given situation with members of your team is unwise, and in some cases illegal. On an individual level, national laws and regulations that establish privacy of information mean that you can't legally disclose protected information about a member of your team without their consent. But even without those laws, you don't want to share information that reveals an aspect of an employee's personal life if that employee hasn't shared the information themselves. From a company standpoint, you may have access to privileged information about your organization's finances or potential legal actions that you're unable to share with your team members, even if they're curious as to why certain changes are being made that affect the day-to-day experience on the job.

REMEMBER

The most important rule regarding transparency is "Don't knowingly lie to your team." If there's a compelling reason why you can't disclose something, simply state that you're unable to share. If this is a true statement, you're in the clear.

However, you should also avoid using this tactic as an easy escape from the harder work of transparency. You may be tempted to keep something to yourself because it may put you in a bad light or necessitate an uncomfortable conversation with a staff member.

When faced with a tough decision regarding what to tell your team, consider the following questions:

>> Will I be violating a pertinent law or organizational policy by imparting this knowledge? (Your HR department can help if you don't know the answer to this question.)

>> Does my team have a right to know this information?

>> What are likely to be the short-term and long-term effects of sharing or not sharing at this time?

Building and maintaining trust

Consistently exhibiting authenticity and transparency is probably the most important component of building and maintaining trust on your team. (I cover these concepts in the earlier section "Exhibiting authenticity and transparency.") And, of course, the key word in that sentence is *consistently.* Consistency is the bedrock of trust.

When you consistently act with the best interest of the organization *and* your people, you earn their trust. They'll repay that trust by unswervingly doing their best work. When you consistently protect the privacy of your employees, they reward you by confiding in you without hesitation. And when you consistently activate diverse viewpoints on a team and reward them for speaking their minds (even when doing so goes against the grain), you always have access to a diverse set of viewpoints that allow the team to make more creative and innovative decisions.

In addition, leaders who earn the trust of their teams do the following:

>> **Keep their commitments:** As a leader, you don't need to make a solemn promise for people to take you at your word. Your status as a leader means anything you say that can be construed as a commitment will be considered a commitment. Even a benign statement of praise like "Keep it up, and you'll go far" can be heard as a commitment to promoting the employee if they continue their current level of performance. Therefore, you must not only strive to keep your commitments but also be very careful not to make one without meaning to.

>> **Have a reputation for being honest and reliable:** Of course, consistency is the best (perhaps the only) way to build this reputation. And you can't really know what people say about you when you're not in the room. But if you're ready to hear the answer, ask colleagues you trust what you're known for in

the organization. Even if the answers are positive, check them against your top five values to ensure you're being seen the way you see yourself. For help determining those core values, check out the earlier section "Applying your core values to lead authentically."

>> **Avoid presenting their opinions as facts:** Unconsciously making their opinion the opinion of the entire team without full buy-in is another trap leaders often fall into. Anyone who disagrees hears a misstatement or, worse, an untruth.

>> **Trust and respect others:** Part of earning trust from other people stems from modeling what placing your trust in them looks like.

>> **Understand that trust must be earned:** In any relationship with a *power dynamic* (one person is more powerful than the other), the individual with less power may be slower to trust. This hesitance is for good reason, especially if powerful figures in their past have misused them. Allow your team to warm up to you, and aim to earn its trust over time.

>> **Accept responsibility for their mistakes:** Consistent behavior doesn't mean that good, competent leaders must be saints. You'll likely fall short of your ideals at times. When you do, apologize to anyone who was affected by your shortcomings, including those team members who may have only overheard a careless word or observed a lapse in judgment.

>> **Lead by example, not by words alone:** Be the team member you seek. If you say you want different viewpoints, be intentional about asking everyone for their opinions. When everyone is pulling late hours, stay with the team if possible, and if you can best serve by standing over the copy machine, do it. If team members see you pitching in, they'll be only too happy to pitch in themselves.

>> **Always try to do the right thing:** A moral compass is a necessity for a trusted leader who leads a diverse team. Such a leader must be self-aware, authentic, and transparent, traits I cover in more detail earlier in the chapter.

Leading change

Any leader looking to make diversity, equity, and inclusion a part of their personal leadership brand leads change at some point in their career. Leaders who seek to move the needle recognize that it's neither easy nor quick but there are some key practices to keep in mind if you want the change to succeed. Several of these practices were first introduced by Dr. John Kotter in 1996, a global management consultant, former Harvard University Professor, and best-selling author *of Leading Change* (Harvard Business Review Press). While they were not developed specifically to lead DEI change — they work on any organizational effort — but I have found them extremely useful in my work.

I have been using Kotter's change model for nearly 20 years to help organizations navigate change, including those that will make a team or organization more diverse and inclusive. In the following sections I describe what I believe to be the most important first steps to leading change in HR and DEI policies and practices and I provide real world examples of how I implemented them in each step. As you review them, conduct an informal analysis of how many of these competencies are resident in your organization.

Creating a sense of urgency

By nature, people don't like change, especially change that moves them from their comfort zones, disrupts their habits, or threatens to take away something that they value or have developed as a habit. If the idea of something new feels threatening, people will tend to resist rather than buy into the need for change. So creating a sense of urgency must be swift and persuasive enough to cause change to happen; otherwise, the value is diminished and complacency can set in.

I've had to lead organizational change on numerous occasions, and I've had to work with the client in creating a sense of urgency. On one occasion when the #MeToo movement started, I was consulting with a client and leading some training on implicit bias. In the midst of the presentation, the national news broke and several of the company's senior leaders were accused of sexual harassment in several offices around the country. A group of women had coordinated with an attorney to file the complaints, and the news got wind of it. Immediately, I pivoted my session and began to discuss the importance of a respectful and harassment-free workplace. I was able to use the fallout and the likely consequences that would result as a way to drive a sense of urgency. The company immediately responded with statements from the president restating their zero-tolerance policy as well as a mandate that all people leaders should go through harassment training to ensure that they understood the seriousness of inappropriate behavior and that they were being responsive to any additional complaints.

Building a coalition

Leading successful change in an organization can never be done solo. It has to be done with a team of people who bring complementary skills, a willingness to work together, and a commitment to achieving success. They must also be influential and well-respected so that those affected by the change will trust the process. When I was implementing a change during a merger and acquisition for a utility company that I worked with, I was tasked with assessing how the cultures of both companies would align, how they would clash, and what significant changes would need to be made once the merger took place. There was no way that I could be successful at this task alone, so I assembled a coalition of leaders from both companies and from across various departments and locations. We all had varying degrees of functional expertise, tenure, and levels of authority with our respective companies, but all of us agreed on one thing: We wanted the merger to be a success and with as little interruption as possible.

Establishing a clear vision and strategy

To get anywhere, it helps to know exactly where you're going. Casting a clear vision is much more than sharing vague notions or positing grandiose ideas. Change can be scary, and many people resist or choose the status quo, so you must paint the picture of the future and describe the reason why it is important to create that future or to go in such a direction. You must also take it a step further and identify the steps to getting there and the benefits that will be enjoyed as a result of the change. And even then, change will probably be a challenging and difficult process for most.

Implementing diversity, equity, and inclusion initiatives is a great example of this. In all of my HR and DEI roles, I was met with resistance from line leaders as well as some staff. For example, when we announced that we would be offering domestic partner benefits at a conservative company the backlash from some leaders was immediate. In another company, I was advocating for a policy to allow flexible work arrangements for all staff, and I got quite a bit of resistance from older workers who felt that performance and productivity would suffer, and that because they couldn't see workers in their seats, they couldn't monitor their work. In response, our team provided a clear vision of why we planned to appeal to a more diverse talent pool that would be more reflective of the customers we served and the communities we were located in. We tied the change back to our company values and provided quantifiable actions that would be taken, how success would be measured, and reiterated the benefits that would come from these offerings. It helped to settle some of the resistance and misinformation.

Communicating the change

It's one thing to establish the vision, but you must also share it with all levels of staff and in multiple ways. It cannot be a one-shot deal; there must be ongoing communications to allow for everyone to process the change and to ask questions. Recently my firm was completing an all-staff inclusion and engagement survey and one of the questions that was asked of the staff was whether they felt that the company's DEI strategy was meeting its stated objectives. Over 80 percent of the staff responded, "What DEI strategy?" Most of them had never been told about it. Needless to say, one of our key recommendations back to the DEI committee was that they needed to socialize the plan across the organization if they wanted staff to buy into it and participate in fostering an inclusive culture. You cannot expect anyone to do anything if nothing has been communicated to them with clarity, consistency, and a compelling reason for the change.

REMEMBER

The reality of change can be a dark, scary place. A leader has to remember that not everyone on the change project shares their point of view; therefore, they have to communicate and overcommunicate what often feels obvious or unnecessary. In a particularly complex change project, many team members aren't aware of what others on the team are doing to help achieve progress, and communicating those activities often falls to the leader as well.

Utilizing strong interpersonal skills

Excellent communication isn't just a matter of speaking well. Leaders who want change on their teams and in their companies — especially culture change that seeks to create inclusion and more opportunities for diverse staff — must also be excellent listeners. Any leader, no matter their unique set of identities, can automatically understand the needs and desires of every community that a diversity and inclusion change effort impacts. Therefore, deep and trusting relationships with each of these communities is absolutely necessary.

Maintaining motivation

In any meaningful change process, a point comes when people are weary: They've been working hard for a long time, they can see no evidence of real progress, and their destination is still a long way off. An excellent change leader not only responds to this moment but also expects it and prepares for it in advance. Consistent reminders of the original inspiring vision can help, but more important are short-term wins, especially those that are easy to accomplish and have a significant impact. These easy wins are extremely valuable at the beginning of any change effort because they're often the impetus for those who are aren't bought in to the change.

Even tasks that have less impact but are easy to implement can help keep the team moving when the more difficult, high-impact tasks are taking most of the team's resources. Obviously, if any tasks have been noted as both difficult and low-impact, skip them unless they're absolutely necessary. These tasks are the ones that will damage your team's morale the most.

Another key motivator for a team managing a large change effort involves rewards and recognition. This step can range from the spontaneous and informal (public praise for a team's hard work, taking the team out to lunch, exposure to senior leadership) to the planned and formal (spot bonuses for excellent work, organization-wide awards, detailed mentions of individual successes in annual performance appraisals).

Finally, a leader's own optimism and work ethic regarding a change process, even when the leader is tired, is an intrinsic motivator for those who follow them.

Focusing on the big picture

Details are important, but this work is usually best delegated to others in the change process. For the change to be successful, a leader must have their eye on the big picture as much as possible. In a diversity and inclusion change effort, focusing on the big picture allows a leader to consistently speak in terms of values, reminding themselves and those around them that *how* they do the work is as important as *why*. Reminding people of the goal and how their individual efforts contribute to that goal is important. An eye on the big picture can be crucial if the work itself begins to drift away from the original inspiring vision due to competing priorities or political realities.

Dealing with conflicts

When many leaders imagine what an ideal team environment may look like, they picture smiling faces, people who are happy to come to work every day, and a sense of camaraderie that makes everyone feel as though they belong. For these leaders, conflict is the enemy of productivity, proof that their attempts to build a happy and harmonious team have failed.

Such leaders are bound to be disappointed. Conflict, whether you relish it or try to avoid it, is an ever-present dynamic in human relations. Too much conflict can make a team environment feel toxic and unwelcoming, so your goal shouldn't be a team that's rife with conflict. But a team with no present conflict is probably either a team producing very little innovation or ideation or a team with plenty of unspoken conflict roiling under the surface because of a smothering culture of niceness. This type of conflict is just as poisonous as the kind that marks a hostile work environment — potentially more dangerous because the team leader doesn't acknowledge or feel it.

Many instances of conflict can, if used correctly, be a catalyst for creativity on your team. Most original ideas come from the intersection of two or more opposing ways of thinking, which is what most conflict boils down to. To capitalize on these opportunities, proactively explore conflicts before they deteriorate into a clash of personalities.

When conflicts aren't driving some sort of creativity or production (for example, a skirmish over working style), you should similarly deal with them sooner rather than later. Many leaders ask their direct reports to resolve such conflicts on their own. This response can be appropriate because it can develop leadership skills among junior employees. However, if they can't or won't come to a mutual resolution, a leader may need to act as mediator. At its core, conflict mediation is simply facilitating a conversation between at least two opposing parties so that each side listens and understands the other points of view.

When mediating conflicts, remain in the facilitator role and allow the parties involved to come up with their own solutions. Only as a last resort should you use your position in the leadership hierarchy to impose a solution, and then you should strive to be fair to all parties.

Sometimes, the leader is more directly involved; in other words, the conflict exists between you and one of your direct reports. Resolving these matters can lead to difficult conversations. In such cases, leaders must strive to separate performance issues (for example, true deficiencies in knowledge, skills, and abilities that are a necessary part of a person's job) from coaching opportunities (such as a failure to complete timecards in a punctual manner or a habit of always speaking first in meetings). These in turn are separate from diversity and inclusion issues, such as the only introvert on a team wanting more time to process information before speaking, a woman who bristles at always being asked to plan team events, or someone finding a recent comment offensive or degrading. These different circumstances require different solutions, but all three demand that leaders resist the urge to simply impose a solution based on hierarchical position. Whenever possible, work *with* your team, not against it.

Using diplomacy and tact

The urge to impose order based on hierarchy is completely natural, although you should usually avoid acting on it. Research has long supported the notion that the feeling of power (the degree to which you can effect change and control your environment) decreases mirror neuron activity in the brain. Mirror neurons are responsible for the empathy I discuss earlier in the chapter.

For those who don't feel powerful, empathy comes very naturally. Quite simply, the less power you have, the more community you need. Empathy allows you to join with others, gain a sense of belonging, and offer that sense of camaraderie to others. The more personal power you attain, the less you need others to achieve your desired results. Therefore, the more power you feel, the fewer mirror neurons you need. That feeling causes a biological reaction in the brain that decreases empathy.

Power is a feeling that can come and go very quickly, depending on context. A CEO who feels very powerful at work can suddenly feel utterly powerless as a patient in a hospital, and a middle manager may feel very powerful in a team meeting full of direct reports at 10 a.m. and much less powerful in a meeting with the C-suite later that afternoon.

I'm not saying that people in power can't be empathetic. However, a person in power must make empathy a conscious choice.

Whenever you speak across a desk with someone who sits above you on the organizational chart, you probably aren't going to lose sight of the power dynamic. Even if you enjoy a good working relationship with this person, their position in the hierarchy won't slip your mind. The same, however, isn't true for them. Enjoying a position of power in the conversation, they may fool themselves into believing that the breezy conversation and occasional exchange of jokes feels more like a conversation between equals, and their decreased mirror neuron system means they likely won't register how differently you're feeling.

In such cases, leaders often speak directly, with no intention to cause offense. But these statements can often feel blunt or overly harsh to you, the person in the room with less power. It's a small act, but repeated over time, these incidents become microaggressions that eventually chip away at your confidence, sense of belonging, and productivity. And because of the power dynamic, the leader in this situation isn't equipped to pick up on any of the subtle signs that this is occurring.

TIP

Pay close attention to diplomacy and tact, especially when giving feedback. Don't dilute the criticism until it's easy to hear and essentially meaningless, but always try to give critical feedback in private (while freely giving praise in public spaces). Also, frame the conversation not only in terms of what went wrong but also in terms of what solutions can now be applied. Above all, make the conscious choice to put yourself in the other person's place, and listen to your words from their perspective.

Applying an equity lens in decision making

The term for this work used to be *diversity and inclusion,* or D and I. Increasingly, the phrase *diversity, equity, and inclusion* (DEI) is gaining traction.

Equity is the quality of being fair and impartial. It's sometimes confused with equality, both of which seek to minimize harmful treatment to different groups. But in practice, the two are very different. Equality is all about giving everyone the same resources, but equity means distributing resources according to need.

Equity, therefore, is about achieving equal results. It isn't concerned with treating everyone the same; in fact, doing so is sometimes directly counter to the goals of equity.

When making decisions on behalf of your team, you need to look at things in terms of equity. Instead of focusing on equality (which, to be honest, is much easier), ask yourself the following:

- » How are my team members different?
- » Do any require accommodations to fulfill their primary job functions?
- » Would a solution to benefit one team member actually make another's job more difficult?
- » Do solutions still exist that would indeed benefit everyone on my team?

Focusing on equity rather than equality helps each team member feel as though they matter and are essential to the team.

Exercising cultural competence

The word *culture* gets tossed around a lot, with many definitions around. All have value, but for the sake of keeping things simple, I like to define *culture* as "predictable behaviors and beliefs among a defined group of people." Culture, therefore, can describe a team, an organization, a region, a community, or a nation. (I talk more about culture in Chapters 6 and 18.)

Cultural competence is the ability to work effectively in a multicultural environment. In today's increasingly global workforce, people are working together on teams with colleagues from very different cultures who are literally on the other side of the world. But even if your work teams and customers are completely domestic, they're increasingly diverse. Communities of color, the LGBTQ community, different faith communities, and communities based on ability each have different, but predictable, beliefs and behaviors that guide how they perceive the workplace and show up at work.

Cultural competence has three central components, each of which builds on the last:

- » Self-awareness around your own cultural background (the beliefs and behaviors that guide your perceptions and actions)
- » Knowledge of other cultures (especially those the leader interfaces with on a regular basis)
- » The ability to adapt, if necessary, to achieve harmony and maximum productivity in the workplace

Check out the following sections for more on each of these components.

For a more detailed look at cultural competence, particularly for multinational organizations, see Chapter 17.

Self-awareness

Author David Foster Wallace tells a comic parable about fish that perfectly describes the invisible nature of culture. In it, two young fish are swimming in the ocean when they happen by an older fish. "Morning, boys," the older fish says. "How's the water?" Only after the older fish has swum away does one of the younger fish look to his companion and ask, "What the hell is water?"

People often think about their culture the way fish probably think about water. Though it's omnipresent in their lives, it's also very easy to take for granted. And they typically don't have to think about it, because it's always just there. But, just like a fish, people can become very aware of their culture when it's taken away from them.

Therefore, being aware of one's own culture takes a bit of work. Suppose you have a new client or customer who doesn't make eye contact. Depending on your culture, you may draw very different conclusions about this client's trustworthiness. A wise leader frames this observation as an open question ("Should I trust this person?") as opposed to a declarative statement ("This person can't be trusted."). If you're a leader from a Western culture (for example, the United States or Canada) you may believe that the person isn't trustworthy without ever thinking about the data that led you to that decision (the lack of eye contact) or the belief that prompted your reaction (direct eye contact is both polite and sincere; those who avoid it have something to hide).

A self-aware leader responds to all interactions that strike them as wrong or bad and check them against their own cultural background in a search for cultural misalignment. If your new client comes from the same cultural background as you do, you may be on to something with your assessment., However, if your new client hails from an Eastern culture (such as China or Japan), their lack of eye contact may be easily explained; they may simply have been exhibiting politeness as they understood it.

Knowledge of other cultures

Although knowing about every culture in the world is practically impossible, a leader should be well versed in the cultures that they engage with on a regular basis. If you work in a country where Catholicism is the dominant religion, you're probably already aware of major Catholic holidays and don't question why many employees show up to work with ashes on their foreheads each year around February or March, for example. However, if you're about to welcome the first Muslim member of your team, you may not be aware of the holidays, traditions, and requirements of practicing Islam, and obtaining this information is your responsibility. The same holds true if you're welcoming someone raised in another country, a person with a different race or ethnicity, a member of the LGBTQ community, or a person with a disability.

How you get the information doesn't really matter as long as you don't make your new employee responsible for everything you need to know. (Internet search engines can be very helpful, but make a real effort to look at reliable sites for your research.) It will mean so much more to your new employee if their new leader has some basic knowledge about their culture on their first day. You should feel free, however, to let your new team member know that you're open to new information they may choose to provide about their community or themselves in general. Always remember that your new employee is both a member of a community as well as an individual and may not adhere to all traditions or taboos that are true for the culture at large.

The ability to adapt

Often, an unspoken rule dictates that members of minority cultures should assimilate to the larger culture they find themselves in. Usually, this assimilation will happen to at least a small extent. However, the leader who is a true champion of DEI will also strive to adapt their own behaviors when necessary.

For instance, if you have members on your team who were born and raised in India, they may be extremely uncomfortable disagreeing with you, their leader, in public. You may believe that dissent is a necessary part of innovation. You can ask these employees directly to act in direct opposition to their culture, but a better course of action is to keep your own opinions to yourself in large team meetings so that your Indian employees can speak authentically without worrying about contradicting you, and to thank the entire team for its robust contributions.

Navigating workplace politics

Closely connected to organizational culture is the topic of *workplace politics* (also known as *office politics*). In essence this is when employees who have power and authority use it to minimize, exclude, or withhold resources from those who have less power and authority, to benefit their own personal and/or professional desires. It's also been referred to as relationship currency and influence capital — and the power these two things give you or don't give you.

For example, maybe everyone in your organization knows that it's best to get your CEO excited about a new initiative before your CFO has a chance to ask how much it will cost. So if you want to set up employee resource groups within your organization (more about ERGs in Chapter 13), something you believe would be good for business as well as beneficial to your increasingly diverse staff, you may decide to tell your CEO about the benefits of ERGs before bringing it up at a meeting where your CEO and CFO will both be present. The outcome you seek may indeed be "self-serving" in that it may help you achieve personal goals, like increasing retention and employee engagement. But on its face, nothing is unethical about this course of action, and it may reap rewards throughout your workplace and your marketplace.

WARNING

And, of course, many forms of workplace politics can compromise your ethics or values. These include the following:

>> **Office gossip:** Even if what is whispered is true, it nearly always takes on a life of its own and is often destructive.

>> **Cronyism:** Offering rewards (bonuses, raises, career advancement) to personal friends rather than the most deserving candidates. This practice almost always puts members of majority communities at a further advantage.

>> **Nepotism:** Like cronyism except that those receiving rewards are family members.

>> **Workplace deviance:** Sometimes known as "office backstabbing." Workplace deviance usually involves saying one thing to a trusted co-worker in private (such as promising a raise or a promotion in exchange for supporting an idea) and then doing the opposite in public (giving the promotion to someone else after the idea has been adopted).

>> **Workplace bullying:** A consistent pattern of abuse that damages individuals or groups socially, psychologically, and sometimes even physically. Bullying tactics are often used against individuals because of a group membership (race, gender, sexual orientation, religion, disability, gender identity, and so on) and can have a profound impact on all members of that group.

Before engaging in a process that feels manipulative or sneaky, check in with your values. Most of the negative forms of workplace politics put already marginalized groups at an even greater disadvantage and can quickly undo any credibility you've built as a champion of diversity, equity, and inclusion in your workplace.

Developing accountability as a leader

So many skills and attributes are necessary in the DEI space, and some of them can be counterintuitive, or at least surprising. No wonder very few, if any, perfect leaders of DEI exist. Even those for whom DEI has become an integral part of their brand can tell you stories of missteps they've made along the way. The good news is that no one expects you to be perfect. But those who look to your leadership do expect you to be fully accountable.

Here are a few tips to keep in mind for developing accountability as a leader.

Consistency matters

When people know what to expect from you and how you'll respond, it enhances engagement, increases satisfaction, and improves decision making, all of which lead to greater productivity.

Being predictable is okay! The reality is that employees want to be led. They want to work for a leader who provides them with guidance and helps them navigate the terrain of uncertainty and change.

Take ownership

Leadership accountability requires a personal commitment to honesty and integrity, and that means owning up to your part when things go wrong, apologizing when you make a mistake, and admitting when you don't know something.

Recently I was expecting a member of my team to complete a project by a certain time frame that was a critical deliverable for a client. As I checked in with him on the status of the project, he responded that he hadn't received a report I'd promised to send and that it was impacting his timeline for completion. I could've sworn I'd sent it, and I insisted to him that I had.

But when I checked my email, there it was, in my drafts and unsent. I had gotten distracted and totally forgotten to send it because of my hectic schedule. I went back to him immediately, told him I was sorry, and owned the fact that the project may get delayed because I didn't follow through on my end.

Then I went a step further. I called the client myself to explain that we needed a few extra days to complete the project due to my hectic schedule. I didn't blame my team member; I didn't make excuses; I owned up to it. Ultimately, the project was completed on time, and the client was very pleased.

TAKING OWNERSHIP BY APOLOGIZING SUCCESSFULLY

So how does a leader apologize in a way that takes ownership? The general rule when making an apology is to be truly sorry. This point sounds so obvious that it may be unnecessary, but all too often people apologize simply because they know their words or actions caused offense, even if they don't know why. Apologizing successfully is much easier when you realize exactly why and how you messed up and are sincerely regretful.

I don't know about you, but I've worked for those kinds of leaders who made mistakes and bad decisions and then deflected by blaming, justifying it, or denying the truth rather than admitting it. That kind of leadership undermines trust, engagement, and communication. In this situation, I had those choices to make. And I chose to take ownership.

REMEMBER

The most obvious form of the insincere apology is any variation on "I'm sorry if you were offended." That little *if* speaks volumes, turning an apology into a conditional condolence that translates to "If you took offense, I'm sorry; but if you didn't think I said anything wrong, then I agree with you."

If you don't know why others your words or actions offended others, find out. If the offense was great enough, someone will be willing to tell you exactly what you said or did and how it made them feel. When you understand that link, you can deliver your apology.

Take full accountability for your behavior. Often, otherwise effective apologies are bungled by a leader's tendency to get defensive, deflect blame, or cover their bases. These impulses can leave their mark in a way that's often painfully obvious to everyone but the person apologizing.

REMEMBER

Perhaps explaining your original intent feels important to you, but it can't serve as an excuse. A sincere apology may not feel like a moment of greatness, but it may be the thing that your team remembers most about you and solidify their respect.

Deflecting in particular can be harmful. *Deflection* can take the form of blaming your actions on someone or something else (unusual stress, a sleepless night, too many glasses of wine at the company party) or inserting information about unrelated virtues or successes into your apology in a feeble attempt to improve your reputation. In most cases, people are already aware of those victories, and the deflection prompts the opposite response, doing damage to your reputation instead.

Commit to change

If your words are ill-chosen or your behavior insensitive, it simply promising not to repeat the mistake may be sufficient. However, you may be able to go farther by publicly committing to a new behavior or announcing a new policy or process that will prevent these kinds of mistakes from ever happening again. Sometimes giving restitution to a wronged party is also possible.

REMEMBER

However you commit to change, what's most important is to be true to your word. Offering a well-crafted apology is a humbling experience, but it doesn't need to damage your credibility. Offering the apology and then repeating the behavior, however, can cause real injury both to those you've offered a shallow, meaningless confession and to you.

Promoting DEI as a Senior Executive/Board Member

Your specific role in promoting DEI will likely change depending on where you sit in an organization. If you're a member of the C-suite or the board of directors or lead a specific function in a company or nonprofit, your role is naturally more strategic and focused on the long-term. In a senior role, you can make changes in policy and strategic direction, and your decisions will drive the culture of an entire organization.

Earlier in this chapter, I define culture as "predictable beliefs and behaviors among a defined group of people." The behavior of your employees, and to a lesser extent your customers and other stakeholders, is driven by the decisions that board members and senior leaders make.

If, for example, the only performance metric for your salespeople is total sales per year, in effect you're telling your employees to sell more at all costs. However, if you also measure and reward repeat customers, you're communicating that customer satisfaction is as important as revenue. That belief will have a direct bearing on behavior and will predictably lead to a more ethical salesforce, resistant to upselling or otherwise manipulating customers to buy more than they need. Rewarding the same staff for expanding into new and diverse markets can incentivize sales managers to hire a more diverse sales staff and learn about the needs of a diverse client base. These behaviors can create a more sustainable customer base and lead to greater commercial success.

This is just one of many examples of real culture change that people at the top of an organization can effect. Here are some other questions that board members and senior leaders should consider:

>> Has your organization defined a specific set of core values for itself? If so, are diversity, equity, and inclusion present? If not, is it time for your organization to make its values explicit? You can read more about determining core values in "Applying your core values to lead authentically" earlier in the chapter.

>> How has your organization institutionalized its values, whether they're implicitly or explicitly stated? What rewards and consequences exist for people who either align with or contradict these values in their behavior?

>> Does your organization have a strategic plan? Are your diversity, equity, and inclusion goals embedded within that plan? What measurable progress in this area do you want to see in three years? In five years?

>> What, if any, current policies and processes incentivize your employees to act out of alignment with the values of your organization?

>> Do your employees at all levels have the requisite skills to create and maintain a culture that exhibits diversity, equity, and inclusion?

>> What systems exist to measure diversity, equity, and inclusion in your organization?

Fostering DEI as a Middle Manager or Supervisor

As a middle manager or supervisor, your sphere of influence is limited to your team, but that influence arguably has a greater visceral impact on your direct reports than the actions of senior leaders and your board do. The idea that "people don't leave jobs, they leave managers" has been repeated so often that it's something of a cliché, but it's a true statement nonetheless.

Research in 2017 and 2018 revealed that employees are more likely to look for work elsewhere when they have toxic management or when their jobs are unsatisfying (for example, the job isn't enjoyable, their strengths aren't being used, or they aren't growing in their careers). Those in the first category are obviously the victims of poor management, but you can argue that managers have a significant role in the departure of the second group as well.

Leaders can't be called effective if they're only effective at leading those who are very similar to them, either in personality or interests or in broader categories such as race, gender, ability, religion, sexual orientation, and so on. To be an effective leader (much less a great one) for a diverse team, you have to adapt your leadership style appropriately to the needs of your staff. This flexibility requires cultural humility, vulnerability, trust, and courage, but more than anything else, it requires a great deal of listening. A good (or great) leader of a diverse team has to know their team well, in all kinds of ways:

>> **Culturally:** What is this person's cultural background? How does their nationality, ethnicity, race, gender, religion, ability, sexuality, and so on inform the way they see the workplace? Do they experience barriers to success that are different from yours? Are political and social events outside the organization affecting some of your team differently than others?

>> **Individually:** What is this person's preferred work style? Do they have work/life integration demands that are different from yours or those of other members of the team? Are they eager to share their point of view, or more reserved? What strategies can you employ to help this person perform at their optimal level?

>> **Performatively:** What are this employee's strengths? How can you keep them motivated by using and building on those strengths in their daily tasks? What are their weaknesses? How can you develop those areas while maintaining confidence and high productivity?

>> **Aspirationally:** What are this employee's goals? How soon do they want to realize these goals? Realistically, does their ideal future align with the goals of the business? If so, how can you help them navigate the system to succeed? If not, how long do you expect them to be with your organization, and can you help them pursue their next steps on good terms?

Building deep and trusting relationships takes effort and time. For more on effectively leading diverse teams, see Chapters 10 and 11.

Championing DEI as a Mentor or Sponsor

Your role as a mentor or sponsor is a much more individualized approach. The two terms are often confused, but the key difference between a mentor and a sponsor is that a *mentor* provides advice and career guidance to their mentee while a *sponsor* advocates for their protégé throughout the organization.

Mentorship

Though a mentor is typically not a mentee's direct manager (in fact, mentors often don't even work for the same organization as the mentee), getting to know the individual members of your team as if you were their supervisor applies to this relationship. (Flip to the earlier section "Fostering DEI as a Middle Manager or Supervisor" for details on knowing your team members.)

Mentoring across difference requires much more listening and reflection than mentoring someone very much like yourself. When mentoring across difference, the most common mistake is passing along advice that worked well for the mentor but wouldn't be effective for the mentee. Behaviors that benefit straight white men, for example, may cause a person of color, a woman, or an LGBTQ person to be perceived as aggressive, pushy, or belligerent.

REMEMBER

Mentorship across difference is a learning experience for both parties, and you must approach it as such. Both mentor and mentee are there to teach the other, and both will hopefully emerge with new skills and strategies.

Sponsorship

A sponsor advocates for their protégé within an organization, so unlike a mentor, a sponsor nearly always works within the same organization and is either senior to their protégé or has access to a greater network by virtue of his/her role and level of influence. Having been a sponsor myself on several occasions, and having had three sponsors in my senior roles, I found that they provided several things:

» First, they spoke on my behalf when I couldn't be in the room or where important talent decisions were being made. They spoke up on promotions, succession planning, stretch assignments, and other activities that would provide me development and visibility.

» Second, they acted as an ally and advocate and spoke up on policies and practices that could have adversely impacted me.

» Third, they provided me a safe place to share the challenges I was experiencing and coached me on how to recover when I had missteps. They also responded to their peers when those missteps were noticed, and they redirected the conversation to my strengths or lessons learned.

To be a sponsor across difference, you must be aware of the barriers to success that may exist for your protégé (both generally and specific to your organization) but may not necessarily apply to you so that you can advocate for their success effectively. Unfortunately, 71 percent of self-identified sponsors in a 2019 study conducted by global consulting firm, Coqual, reported that their protégés share their gender or race. Therefore, when sponsoring talented employees in your organization, pay attention to difference. If most of the leaders in your organization share your key identities, your sponsorship may be vital to helping your organization as well as your protégé by helping create a more diverse set of leaders in the future.

» Becoming an organization people want to work for

» Knowing how inclusion can drive creativity and innovation in your company

» Ensuring your staff are safe and healthy

» Providing an environment where employees feel valued and engaged

» Keeping employee complaints and lawsuits to a minimum

» Retaining talent and top performers

Chapter **4**

Making the Case for DEI

D iversity, equity, and inclusion have long correlated to organizational success in the forms of profitability, productivity, innovation, and talent engagement and retention. In this chapter, you discover examples of how DEI enhances performance in these areas and how you as a leader can contribute to furthering your organization's performance through effective DEI practices.

Making the case for DEI has been an ongoing conversation for decades. As a former chief diversity and inclusion officer (CDIO), I was often asked to do so as a first step in my role so that I could justify my request for securing more staff, dollars, and other resources. What was disappointing was that after a decade of seeing the demographic shifts and the proliferation of the role of CDIOs, I would've thought that this need was obvious. Being asked to "prove" that DEI should be an important organizational priority became a red flag that the company wasn't as serious as it touted publicly about its commitment to DEI or that it was so out of touch with the realities of the changing workforce that it needed to be educated and convinced. Many of my DEI colleagues who are CDIOs still share their frustrations of going through these futile exercises of "making the case" only to be met with resistance and denied necessary resources.

Even today as a global workforce consultant, I get requests from many of my clients who are just starting their DEI journeys (yes, just starting) that I help them make the case to their senior leaders so they can justify the costs of implementing a DEI strategy and hiring a consulting firm as a partner. So because companies are still asking, I've written this chapter to provide a detailed explanation of how DEI enhances organizational performance.

REMEMBER

When diversity wins, you win and your organization wins; it really is that simple. The challenge is determining what specific DEI practices your workplace needs to implement, update, discontinue, or expand.

Recognizing DEI's Impact on Organizational Success

Research has proven over time that DEI programs and practices contribute to overall organizational success, such as increased profits, employee satisfaction, innovation, and positive brand reputation in the marketplace. In turn, the companies that lack diversity are likely to suffer downturns in these same areas. For example, well-known and highly profitable Fortune 100 global companies often experience public scrutiny because of their cultures of fear, retaliation, or distrust and/or their leaders' inappropriate actions or insensitive comments. Some of them are exposed through videos that go viral, social media protests, public lawsuits/settlements, or lists ranking the worst companies to work for. In today's digital world, a company's commitment to DEI can be traced and used as a competitive advantage (or disadvantage).

In addition to sharing the practical outcomes specific to the organization to convince executives of the impact of DEI, I also draw on the extensive research and external data that proves DEI's value and effects. Over the years, many global consulting and research firms have shown that DEI programs and practices equate to increased organizational performance across industries, sectors, and countries. Data that has been tracked across industries and comes from large samples of respondents helps enhance the organizational proof. Here are some examples from across the globe you can reference.

A 2019 study of 162 organizations in India analyzed the relationship between diversity management and DEI practices related to recruitment, selection, training and development, compensation, performance management, and organizational performance. Findings published in the *Journal of Asia Business Studies* include the following:

>> DEI practices positively influenced and impacted organizational performance.

>> Equity practices were the main influencer between DEI practices and organizational performance.

>> Senior management support was necessary to implement equity- and justice-based DEI management practices.

>> Organizations should establish company-wide equity- and justice-based procedures.

A 2017 Malaysian study published in the *American Journal of Social Sciences and Humanities* included 100 nonfinancial firms. It found that companies with greater gender diversity on their corporate boards had positively impacted financial performance.

McKinsey & Company conducted comprehensive research over a period of five years on DEI spanning over 1,000 companies in 15 countries: Brazil, Mexico, the United Kingdom, the United States, Australia, France, Germany, India, Japan, Nigeria, Singapore, South Africa, Denmark, Norway, and Sweden. It analyzed five indicators of DEI practices:

>> Diverse representation: Gender and ethnicity

>> Leadership accountability

>> Equity

>> Openness

>> Belonging

The findings stated that companies with gender diversity in executive leadership were 25 percent more likely to achieve above-average profits than companies who didn't have as much gender diversity in the C-suite were. In short, the greater the gender diversity representation within executive leadership, the greater potential to outperform financial goals. Here are other key findings from this research:

>> Companies whose executive leadership teams are made up of more than 30 percent women are likely to significantly outperform companies whose leadership is 10 to 30 percent women. But the companies in the latter group did outperform those with even fewer or zero women executives.

- ≫ Companies with the most gender-diverse leadership have 48 percent higher performance than those with the least gender-diverse leadership.

- ≫ Companies with higher levels of diversity have an increased potential and likelihood for financial performance.

- ≫ A common thread for the companies winning and leading with DEI is a systematic approach and bold action to strengthen inclusion.

Finally, the McKinsey study identified five standards for increasing DEI efforts and organizational performance:

- ≫ Making sure diverse talent is represented at all levels

- ≫ Holding leadership accountable for DEI

- ≫ Making the processes for promotions and so on fair and transparent and working to eliminate bias from those processes

- ≫ Creating a culture of openness and nondiscrimination, including targeting microaggressions

- ≫ Supporting all types of diversity

Becoming an Employer of Choice

Companies have come to realize that a key driver to attracting and retaining top talent is being known as an employer of choice or a great place to work. A variety of outlets compile lists of desirable companies, include the following:

- ≫ *Fortune* magazine's Most Admired Companies

- ≫ DiversityInc's Top 50

- ≫ Best Places to Work presented by the Great Place to Work Institute

- ≫ *Forbes* magazine's America's Best Employers for Diversity

- ≫ Working Mother 100 Best Companies by Working Mother Media

- ≫ 50 Best Companies for Diversity by *Black Enterprise*

- ≫ Glassdoor's Best Places to Work

So what does building a positive employer brand and being a great place to work take? Here are some attributes that companies who consistently appear on those lists share:

>> **Fairness:** Companies where employees feel like everyone is getting a fair opportunity and a level playing field consistently report more positive employee experiences.

>> **Trust:** Managers' and leaders' actions align with their words (they walk the talk).

>> **Safe space:** Ideas and diversity of thought are solicited and valued.

>> **Value alignment:** The company has a clearly articulated purpose, mission, and vision that align with its values.

>> **Communication:** Open and timely communication is key.

>> **Leadership accountability:** Leaders are held to the same standard as everyone else.

>> **Employee growth potential:** Growth opportunities are available for ongoing developing new skill sets and competencies.

>> **Benefits:** Competitive pay and non-compensatory benefits such as recognition, health and wellness programs, and flexible work arrangements are important factors.

>> **Care:** Workers want a caring and socially responsible company that gives back to its employees and the communities they serve and that contributes to making the planet better.

Which of these attributes does your company have that qualify it to be an employer of choice? Where can it improve?

Leveraging Inclusion to Drive Innovation and Creativity

Simply put, companies need diverse talent and diversity of thought and experience if they want to change, grow, and innovate. As the world changes, the demographics shift, and the marketplace, communities, and customers become more diverse, people are demanding that organizations they work at, do business with, and support look more like them and reflect their values. And the only way to get this outcome is to embrace, value, and leverage diversity. It has been proven to enhance creativity. It contributes to better outcomes to complex problems and to better decision making. Diversity can improve companies' bottom lines and lead to new discoveries and breakthrough ideas.

If you employ a wide range of people from various backgrounds, ages, levels of education, sex, LGBTQ etc., you're inviting a wide range of experiences, points of view, beliefs and ideas into the mix. Regardless of industry, field, or sector, the organizations that seek diverse viewpoints — across ethnicity, gender, age, experience, thinking, etc. — experience higher rates of innovation. Innovation occurs when all of these attributes come together to solve problems and create new products and services.

While technology companies are often touted for their innovation, other companies such as 3M, Merck, Tesla, DuPont, Toyota, Pfizer, Moderna, Disney, and SalesForce, etc. continue to be recognized on lists like *The World's Most Innovative Companies* by Forbes and Boston Consulting Group's *Most Innovative Companies of 2021.* Each of these companies have either streamlined processes to increase efficiencies, invented and launched new products in record time, made investments into future technologies that advance entire countries' interests, and that have integrated systems, leadership, and processes.

Formal innovation processes, roles, and skills are also critical to propel ideas and creativity toward execution, which is where value is delivered. I've worked with or know the head of HR or DEI at a number of these organizations I mentioned above and here are some common denominators they share for bringing out more innovation and creativity. Consider how you can use these to foster innovation in your own organization:

>> Host ideation sessions and brain-a-thons at all levels that open possibilities and new creative ways of doing things — that remove any limitations and constraints on ideas.

>> Allow for admissions of failure (without retribution or blame), such as ideas, projects, and programs that went awry. Then ask for lessons learned and what course corrections were and will be made next time.

>> Be consistent in inviting workers to utilize a suggestion box — and then publicize those ideas that were shared and implemented.

>> Engage your employee resource groups (ERGs) for ideas and solutions, particularly regarding new products and services for diverse markets. You can read more about ERGs in Chapter 14.

>> Benchmark against other organizations and identify leading or competitive practices that may work for you.

>> Provide the budget, coaching, equipment, and other resources needed to carry out new and innovative ideas.

TIP

As a consultant, one of my go-to resources is Coqual (formerly the Center for Talent Innovation). It stays on top of these kinds of trends and conducts cutting-edge research on the effects and benefits of DEI. Its study to discover how leaders and organizations can create a culture that fosters innovation and creativity found that productivity and profit were the outcomes of leadership investment into employee engagement. By cultivating difference and disruption, as well as encouraging open communication, it found that "true innovation thrives in organizations with an inclusive culture that values diverse ideas."

That means that you have to attract and hire workers who bring diverse backgrounds and perspectives; you have to diversify the seats at the decision making table, and you have to invite that diversity of thought. But don't stop there. You also have to value diverse ideas and even be willing to allow for the sharing of opposing/divergent thinking. These steps are what really require a paradigm shift and more education and skill building for leaders to learn how to exercise more cultural sensitivity, emotional intelligence, and inclusivity. These competencies and skills are what build more inclusive workplace cultures that enable *all* talent to feel valued and as though they have a sense of belonging and an opportunity to succeed.

I talk more about a culture of inclusion in Chapter 18.

Enhancing the Safety, Health, and Wellness of Staff

Today more than ever, the need to focus on the safety, health, and wellness of staff can't be understated. Even before the COVID-19 pandemic, the prevalence of mental illness among adults was increasing, as was the creation of corporate health and wellness programs. The most common of these include weight loss programs; gym memberships or onsite exercise programs; onsite health screenings for high blood pressure, cholesterol, and obesity; stress reduction; smoking cessation; and nutrition education.

Safety programs include CPR, self-defense, emergency response, and workplace violence. Though safety has traditionally been a regulation-based entity within an organization, employee safety, health, and wellness programs are a trifecta! They are not necessarily independent of one another but rather a collaborative effort that's a cornerstone to an inclusive organization.

REMEMBER

Companies must integrate the improvement of workplace wellness while decreasing the potential for workplace injuries and illness. Workplace health and wellness programs have seen significant increases over the past several years, and numerous research studies have found that healthy employees are highly productive, have reduced absenteeism, and have higher morale and greater loyalty to the company.

With that in mind, here are a few steps that HR departments can use in establishing a comprehensive wellness program. These efforts address not only employees' health and wellness but also organizational factors such as work environment, training and leadership, and corporate values.

» **Conduct a climate survey or health risk assessment among your employees to identify current health, wellness program needs, interest in participation, and expectations.** This analysis can occur through an anonymous online platform or through focus groups and one-on-one interviews. Also assess the usage and satisfaction of your current healthcare program, including your employee assistance program.

» **Establish a health and wellness committee — a group of leaders from across the company who can represent the interest and needs of various staff and locations.** They can also contribute to some of the other steps in this list.

» **Identify some best practices among other companies regarding what's working, what's not working, and how you can leverage existing resources available.**

» **Develop a strategy for your wellness program and solicit the support and input from senior executives as well as other key stakeholders.** Your health and wellness committee should participate in this process. Conduct a cost/benefit analysis because funding is an important consideration for how broad the services can be.

» **Provide education and training for physical and regulatory safety measures.** Create an environment for having conversations about mental health and fostering a "safe to speak" and psychologically safe culture.

» **Devise an organizational communication plan, including an internal website with resources, tools, and education for staff to access.**

» **Implement and evaluate the utilization of, effectiveness of, and satisfaction with the program and report results to senior leadership and staff.**

REMEMBER

As of this writing, the COVID-19 pandemic is still ongoing. As the world recovers from the global crisis and adjusts to a new normal of working, living, and doing business, organizations can't be slack in recognizing the extensive emotional, psychological, and physical toll it has taken on workers.

Improving the Employee Experience and Encouraging Engagement

The buzzword "enhancing the customer experience" has been around for years, but the notion of the *employee experience* is relatively new. While studying the guest and host experience, an HR leader in the travel industry discovered that the company could apply this framework to its internal activities. Many of the company's internal functions were outsourced, which made employees' experiences inconsistent. From that point, the HR leader took on the new role of global head of employee experience. Today, many companies have adopted this practice and are striving to implement programs geared to enhancing the employee experience.

Creating a positive employee experience

What does your organization do to create a positive employee experience? What do you do as a leader do? Here are some example practices you can implement. I realize that many of them seem incredibly simple, but leaders often underutilize them.

>> **Create meaning and purpose.** Workers want to feel the work they do is tied to something significant and bigger than they are.

>> **Provide clear objectives and goals for achieving performance.** Ensure that these markers are aligned with the company's values and that you're living the values.

>> **Identify worker potential and help workers grow and develop new skills.**

>> **Recognize and appreciate good work.** Workers want to hear "thank you" more than leaders think, and they like creative and fun ways to show appreciation.

>> **Give the "what" and "why" of tasks and leave the "how" to your staff.** People want autonomy and freedom to figure things out versus being micromanaged and/or prescribed that something has to be done a certain way.

>> **Admit when you make mistakes and use them as teachable moments for the team.** Allow the team to do the same and to share their failures and how they course-corrected.

>> **Treat each person as an individual and appreciate their uniqueness and diversity.**

>> **Allow flexible work arrangements.**

Seeing increased engagement

As you enhance the employee experience (as I discuss in the preceding section), increased employee engagement is a natural outcome. *Employee engagement* occurs when a company meets a person's psychological (emotional and social) needs so that they can excel in performance and productivity and connect to a higher purpose.

And that couldn't be more needed now. A number of research and consulting firms I've worked with over the years (such as Gallup, SHRM, Workhuman, Willis Towers Watson, and so on) have been surveying and tracking employee engagement for decades. Since 2016, the number of workers who report being highly engaged at work lags between 34 and 36 percent. Think about it. If only 36 percent of workers are highly engaged, that means that over 60 percent of people in your organization are disengaged, feeling unsupported, or detached altogether. I like to say these people quit a long time ago but just didn't leave.

REMEMBER

The main reasons that employees disengage are poor leadership experiences, toxic workplace cultures, lack of growth and development opportunities, unfair and biased treatment, and low or perceived unfair pay/compensation.

You can increase employee engagement in ways very similar to those I describe for creating positive employee experience in the preceding section. Here are the best practices I've used that have seen short- and long-term payoffs:

>> Give clear, compelling direction and vision that empowers employees.

>> Make retention strategies personal, not one-size-fits-all.

>> Offer meaningful and challenging work.

>> Invest in leadership development and people manager training.

>> Provide open, honest, and balanced feedback/coaching.

>> Maintain a focus on career growth and development.

>> Allow more flexibility.

>> Closely examine underperformance.

>> Recognize and reward high performance. Know what motivates your people.

>> Practice the platinum rule: Treat people the way *they* want to be treated.

>> Build inclusion into all your business processes.

>> Encourage participation within your employee resource groups (if applicable).

>> Conduct stay interviews. Be proactive in asking employees what they need, how you can better support them, whether they plan to stay at the company a year or two from now and why/why not, what challenges they face, and so on.

Review this list and check all that you're currently doing. Then make a separate list of those that you'll commit to implementing over the next 12 months.

Minimizing Employee Complaints and Lawsuits

You may be wondering what employee complaints and lawsuits have to do with DEI. At times, employee complaints and ultimately lawsuits result from employee dissatisfaction, employee disengagement, and underperforming organizations. One thing is clear: Organizations must clearly understand the laws that govern employment. The following are tips that your organization can use to safeguard from internal legal issues:

>> **Establish and maintain clear policies and procedures regarding employee incidents, employee grievances, termination procedures, and performance improvement.** Make sure these policies are accessible and readily available for all employees, including distribution during onboarding.

>> **Provide proper and appropriate training for all employees critical to their job functions.** You should also train workers so you ensure they understand the polices in the preceding bullet.

>> **Enact accountability measures to make sure all employees across teams, departments, units, and management levels receive fair and equitable treatment.**

>> **Maintain open communication regarding roles, responsibilities, and expectations and create an open-door policy with leaders.** Keep confidences and trust so that open communication can take place freely.

>> **Know the labor laws of every country, region, and locale in which your company operates.**

Avoiding the Revolving Door and Turnover of Top Performers

Having a top performer leave your company for a better opportunity can make your stomach do cartwheels. Why wasn't your company the "better opportunity"?

TIP

When your best people leave, pay attention to what they share in their exit interviews as to why they're going. What you take away from an exit interview can help you do differently going forward.

Having been one of those high performers who made the decision to leave my company, and having dealt with high turnover in multiple companies over my HR career, here are some of the most common lessons learned:

>> **Turnover is expensive.** The immediate cost of the exiting employee's lost productivity and the time and expense of acquiring and training new talent adds up quickly.

>> **Retention starts with onboarding.** I talk about the employee experience earlier in the chapter. Employees need to feel celebrated and appreciated when they come in the door. For example, the former CEO of one of the world's busiest airports would personally greet each new employee with a balloon bouquet, sweet treats, and a personal message welcoming them to the organization. This small gesture proved to be a major factor in making employees feel as if they belonged to the organization from day one.

>> **Remember culture, connection, and contribution.** In particular, the culture of the organization has to be inclusive, appreciate diversity, create a sense of belonging, and strive to be a great place to work.

>> **People don't leave bad jobs; they leave bad leaders and toxic cultures.**

Consider these questions for your organization and place a checkmark beside those that apply:

❏ Does the culture demonstrate value for employees and their unique attributes and offer career growth opportunities?

❏ Do employees feel connected to the culture?

❏ Are leaders good at creating and maintaining connection?

❏ Do employees feel as if the work they do is meaningful and contributes to the organization?

❏ Are leaders trained and developed to be able to lead more effectively across difference?

Chapter **5**

Hiring a Chief Diversity, Equity, and Inclusion Officer

Like many of the other aspects of DEI, the role and responsibilities of the Chief Diversity Officer have evolved over time. When I assumed my first role in DEI in the 1990s, neither the *E* nor the *I* was a part of the title. We didn't even have job descriptions for them. I was first asked to take on the role because I was the only Black female in my division, and most of my colleagues back then had the same experience. The role mainly existed in large or mid-sized companies, mostly for-profit organizations, and it didn't have the broad reach and global responsibilities that it has today, both inside and outside the organization. It wasn't even considered a profession.

Today, the role couldn't be more important. Even before the COVID-19 pandemic hit, the role of the Chief Diversity, Equity, and Inclusion Officer (CDEIO) was gaining greater tracking thanks to significant demographic shifts, the war for talent, the impending skills shortage, and the need for more inclusive workplace cultures. But that pandemic forced countries around the world to face the harsh realities of healthcare, educational, socioeconomic, and workforce disparities that it exposed in 2020. Women, Black and brown people, people with disabilities, and people over 60 years old were hit the hardest by furloughs, job loss, and COVID-19 illnesses and deaths. The racial and civil unrest following the murders of George Floyd, Breonna Taylor, Ahmaud Arbery, and others exploded, and the DEI work took front and center like never before.

In this chapter, I introduce you to the role of the CDEIO and its responsibilities and help you recognize when you need to hire one and how to position that person in the organization for success.

Tracing the Rise of the Chief Diversity, Equity, and Inclusion Officer's Role

Global calls for greater equity, inclusion, belonging, and accessibility have corresponded to a significant rise in the number of companies seeking CDEIOs. In Standard & Poor's 500 index, researchers found that the hiring of Chief Diversity Officers tripled over a 16 month period, with an average of about 12 new positions filled each month. Of that group, more than 60 firms reported hiring their first ever CDEIO after May 2020. LinkedIn Workforce Data reports show that jobs with the title "head of diversity" increased 104 percent from 2015 to 2020.

Consider also that discrimination lawsuits, complaints, and the public naming and shaming of companies on social media have become more prevalent. And anecdotally, my inboxes on both email and social media have been flooded with requests for me to consider applying for a specific CDEIO role or to provide recommendations to fill the many vacancies that now exist. Even diversity program budgets and CDEIO salaries have seen an increase; that's good news because I've witnessed over the years that in lean times, the office of DEI and/or HR is among the first to get cut.

Other factors that have greatly influenced the rise of CDEIO roles include demographic shifts in the workforce and the marketplace (see Chapter 2), the increased focus on employer brand and reputation (including the benefits of appearing on great-place-to-work lists), and pressure from inside (board members and staff) and outside (customers, community groups, and advocacy groups).

REMEMBER

A significant surge in hiring for DEI professionals and leaders is only part of the process; a great amount work still needs to be accomplished. Prospective employees are no longer focused only on finding the right job. Rather, they're also looking for the right culture and conditions to work in, the right leader to work for, the right team to work with, and the right type of work that challenges them and enables them to grow and to do something meaningful. And much of this consideration is tied to the role and responsibility of the CDEIO and human resources.

Knowing When It's Time to Hire a CDEIO

In order to effect real change with DEI in the workplace, the role of the CDEIO must be carefully planned, selected, and supported. With the huge increase in CDEIO hires over the past few years, many organizations are feeling pressure from their stakeholders (employees, clients and customers, investors, suppliers, and the community) to have a visible commitment to DEI. On average, most positions come about because the organization is reacting to key events such as the following:

>> Difficulty in finding diverse talent

>> High turnover, particularly among marginalized and underrepresented groups

>> Low employee engagement/low scores on employee satisfaction surveys

>> Employee complaints/lawsuits/settlements

>> Protests and national movements that put pressure on companies to act

>> Viral social media activity regarding something leaders have done

I know these motivators firsthand. One of my roles came as a result of the company's having settled a multimillion-dollar class-action lawsuit; it was under a *consent decree* (which settles a suit without admission of guilt or liability) that required it to hire this role. Others hired me because they'd received pressure from stakeholders, they wanted to comply with new laws and regulations that required them to reach more underserved markets/customers, or their boards had made the calculation that they needed to be more progressive in their DEI efforts if they wanted to remain relevant and be considered a resource for their members.

Which of these companies are you? Why did you hire your CDEIO? If you don't have one and are considered hiring one, what are the reasons?

TIP

When hiring a CDEIO, here are a few questions to consider:

>> What's necessitating that you hire this role? What problem(s) are you trying to solve?

>> What's your organization's level of readiness for hiring this role? Think about it on a scale of 1 to 10, with 1 being "not ready at all" and 10 being "completely ready". Consider why you rated the way you did and what your organization needs to do in order to be more ready.

>> If someone occupied that role in the past, what worked well and what didn't work? Think about how you can address/have addressed what didn't work.

>> To what extent do you have buy-in and support from your senior executive team/board of directors (if applicable)?

REMEMBER

Fostering a culture of inclusion, belonging, and high performance is *not* the CDEIO's job. Rather, it's every person's job. The CDEIO provides the vision, strategies, tactics, and expert consulting for how to achieve this goal.

Considering the Best Candidate for Your Organization

When searching for the best candidate for your organization, keep in mind that DEI work really took root in the 1980s and is still evolving. Diversity training was facilitated in the workplace in the 1980s as means to comply with laws and to prevent civil rights lawsuits. Also consider that DEI programs haven't always had adequate staffing, budgets, and organizational commitment. In fact today, many organizations are still asking for proof of the business case and that DEI work is worth the investment. (If that situation sounds familiar to you, check out Chapter 4 for help providing that evidence.)

There has been a lot of talk about who should be hired into the CDEIO role and what qualifications they need. Should they come from HR? Should they come from operations? Should they be a person of color? A woman? A person with a disability? Can they be a white male?

REMEMBER

Here are a couple of points to keep in mind when choosing a CDEIO:

>> The CDEIO should be an influential leader and champion for people within the organization, have a working knowledge of how the business operations run, and be highly respected.

>> A CDEIO does *not* have to be a career HR professional. I happen to be one, and it has served me well because 70 to 80 percent of the work falls on the people side of the business. But that was my journey. Others of my colleagues have come from sales, marketing, operations, finance, community outreach, and so on.

My advice is to seek out leaders with broad backgrounds that include being a change agent, influencer, strategic thinker, and results driver and having the ability to create metrics and drive accountability. The potential CDEIO must be able to effectively communicate across all levels and units of the organization. Consider individuals who have been informal DEI champions or who have served as an executive sponsor for an employee resource group (ERG). An integral part of the CDEIO role's success is that whoever fills this position knows the good, bad, and ugly of your organization's DEI journey.

Here is a representative example of a job descriptions of a CDEIO that will give you an idea of the types of functions, qualifications, and responsibilities for this role.

Chief DEI Officer

Job Summary (basic description)

The Chief DEI Officer will work with Human Resources, Professional Development, Business Development, and other business services functions to develop a DEI strategy that will be presented to the Board of Directors, and other key stakeholders and will support implementation of the strategy.

The CDEIO is responsible to ensure that all policies, systems, processes support the organization's DEI strategy, are inclusive and equitable, and ensure DEI goals are embedded into every business function.

The Chief DEI Officer will also work directly as a liaison to the DEI Committee.

Essential Functions

Develop and implement the organization's DEI strategy and programs to:

- ○ Enhance representation of senior leadership
- ○ Champion a culture of inclusion and belonging
- ○ Eliminate inequities and barriers to success.
- ○ Attract, retain, and advance top talent from underrepresented backgrounds.
- ○ Design and implement talent management processes and systems to increase diversity of leadership team over time.
- ○ Lead implementation of strategic DEI initiatives.
- ○ Represent the organization at external events; speak at DEI conferences and other events that advance our organization's diversity efforts; maintain relationships with minority organizations and participate in industry DEI forums and seek opportunities to work collaboratively with other Chief DEI Officers within our industry.
- ○ Work with ERGs to develop annual strategic plans, including requesting any budget funds, and identify opportunities to continuously improve their operations and effectiveness.
- ○ Partner with Human Resources to ensure that DEI is integrated and implemented in policy development, employee development, surveys, performance management.

(continued)

(continued)

○ Develop metrics for measuring the effectiveness of DEI initiatives and assess the outcomes of those initiatives; benchmark our organization's DEI initiatives against evolving best practices in our industry.

○ Work with the Communications Officer to develop and distribute internal messaging regarding DEI across the organization; ensure DEI communications reflect our values and are aligned with our priorities.

Qualifications/Skills Required

○ 10+ years of DEI experience in a professional services environment, including at least 3 years in a leadership role

○ Exceptional influencing skills

○ Excellent verbal and written communication skills

○ Skillfulness in motivating and coaching others

○ Strong business acumen and ability to communicate effectively across all levels

Educational Requirements

○ Bachelor's degree in a related area or equivalent experience or training

○ Advanced certification in DEI desired

As you can see from this example, the role of CDEIO is no small or easy task. It has evolved into quite a large role with broad visibility, responsibilities, and impact. In fact, the role is now certifiable (meaning you can become a certified practitioner, like me) and can be deemed a degree program. I know this because I used to be a guest lecturer for Georgetown University's master's program for Diversity & Inclusion Management. Yes, you can get a master's degree in DEI at numerous colleges and universities; some also offer it as an undergraduate degree and certificate program.

Positioning the Role at the Right Level

To whom the CDEIO should report is one of the most common questions I get when working with clients who are considering hiring one. Popular options include the CHRO, CEO, COO, and president. In my typical HR-speak, my response is "it depends."

Reporting to the CEO may feel like a huge badge of honor, but if the CEO is unavailable and uncommitted, it can derail your success. Likewise, you can report to a CHRO who's clueless about the importance of the work and deprioritize it because they think the work of HR is significantly different and more important.

REMEMBER

Whomever the CDEIO position reports to, they should have a dotted line and a direct line to both the CEO/president and the CHRO. If that isn't how the organization is structured hierarchically, then the CDEIO needs access to the CEO/president for frequent meetings and updates. The position should be set up for success from its inception and have executive support upfront.

I remember reporting to a CHRO in one of my roles with no dotted line to the president. The CHRO was supportive of my work and gave me a lot of autonomy, but I could see clearly that she wasn't knowledgeable about the DEI work and thus was uncomfortable articulating the DEI strategy and metrics and asking the president for the specific budget and resources requests I needed. It slowed my progress and caused me a lot of added pressure to get work done with little support from the president. If I'd had a dotted line to the president, I could've spoken for myself.

In other instances, the CDEIO role may report farther down in the organization, which may not allow them to have access to the CHRO or the CEO/president. In those situations, I recommend assigning an influential senior leader in the organization as a champion or advocate for the DEI efforts to ensure they get the support and traction they need. To foster meaningful and impactful change within the organization, the CDEIO must have a seat at the senior leadership table in the C-suite.

The following list illustrates the interdependencies of the CDEIO role and gives guidance on how to partner productively across the organization. These are the key areas where the CDEIO needs to have relationships established:

» **Marketing:** How do you communicate with and expand your marketing efforts? How is DEI integrated into this functional area?

» **Corporate social responsibility:** What type of nonprofit organizations does your organization support? Who are the people you serve? How do you serve?

» **HR/recruiting/selection/onboarding and retention:** How does DEI integrate with these HR functional areas?

» **Procurement/supply chain:** Does your organization have a supplier diversity program? How do you spend your corporate dollars in procurement?

» **IT:** Are your technological services accessible to all?

» **Learning and development:** Is DEI integrated in how employees' professional development is facilitated? Is career progression available for all roles?

2

Examining DEI in the Workplace

Evaluate how equitable and inclusive your organization's culture is based on the employees' experiences.

Identify ways you may be perpetuating biases, stereotypes, and microaggressions.

Track your company's mission, vision, and values to DEI goals. Create and communicate a DEI plan.

Chapter 6

Assessing Your Organization's Culture

The topic of company culture has been active in some organizations for decades, but it's now a global issue as more institutions are addressing organizational health. Company culture can make or break your brand and reputation among customers and top talent. It can impact employee productivity, engagement, creativity, and retention, and it can affect bottom-line profits and company success. At the very least, employees are demanding workplaces that are more inclusive, welcoming, and respectful; that create a sense of belonging; and that are free from harassment.

For some companies with legacy cultures (those that have passed down traits, practices, and stories from generation to generation) and others that have existed for more than a century, this change to the management process is extremely hard. But it's necessary in this era of accelerated change, increased competition, and overwhelming complexity, where the global workforce and marketplace is much more diverse, multicultural, and multigenerational and works more virtually. I cover these demographic trends in Chapter 2; this chapter builds on these realities and helps you understand why and how to conduct an organizational assessment and what to do with your findings.

You're never really done improving your overall culture; every organization always has room to grow and improve. I recommend conducting DEI organizational assessments every 12 to 18 months to help maintain a healthy culture and try to identify new ways to keep employees engaged, motivated, retained, and eager to do more.

Exploring What Culture Is

Culture is the collective behavior of all the people who are part of the organization formed by the norms, values, behaviors, and attitudes that the company rewards or holds in high esteem. Culture is the soul of a company, which means it can determine whether the business succeeds or fails. You can compare it both to a living organism that's continuously influenced by individuals and to the wind. You can't see it, but you can see and feel its effects. When it's blowing in your direction, it makes for smooth sailing. However, when it's blowing against you, everything is more difficult.

WARNING

Often, leaders ignore culture unless the workplace becomes toxic. Over the past few years, the news has been filled with stories of companies engaged in misdeeds that become public. And almost always, the stories attribute the actions to cultures that allow or even encourage the underlying behaviors. The companies experience damage to their reputations while also harming employees and, in some cases, society at large.

Every employer wants to think it has a great company culture, but that doesn't mean it does. What you see in your role as a CEO, chief diversity officer, or HR manager often differs from what actually goes on day to day between employees. Even healthy cultures always have room for improvement. That's why performing an organizational assessment is imperative — to check the pulse of how the staff is experiencing the culture, how strong or weak your culture is, and in what ways you can transform your culture into one of inclusion, belonging, and high performance.

TIP

You can assess your culture in multiple ways. The most common options include these:

>> Hire an outside firm that specializes in strategic and tactical organizational culture transformation

>> Have HR conduct anonymous surveys with employees

>> Set up individual employee interview/focus groups at all levels to see what they think

>> Schedule open town halls to start discussions around company culture and improvements

Using Benchmarks and Other Industry Standards

Across all sectors and industries, organizations are always looking for ways to remain relevant, reflect best practices, and/or outperform their top competitors. *Benchmarking* is one of the processes they use to determine the best standard of performance based on other companies' success. This process often involves studying competitors' products, services, policies, and practices to examine how they achieve a high level of performance.

It also works for human resources and DEI. Here's an example of how I first used benchmarking for a business need.

When I was completing my PhD program in business and organizational leadership in 2007, I conducted my first benchmarking study as a part of my dissertation study. At the time, I was a chief diversity officer (CDO) for a global utility/energy company in the Northeast, and I studied ten of the largest utilities in the United States. I benchmarked their companies' commitment to diversity and inclusion, the activities they implemented, what levels of support they had in resources and budget, and how they were tracking and measuring the impact of their DEI initiatives. It was the first of its kind for the company, but it documented what its competitors were doing in this space and how they were doing it. I was able to use that data not only to complete my doctoral program but also to build a strong business case for my DEI efforts. As a result, I was able to secure additional resources in my role as CDO so that we could catch up to our competitors.

Whatever methods or sources you use to benchmark, getting an understanding of where your organization stands in the marketplace and how far it needs to go to become more competitive, relevant, and successful is what's most important.

When my firm conducts organizational assessments for our clients, we use not only our team's expert knowledge and experience but also industry standards and benchmarks that have been designed and vetted by reputable organizations such as the Society for Human Resource Management (SHRM), which serves over 300,000 HR and business executive members in 165 countries. We use the SHRM Competency Model, which according to the society "provides the foundation for talent management throughout the HR lifecycle and helps organizations ensure that HR professionals are proficient in the critical behaviors and knowledge necessary to solve today's most pressing people issues and strategies." (You can view this model and additional materials at `www.shrm.org/learningandcareer/career/pages/shrm-competency-model.aspx`.)

Additionally, we use the Global Diversity, Equity, and Inclusion Benchmarks (GDEIB), shown in Figure 6-1, because they were vetted by 112 global DEI experts and 3 authors (I'm honored to have been selected to be one of those experts). It contains 275 benchmarks that encompass 15 categories with 5 progression levels: Inactive, Reactive, Proactive, Progressive, and Best Practices. It offers a systemic perspective on managing diversity and promoting equity and inclusion, and it guides organizations on how to impact systemic change in addressing all DEI issues. (Visit `centreforglobalinclusion.org` to find out more.)

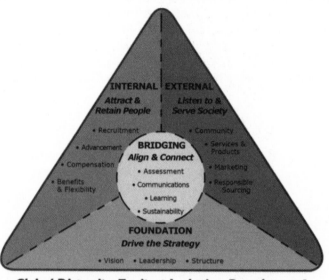

FIGURE 6-1:
Global Diversity, Equity, and Inclusion Benchmarks.

Adapted From the Global Diversity, Equity, and Inclusion Benchmarks: Standards for Organizations Around the World. Copyright 2021 Yvonne Kegomoditswe Molefi, Julia M. O'Mara and Alan Leon Richter. Used with permission. All Rights Reserved.

Additionally, we benchmark other models and frameworks from reputable consulting and research firms that study trends and best practices in HR, and we seek out companies that consistently appear on best-place-to-work lists because most of the scoring and ratings for these lists are tied to talent, workplace culture, and DEI.

REMEMBER

Benchmarking shouldn't be a one-time exercise but rather an ongoing business process that lets your company close any gaps and deficiencies that may jeopardize your ability to remain relevant and competitive in your industry, the marketplace, and the communities you serve. Additionally, it doesn't mean blindly copying what your competitors do. It simply means understanding what the acceptable standard in the industry is.

This due diligence benchmarking process forms the basis for assessing an organization. You can use it in the assessments and document reviews I discuss in the rest of the chapter to help you identify measures of success and create a DEI plan (which I discuss in Chapter 8).

Conducting Document Reviews of Policies, Processes, and Strategies

The *document review* is a process that provides initial insight into the organization's patterns, processes, practices, and language as they relate to DEI. Obtaining a baseline understanding of your organization's strengths and development areas is important because it gives you a snapshot of the current state and provides something to compare the progress of your DEI efforts against.

REMEMBER

Use both qualitative and quantitative (as well as internal and external) methods to assess the current climate in your organization. The assessment process focuses on identifying the effectiveness of your formal diversity and inclusion efforts and how they support or create barriers to equity within your organization. It also helps you find formally or informally sanctioned behaviors that can also prevent underrepresented employees from fully engaging.

A document review starts with a punch list (such as this one) of requested documents:

» **DEI Vision, Strategy, and Business Case**

- Mission, vision, and values
- Strategic or operating plan
- EEO statements, goals, and affirmative action plans
- HR strategic plan
- Diversity and inclusion strategy or plan
- Organization charts

» **Leadership and Accountability**

- Board of directors
- Past board and executive retreat agendas

» **DEI Structure and Implementation**

- Office of DEI staffing structure and budget
- List of DEI council/committees and associated charters
- Review of intranet site
- List of DEI council/committee/network activities
- Senior executives as sponsors/champions

» Recruitment and Selection

- Candidate sourcing and recruiting process (requisitions, internal/external job postings)
- Tracking open positions
- Diversity recruitment strategy
- Process for posting jobs (internally and externally)
- Selection process (internally and externally)
- List of sources used for recruiting diverse talent (agencies, job sites, search firms, colleges, and so on)

» Advancement and Retention

- Performance management process
- Sample performance appraisal
- Progressive discipline policy
- Termination practices
- Exit interview data for past years including demographics
- Succession planning process and list of candidates (including demographics)
- Promotion rates and demographics

» Job Design and Classification

- Job families and descriptions
- Demographics of new hires
- Employee turnover by demographics

» Work Life and Benefits

- Compensation guidelines and pay increases
- Benefits package (employee leave, short- and long-term disability, child-care, parental leave, flexible work policy, retirement plan, and so on)
- Health and wellness (employee assistance program and partner benefits such as gym memberships, yoga classes, and so on)

The following are a few examples of how some of the documents requested may be evaluated:

» DEI Vision, Strategy, and Business Case

- Does your organization have a comprehensive DEI strategy that includes a mission and vision?

- Does it align with the overall business strategy?

- Is your DEI statement visible to your customer base (if applicable) and employees?

- Does HR have a strategic plan that includes DEI initiatives for each of its practice areas?

» Leadership and Accountability

- Does the board and senior leadership team include diverse representation?

- Does the organization have a clear vision of the business impact resulting from lack of representation?

- Are leaders being held accountable for implementing the organizations DEI goals and achieving results?

» DEI Structure and Implementation

- Do DEI initiatives have dedicated support at the senior level of the organization?

- Do teams, committees, or networks within the organization champion DEI efforts?

» Recruitment and Selection

- Is a process in place to attract and retain diverse talent?

- Do measures of success exist throughout the recruitment process?

» Advancement and Retention

- Are processes in place to ensure that talented employees have equal access to advancement?

- Is the onboarding process effective?

>> **Job Design and Classification**

- Does the organization review job requirements and performance standards at regular intervals?

- Does the organization analyze compensation to ensure females and people of color are compensated equitably?

>> **Work Life and Benefits**

- Does the organization assess benefits and services on an ongoing basis to ensure they meet the needs of a diverse population?

Conducting Leadership Assessments

Understanding where your leaders are in their DEI development, commitment, and ability to work effectively across differences is an important step to take early in the organizational assessment process. This can take the form of conducting stakeholder interviews or using survey instruments.

Stakeholder interviews allow you to discover critical insight into what leaders at the highest levels of the organization understand and how they view and prioritize DEI initiatives and strategies. They're conducted with select senior leadership in the organization, which can include the president/CEO, board members, senior executives, and other key leaders. Utilizing a specific set of questions in a confidential setting, leaders provide thoughts and insights that inform, guide, and direct DEI efforts going forward. The following are examples of questions/prompts used in a 60-minute interview:

>> Describe the culture of your organization.

>> What can the organization do differently over the next 12 months to be more inclusive and to demonstrate greater value for diversity?

>> What are some perceived or real obstacles in your organization that may prevent it from achieving greater inclusion?

>> As a senior leader, what role will you/do you want to play to ensure long term sustainability of DEI initiatives in your organization?

Leadership surveys can provide a framework to gauge cultural competence among your leadership team. They give the organization and individual leaders valuable intel on how their attitudes, beliefs, and unconscious biases weave their way into the organization and teams and create formal and informal barriers to success. These surveys also provide the organization with a broad overview of leadership training and development needs.

Several of the surveys that I have used include the Intercultural Development Inventory (IDI) created by two industrial organizational psychologists, Drs. Mitch Hammer and Milton Bennett; the Inclusion Skills Measurement (ISM) Profile developed by Dr. Helen Turnbull; and the Global Diversity Survey developed by Dr. Alan Richter.

Other popular tools you can use to assess leaders' differences in thinking, personality, and leadership styles include the Myers–Briggs Type Indicator (MBTI), DiSC Personality Profiles, CliftonStrengths (formerly StrengthsFinder), the Predictive Index, and the Hogan Assessments.

Conducting a Staff Inclusion and Engagement Survey

The *inclusion and engagement survey* is a very effective tool designed to help organizations foster a culture of inclusion and high performance where every employee feels valued for their contributions regardless of their background, ethnicity, culture, gender, language, organization, level, or other diverse characteristic. The all-staff inclusion and engagement survey provides invaluable feedback from employees regarding their lived experiences and perceptions as well as their suggestions for improving the culture. Results from the survey lay the groundwork for the next step, conducting focus groups, which I discuss in the following section.

The surveys include both quantitative and qualitative questions. The number of questions varies, but on average you're looking at 30 to 50 questions divided into several categories specifically designed to uncover areas that have the greatest impact on DEI. These categories may include feedback, employee development, fairness/respect/diversity, workplace flexibility, communication, and compensation. Employees usually take 20 to 30 minutes to complete the survey depending on the number of questions.

TIP

I've found that including five to seven write-in comments sections yields invaluable insights, examples, and greater context of issues identified in the culture.

The following gives some examples of questions typically asked on inclusion and engagement surveys:

>> My manager values diversity, equity, and inclusion.

>> Senior management values diversity, equity, and inclusion.

>> The company provides training programs that promote diversity, equity, and inclusion, including the understanding of differences, biases, and mitigation of unconscious bias.

- » The company works to attract, develop, and retain people with diverse backgrounds.

- » The company workforce across all levels represents the diversity of the community that we work in and serve.

- » I feel a sense of belonging within the company.

- » I'm comfortable sharing my perspectives and ideas without fear of retaliation in this organization.

- » Cultural holidays are mostly accommodated even if they aren't the holidays of the majority.

- » Senior management leads by example and proactively looks for opportunities to communicate the division's DEI values.

- » I have the same opportunities as my coworkers to enhance my professional growth in the company regardless of my background and difference.

Conducting Employee Focus Groups

You can conduct all-staff *employee focus groups* after the results of the inclusion and engagement survey are in. (Read more about that survey in the preceding section.) Focus groups provide the organization with real-life employee experiences and may help to uncover hot-button issues that arise from internal or external cultural topics. You can also use them to solicit recommendations for how the organization can improve in its efforts to be more diverse, inclusive, and equitable.

Focus groups should be small enough that everyone has time to share (10 to 25 people is a good size). I suggest limiting the sessions to 1.5 to 2 hours and between 10 and 12 questions. Here are a few examples of the types of questions you can use:

- » What three words would you use to describe the culture?

- » What are the strengths of the culture?

- » What can be improved?

- » What does it take to be successful?

- » Does leadership focus on DEI? If so, what does it do best?

- » How can DEI awareness enhance communication and trust between management and staff?

> » Being unwilling to change the status quo
>
> » Allowing stereotypes, microaggressions, and prejudices to rule the culture
>
> » Failing to see the true value of everyone on the team
>
> » Resisting feedback

Chapter **7**

Exposing Common Organizational Barriers to DEI

When deciding to make large-scale change, people from Western cultures often think in terms of what they must build to create the change they want to see. In the case of DEI, this approach may mean setting up an Office of Diversity, Equity, and Inclusion; hiring a chief diversity officer; conducting diversity and inclusion training; setting up a diversity council; and so on.

People from Eastern cultures have a different view of change. They believe that change is inevitable and not for humankind to make. The best we can do is influence the change. If you think about it, the world is changing — becoming more diverse, more global, more interconnected. And your companies and teams certainly feel these changes each and every day. So why don't diversity, equity, and inclusion just happen naturally? Why is the change so slow, and why does the work feel so hard?

Perhaps, in addition to the changes you build, you can also approach change another way: by removing the barriers to the changes you want to see. In this chapter, I don't write about the things you can start doing but rather the things you can stop doing, or at least do a little differently. That doesn't mean that what I discuss is easy; breaking an old habit is sometimes even harder than starting a new one. But some of your old habits may be getting in the way of allowing your organization to move in the direction of greater diversity, an experience of equity, and the feeling of true inclusion for your employees.

Looking for the Culture Fit

When evaluating job seekers or candidates for promotion or career-enhancing opportunities, people are often more comfortable with some than with others. This comfort encourages them to afford greater opportunity to those comfortable people — usually those who have a lot in common with them. When they don't feel an immediate ease with an individual, they experience that feeling as though something doesn't quite fit together. And it's that very notion of "fit" that stands in some people's way. Obviously, when those who seem to fit are also those who primarily belong to dominant identity categories (race, ethnicity, gender, sexual orientation, religion, and so on), this reliance can send your organization's DEI efforts sliding backward.

WARNING

Whenever I hear the words *culture fit*, I immediately have questions. So often, the term has nothing to do with organizational culture at all but is instead all about comfort. Remember, a little bit of friction creates sparks — and those sparks may yield the creativity and innovation that your company needs to outperform the competition. Doing things in a new way isn't supposed to be comfortable! And always doing things the old way won't get you very far in today's competitive marketplace.

REMEMBER

This isn't to suggest that "culture fit" isn't a valid concept. But when determining culture fit, be aspirational. In other words, look for the people who fit the culture you aspire to, not necessarily the culture that you have today. In fact, some companies speak in terms of "culture add" to establish this philosophy in daily practice.

For instance, if your team's future success relies on teamwork and collaboration, then perhaps the hard-charging, independent thinker (who may be fantastically successful elsewhere) isn't the best person for your team. Or, if you work in an environment where safety is vital, you may be correct to promote those who can work in a routine of checking and double-checking rather than those whose spontaneity borders on recklessness.

Finally, if you want your team to be open-minded, creative, willing to take calculated risks, then perhaps the best "culture fit" you can hope for are those who have viewpoints, areas of expertise, and opinions that aren't already represented on your team.

TIP

Rather than using "culture fit" to screen out candidates for jobs and promotions, consider being proactive about finding individuals who indeed fit the aspirational culture of your workplace. You can do so by

>> Clearly defining your culture, both in terms of your organization's values and the day-to-day behaviors that you believe will lead to business success

>> Communicating these norms and values as a part of your company's brand

>> Making your company's aspirational culture a key part of the onboarding process

>> Talking about your organizational culture with your team and letting employees know exactly what's expected of them

>> Rewarding employees who exhibit the organization's norms and values and providing constructive feedback when employees fall short

Resisting the Value and Need for DEI

Often, the biggest barrier to diversity, equity, and inclusion is simply an unwillingness to change. This desire to cling closely to the status quo sometimes shows up as overt hostility to DEI work but more often appears in the form of skepticism ("Do we need to do this?") or pessimism ("Might this make us worse rather than better?").

According to the classic Beckhard–Harris model of change, for any change initiative to succeed, the level of dissatisfaction (D), along with a clear vision for the future (V) and defined first steps (F), must be greater than the resistance to change (R). To put it in math terms, $D \times V \times F > R$.

Handling resistance

People generally experience *skepticism* about DEI work as a feeling of contentment about the way things currently are: "If nothing is broken, why fix it?" Of course, the idea that "nothing is broken" is usually demonstrably untrue to the marginalized people within your organization, but if they don't exist in sufficient numbers or aren't present in enough positions of power, their dissatisfaction with the status quo may not be enough to spur change forward.

Pessimism is a resistance to change that must be reduced for any change initiative to succeed. The basis for pessimism about DEI work is most often a misplaced belief that increasing diversity in an organization automatically means lowering standards of quality. Quite frankly, this belief is offensive to many (including me) because the only way to justify it is through believing that people who belong to dominant groups (white people, men, heterosexual and cisgender people, able-bodied people, people who practice the dominant religion, and so on) are smarter and more talented than those who don't.

However, even those who don't overtly believe in the supremacy of dominant groups can find themselves feeling pessimistic about DEI work based on a belief that the work is simply too difficult. "We can focus on that next year," some say, after another important goal has been accomplished.

Because skeptical and pessimistic arguments are often phrased as pseudo-intellectual debates, perhaps the first best tactic to counter both is data. You can find a wealth of research that proves that the combination of a diverse workforce and an inclusive work environment yields substantial benefits, including greater profits, lower turnover, more innovation, *and* higher quality. Having this data at your ready disposal is invaluable to you when you encounter skepticism or pessimism from others in the organization.

Overcoming fear

No matter how the arguments against DEI are framed, they're never entirely scientific. What underscores most skepticism and pessimism regarding DEI work (see the preceding section) is fear.

REMEMBER

An intellectual argument may win a few battles, but it will never end the fight unless you also take steps to address the fears that many powerful people harbor about creating a more diverse and inclusive organization. Here are few examples:

>> **Fear of change:** There's an old saying that only wet babies like change. And in truth, even wet babies who love their dry diapers typically don't enjoy the process of change much. Change can be difficult, and a few mistakes along the way are certain; those who are highly invested in a self-image of competence and success can be very threatened by even the idea of large-scale changes and the gaffes and blunders that inevitably follow.

>> **Fear of moral judgment:** In her famous work, *White Fragility,* Robin DiAngelo points to a very curious phenomenon among (mostly, but not exclusively,

American) white people: that for many, being called a racist is far worse than participating in a racist system. The same dynamic is likely true among many other dominant groups. Not embarking on DEI change initiatives keeps conversations about power, privilege, and the "isms" (such as racism, sexism, and ableism) at bay and allows those in dominant groups to continue seeing themselves as pillars of morality, without privilege or bias.

>> **Fear of hardship:** Although people who advocate for DEI often say that "everyone wins" when opportunities for all are increased, the detractors of the work envision a future where people are hired, promoted, and appointed to leadership roles simply because of their identities, resulting in discrimination against privileged groups. These cynics are mistaken about the nature of future opportunities, but they're correct when they suppose that they, with their privileged identity, may have less of a chance of being CEO one day. The hard truth is that not all straight white men benefit from the status quo, just the mediocre ones who may not rise as quickly or as high when more talent enters the pipeline and is taken seriously.

>> **Fear of failure:** For some, DEI work feels scary simply because it isn't always successful. For every organization that has invested in its workforce and its culture with tangible results, you can find another that tried but didn't succeed. Some business leaders are naturally risk-averse, and the DEI journey is never without risk. The only thing certain about these programs is the eventual demise of organizations who don't get it right — either because they fail or because they never even try.

Assuaging deep-seated fears is never easy, but if too many people in your organization are allowing their fear to show itself as skepticism or pessimism about the work, then it can sink a change effort before it has even begun. If an organization isn't ready for change, actions must be taken to both increase dissatisfaction with the status quo and lower the resistance to change. This shift can often take place simply through a force conversation. Diversity workshops that are highly interactive can give voice to those who are already dissatisfied, moving some skeptics to become allies. Town halls where senior leaders share their commitment to DEI, along with compelling arguments on why doing nothing isn't an option, can convince some in an organization that they have more to fear from doing nothing than they do from acting.

Many people, especially those in corporate, for-profit organizations, aren't used to enacting strategies designed to create emotional shifts in their formal, buttoned-up workplaces. But contrary to popular belief, human beings don't leave their emotions at home when they show up to work, and these strategies prove to be as important as any other in your DEI journey.

Perpetuating Microaggressions, Stereotypes, and Prejudices

A particular barrier to DEI success takes the form of harmful attitudes and behaviors. People from marginalized groups experience microaggressions, stereotypes, and prejudices on a constant basis, and for them, hearing senior leaders tout their commitment to DEI can be very difficult to believe. For them, it's often a case of their employer talking the talk, but not walking the walk — or living the company's values. For example, when the CEO gives a speech about the importance of diversity but direct supervisors are still overlooking marginalized people for promotions, minimizing their contributions, or showing favoritism to those who are most like themselves, it undermines trust that the company is really committed to DEI. Ditto for running ad campaigns celebrating Black History Month, Disability Awareness Month, Women's History Month, Pride Month, and so on when colleagues are still allowed to crack jokes about a person or make insensitive comments with no real consequences. It contributes to a toxic workplace culture.

Taking a closer look at microaggressions

The term *microaggression* was first coined by Dr. Chester M. Pierce back in the 1970s. Psychologist Derald Wing Sue defines microaggressions as "the everyday slights, indignities, put downs, and insults that people of color, women, LGBTQ populations, or those who are marginalized experience in their day-to-day interactions with people." The name may suggest that microaggressions are no big deal, but although each behavior may be viewed as a small thing, the cumulative impact of microaggressions over time can be very damaging.

This effect makes combatting microaggressions especially difficult for the targets to do without being viewed as "overly sensitive" or "angry about everything." In fact, microaggressions are often intended as compliments (telling someone they're "articulate" as though it's a surprise they speak English fluently or that they "don't *act* gay"). Therefore, the organization is responsible for teaching its staff about microaggressions and making its expectations regarding treating others with respect clear. Expecting those who are already marginalized to police others' well-intentioned behavior, possibly setting them up for further backlash, is unfair.

Table 7-1 outlines common microaggressions I've seen and heard used on a daily basis (and many of which I've personally experienced over and over). As you look at this list, try to identify the ones you've heard used in the workplace. Have they been directed toward you? How did it feel to hear them? How did you respond?

TABLE 7-1   **Common Microaggressions and the Messages They Send**

Microaggression (Comments and Behaviors)	Message It Sends
"Where are you from?" or "You speak English well."	Assuming one doesn't belong or is not from your home country
"I don't see your color."	Denying a unique attribute of a person
"You are so articulate!"	Assigning intelligence based on ethnicity
"I'm not racist. Some of my best friends are black."	Denial of racism and an attempt to justify it
"Why do we have to lower our standards to hire more women and people of color?"	The playing field is already level, and there is equal opportunity for all who work hard for it
Continuously calling someone the wrong name (especially when they have corrected you)	Devaluing the person's origin/ethnicity
Rolling your windows up or hitting the door locks when you see a black male crossing in front of your car	Assuming that they are dangerous
Following a person of color around in the store, or assuming that they cannot afford an expensive item	Assuming that they are a criminal; assuming they are poor
Assuming an Asian person is good at math and science or being surprised when a black person is an engineer, scientist, or mathematician	Assigning intelligence based on ethnicity
Not promoting a woman because you assume that she will start a family	A woman couldn't handle the job or is not cut out to be a mom and a professional
Dismissing or overlooking a comment made by a young professional, a woman, or a minority	Minimizing experience based on age

Sniffing out stereotypes and prejudices

According to the American Psychological Association (APA), *stereotypes* are beliefs or expectations about the members of a group or social category. Stereotypes generally don't allow for natural human variation within a group.

Microaggressions, which I discuss in the preceding section, are often based on harmful stereotypes. For instance, telling someone in a minority ethnic group that they speak English very well assumes at least a couple of things:

>> That "good English" is unusual from someone of their background

>> That English must not be their first language

To the recipient of this "compliment," it's a reminder that they're perceived to be an "other" within their community, even if they were born in the United States and speak only English. The stereotype that informed this microaggression is that people from this group aren't *really* American in the same way people from the dominant group are. Instead of feeling good about their linguistic skill, this person is likely to leave this interaction feeling insulted and excluded.

The APA defines a *prejudice* as "a negative attitude toward another person or group formed in advance of any experience with that person or group." Like stereotypes, a prejudice places a person's identity marker above their basic humanity. These overtly negative assumptions can be very damaging and even dangerous. A former colleague of mine who uses a wheelchair tells a story about a work lunch where the person next to him began to cut his food in tiny pieces without asking, based on the prejudice that having a disability in his legs rendered him completely helpless in all other aspects of life. Men who harass women sexually in the workplace are usually operating under the belief that a woman's sexuality should always be available to the men around her — or even that women are merely sexual objects, not human beings with intelligence or dignity.

WARNING

Obviously, sexual harassment is a severe act, not a microaggression, but some organizations and industries, particularly those where women are starkly underrepresented, are rife with this kind of behavior. Organizations and leaders must make a real effort to combat especially the sexist stereotypes and prejudices that exist within their company walls in an effort to stave off the words and actions that result from them, be they annoying or truly destructive. Unlike many microaggressions, the potential for litigation and consequences is very probable.

Overlooking Hidden Figures Who Are Overperforming but Undervalued

The award-winning movie *Hidden Figures* portrayed the race between the United States and Russia to put a man in space. NASA found untapped talent in a group of three brilliant female African American mathematicians — Katherine Johnson, Dorothy Vaughan, and Mary Jackson — who overcame gender and race bias to make space history. The movie generated conversations and articles all over the world about leadership, inclusivity, how to shine at work, and how to identify hidden figures in your organization.

Hidden figures are workers with great potential but minimal opportunity to showcase their talent. They may be in the minority (based on their unique and diverse identities). They may not speak up or boast about their results, but they're working hard, making sacrifices, and keeping their heads down, and they're invested in the company's success.

In my work with clients, I find that too many leaders are still overlooking these hidden figures on their teams or in their divisions because they have people they consider their favorites or their "star performers," and their biases or blind spots cause them to default to what's comfortable, common, and known to them. They also spend a lot of time trying to get the underperformers back on track for their sake and the company's, so naturally something gets overlooked. And in this case, it's the talent that you also don't want to lose.

Who may be the hidden figures on your team? Is it possible that you have people in your organization who are overperforming but undervalued? Who do you keep selecting as your "go-to" resources? Have you considered that others on your team may have the answer or solution? Or that others are screaming with their hands in the air, "Pick me, pick me!"

TIP

If you do identify some hidden figures, ask yourself these questions about them:

>> Do you know how they typically spend their workdays?

>> What are their career aspirations?

>> Are they working against clear and easily measurable goals? If so, how would you rate their success? (If not, why not?)

>> Do they speak up in meetings? If so, what value do they add? If not, do you interpret their silence as a lack of anything to contribute?

>> If they left your team tomorrow, what skill gaps would exist? How long would you need to find and upskill someone to replace them?

REMEMBER

No one likes to be taken for granted. An organization that promotes diversity, equity, inclusion, and belonging well advances these values for everyone at the organization, not just those who call attention to themselves.

Minimizing the experiences and contributions of underrepresented talent

The hidden figures in your teams may also belong to marginalized groups who are underrepresented in your company, and that's not a coincidence. Often, children who belong to marginalized groups are coached by their parents not to call attention to themselves. "Just keep your head down," they may have been told, "and let your work speak for itself." This mindset occurs because calling attention to yourself when you're already the target of unfair stereotypes and prejudices often brings more negative attention than positive attention. (You can read about stereotypes and prejudices earlier in the chapter.)

Publicizing their accomplishments usually brings members of dominant groups mostly acclaim, but it often gets those outside the dominant groups accused of arrogance, false pride, self-promotion, or even deceit. Sadly, these patterns often persist in the workplace, causing the people of color, women, LGBTQ people, people with disabilities, or other disenfranchised identities to avoid announcing their successes while still hoping that the quality of their work will be noticed.

Unconscious bias also plays a role in this phenomenon. As I discuss in detail in Chapter 15, *biases* are implicit decisions that your brain makes on your behalf. One bias (among hundreds identified by psychologists and social scientists) is known as *performance bias,* which judges people from dominant groups (for example, white, male, heterosexual, able-bodied) based on perceived potential while judging others based solely on accomplishments. In other words, everyone, regardless of identity, can experience a tendency to force people from marginalized groups to prove they can do something but assume people in dominant groups can do it.

Performance bias affects not only evaluators but also those being evaluated. Because of the way they've been consistently treated, people from marginalized groups are less likely to believe they'll be good at something they've never tried, whereas those who belong to multiple dominant groups may overestimate their own untested potential.

To combat this type of bias, organizations should decide how much perceived potential should matter and then standardize promotion criteria in a way that forces equitable behavior. Without a deliberate and enforced structure, organizations are liable to slip back into performance bias without realizing they're doing so.

Relying on favorites and go-tos

Do you have a star performer on your team that you can always trust in a pinch? That's understandable. As a leader, you never know when an emergency will happen, and you need to know who to turn to.

But leaders can easily become over reliant on their star performers, handing them every high-profile or challenging assignment even when it's not an emergency. This habit can be bad news for the hidden figures on your team who are often ready for a stretch assignment that never comes their way, but it can also tax your star performers, who are juggling multiple projects while the rest of your team sits idle.

Wanting to keep your star performers busy is natural, but the next time you put them on a great assignment, consider asking them to act as a mentor for another team member. If your star performer has never been a people leader, you can take advantage of their excellent skill set while providing stretch assignments for them and for another member of your team who will benefit from the high-profile, challenging work.

Silencing and Ignoring Employee Complaints

A big mistake leaders often make is failing to listen when teams tell them that something isn't working. Lodging a complaint, even informally, generally takes some courage for an employee, and when you hear dissatisfaction, you need to respond. Unfortunately, staff members who do complain are all too often ignored — or worse, leaders do respond, but by swiftly communicating their displeasure. Those employees aren't likely to speak up again after the bonds of trust have been broken.

Obviously, you can't respond to every complaint in a way that completely satisfies every complainant. Some ideas for improvement will be unrealistic or conflict with the mission, values, and vision of your organization. However, many employee complaints are entirely valid, and for everyone willing to make a complaint, many other employees are typically in silent agreement.

In these cases, giving your employees a fair listen is important. This point is especially true for employees from marginalized groups because harmful stereotypes about disenfranchised communities are often exacerbated when a member of a group steps forward with something negative to say, and these groups are far more likely to remain quiet. As a leader, inequities, microaggressions, and all policies, processes, or behaviors that lead to exclusion are your responsibility, whether they reach your ears or not. If these dynamics exist on your team, hearing about them is far better than not hearing about them.

Because making a complaint requires so much bravery to begin with, a system where employees can give feedback anonymously if they want to (perhaps online), is best. Making it easier for your staff to complain may seem counterintuitive or foolhardy, but doing so makes spotting trends among the members of your team much easier. You can also encourage staff to give both positive and negative feedback and to attach suggested solutions to negative feedback when possible. Positive feedback and suggested fixes to perceived problems not only make the feedback easier to read but can also be extremely valuable for leaders. Knowing what your staff is excited about or grateful for makes you far more likely to replicate those successes, and hearing solutions that you may not think of just brings more creativity and innovation to the workplace.

TIP

When you launch your diversity, equity, and inclusion programming, people will likely complain. But even those complaints need a response, even one just to say that the organization is proud to work toward its DEI goals. The complainant likely won't like that response, but it will mean a great deal to a great number of your staff and make your intentions very clear.

REMEMBER

Feedback is truly a gift, especially negative feedback that a leader may take personally. Ultimately, your team's productivity, culture, and sense of belonging are your responsibility, and any knowledge that can help you navigate these dynamics does make that job easier, even when it feels hard.

Chapter **8**

Positioning DEI as an Organization's Strategic Priority

Proclaiming the importance of diversity, equity, and inclusion for your organization without a strategic plan is like packing for a vacation but having no place to go.

In the early days of DEI consulting, organizations commonly spent thousands of dollars on DEI training for their employees. Senior leadership attended only abbreviated sessions, if any. After a while, employees who had taken the training would move on to other organizations, and new employees would then take the same training. It was a continuous cycle. However, the training never resulted in any real organizational change. Why? Because the training was just a stand-alone program, not part of a strategic plan for change.

REMEMBER

Looking for a quick solution or bringing in someone to lead a "flavor of the month" topic discussion may be tempting, but training alone that isn't tied to a long-term DEI culture strategy may be a big waste of money. You save money in the long run by spending money in the beginning to develop a DEI plan. Too often, organizations spend money on diversity-related training, anti-bias education, and diversity, equity, and inclusion events that go nowhere. Without a DEI plan, no real change happens.

Without investing in a DEI plan, you end up wasting money, time, and resources because no one knows where they're going after the training, why they're taking it, or how it impacts them and their work.

In this chapter, I talk about how to integrate DEI into your organization's strategic plan, how to create a DEI plan, and how to align it with performance goals and objectives. I also walk you through how to share the plan across the organization.

Embedding DEI into the Organization's Mission, Vision, and Values

I was at an event with the CEO of a mid-sized organization who spoke at some length about how important DEI was to him. He told me he was working on recruiting a more diverse workforce but couldn't attract enough people. Later, when I looked up the company's website, I found no mention of diversity, equity, or inclusion in the About Us section on mission, vision, and values. And no one in leadership reflected visibly diverse demographics. That told me a lot about how serious the company was about diversity. But that's exactly what top talent is looking for. If no one looks like those you're trying to attract to work at your organization and the mission, vision, and values don't even mention DEI, you'll have hard time convincing anyone about how serious you are.

When you create a DEI plan for your organization, it needs to align closely with your organization's strategy. This match helps people see DEI as a critical factor for organizational success. And the best way to do that is to begin the process by embedding DEI into your organization's mission, vision, and values.

Doing so reinforces to your employees, job seekers, customers, and potential customers what you believe as an organization, where you're going, and what's important to your organization. It also demonstrates that you have a strategy and a commitment to taking action, something more and more customers are demanding from companies they do business with.

Consider these questions:

>> Why is DEI important to you?

>> How can it help you thrive or grow as a business?

>> Do you follow a business-to-consumer model that must appeal to an ever-changing customer base in order to succeed? If so, you need people within your organization who mirror your desired customer base, and they need to work in a culture that values their input.

>> Do you depend on innovation to compete in the marketplace? If so, you need to assemble diverse and dynamic teams that are more creative and inspired than your competition.

>> Are you a nonprofit or educational institution that exists to serve your community? If so, you need the diversity to understand your community's needs.

>> Are you in the business of providing healthcare, law enforcement, business loans, housing, and other similar industries where studies have shown to have significant disparate treatment? If so, you need to understand how to address and mitigate those disparities.

REMEMBER

Whatever your organization exists to do, a commitment to DEI will likely help you do the job better and reach a broader market. If you can make the connection clear in your mission, vision, and values, then the DEI plan you create from that won't be something that pulls focus away from your essential business functions but rather is directly tied to them.

After you've embedded DEI into the organization's mission, vision, and values, examine the rest of your organization's strategic plan and make sure that the goals, objectives, and measures for success it contains are aligned with the renewed focus on DEI. The following are some tips that can help you carry out this alignment more effectively:

>> Don't just say you value diversity, equity, and inclusion and leave it at that. Explain what you mean and why.

>> Identify the need for DEI in your workforce (your people), your workplace (the company culture), and the marketplace (customers and stakeholders) and communicate these needs as a business imperative.

>> Articulate why DEI is necessary in order for your organization to reach its vision. Include language in the vision statement that directly mentions diverse employees, customers, students, patients, and so on and the inclusive culture your employees need to achieve their goals

>> Ensure that respect for difference or equitable access to resources, opportunities, and success are laid out in your organization's core values.

REMEMBER

When you include DEI in your mission, vision, and values, you'll be expected to show the actions you're taking now and the actions you plan to take.

Creating a DEI Plan

When you've planted the seeds for effective DEI in your organization's mission, vision, values, and strategic plan, you're ready to create a plan specific to DEI. Basically, a DEI plan presents a vision for the desired state of the organization, identifies the current state, and then creates a plan to get from that point to the goal point.

A DEI strategic plan is your road map to create an inclusive culture that supports diversity, equity, and inclusion in every system and process. Training alone is just a one-time event. Employee Resource Groups (see Chapter 15) that operate outside of a strategic plan can quickly devolve into social clubs as opposed to hubs for culture change or informed business decisions. Implementing the right strategic plan means that as people come and go — even the CEO — you have a brand and a culture that attracts, hires, and retains people who can excel and contribute their genius.

The right strategy helps you identify your strengths and challenges and determine where you need to direct your time, energy, and money to get the results you want. DEI isn't a set-aside. It must be integrated into all your business systems and processes. DEI as a strategic business priority is essential to be able to serve your diverse customer base, do business with people across the globe, and create a culture where employees from diverse backgrounds can thrive and be successful.

REMEMBER

For a DEI plan to be successful, it should include key stakeholders from across the organization. Otherwise, it may be perceived as one person's plan, not that of a broad group of leaders. You can't develop a successful DEI plan in a vacuum, void of the organization's mission, vision, values, and its goals and objectives. You have to position it as an *enabler*, meaning a DEI plan alone doesn't drive sustained change. It should be integrated into every aspect of the operation, from the HR function to the marketing and branding initiatives to the organizational communications to the social responsibility activities and so forth.

TIP

Bring in an outside consultant to facilitate this process because they bring objectivity and expertise in DEI and group dynamics. Doing so also allows everyone with a stake in the outcome of the plan to participate fully.

I've facilitated DEI strategic planning sessions for countless organizations and highly recommend that the participants include the following types and levels of leaders: the president, CEO, the head of human resources, the chief diversity and inclusion officer, division and regional leaders, DEI council members, employee resource group sponsors, and sometimes members of the organization's board of directors/trustees/governors. Having these levels of leaders involved in the process is important regardless of whether you're a for-profit or nonprofit because the strategic plan should represent multiple voices, perspectives, and experiences and be a collaborative and cross-organizational initiative.

Starting with a vision for the future

In the DEI planning session, the first step I take is to guide the group through a visioning exercise. I ask leaders to consider the following questions as a starting point for envisioning the future state. How would you answer these for your organization?

>> With no limitations, such as budget, staff, or fear of failure, what do you want to accomplish with regards to DEI in three to five years?

>> If you achieved those accomplishments, what would success look like?

>> What values and guiding principles do you need to live by to realize those accomplishments?

>> Considering your DEI journey thus far (over the past two years), what accomplishments are you most proud of?

All ideas are captured, and none are shot down. We work in groups to identify common themes and alignment with any organizational assessments that occurred prior to the session. This activity can take a few hours to facilitate, and I consider it part one of a series of sessions.

REMEMBER

Knowing where the organization is currently is essential so that as you envision the future you know where you need to focus your energy, resources, and budget dollars. After the visioning exercise, I often lead the discussion with a whiteboard exercise describing the current state. I don't start with that exercise because I like to keep the focus on what's possible and not be limited with what can't, hasn't, and may not change. That kind of negative energy often derails the conversation on what the future can look like, but I do believe talking about the current state in this first session is important.

TIP

Refer to the strategic plan throughout and keep these tips in mind when the brainstorming is complete:

» Ensure that the resulting statements support the organization's overall mission, vision, and values.

» If you're working in an organization with locations around the world, be sure that statements are applicable to all key geographies but broad enough to allow for relevant local interpretation and implementation.

» Determine what success looks like in every system and process. Describe success in observational ways (for example, not just how people would feel but how they'd behave and what results they'd achieve).

» Create a section for each goal with a specific action along with milestones for achievement.

» Identify success metrics for each area and for individuals, managers, and departments/teams.

Taking the steps to make it happen

After you have a vision for the future (as I discuss in the preceding section), follow these steps to develop your DEI plan:

1. **Establish norms.**

   Begin by agreeing on specific ground rules for your work together. Here are a few that I recommend:

   - **Listen first to understand and then to respond.** Especially when hearing a viewpoint that you don't immediately agree with, take the time to consider the other person's point of view. Treat their opinions as just as valid for them as yours are for you.

   - **Lean into discomfort.** Conversations about DEI aren't always easy. If the conversation makes you feel a little uncomfortable, you're probably learning something.

   - **Make sure everyone has a voice.** Everyone who has been invited has value to add. In this room, viewpoints that come from leaders aren't inherently more valuable than those coming from people elsewhere in the hierarchy.

   - **Honor confidentiality.** So everyone can feel free to say what's truly on their minds, let's agree to keep these conversations confidential. Take what's learned here, leave what's said here.

- **Assume positive intent.** Operate from a mindset that people come with different experiences and perspectives. Assume that they're coming from a sincere place, with good intentions, and that they're invested in a positive outcome.

These are good core ground rules to start with. Always ask the group whether it has others that should be added to the list. Receive a verbal or visual cue from every member of the group that they agree to abide by these group norms.

2. **Review previous work.**

This information may include prior DEI plans; your mission, vision, and values; statements from leadership about DEI in the organization; and so on. If you can build on what came before instead of starting at the beginning, you increase the likelihood that your employees will be motivated by the work ahead.

3. **Conduct a SWOT (strengths, weaknesses, opportunities, threats) analysis.**

Brainstorm (in small groups at first, if that's helpful) your organization's current strengths, weaknesses, opportunities, and threats. As you build your plan, focus on capitalizing strengths, diminishing weaknesses, seizing opportunities, and mitigating threats.

TIP

During this portion of the work, I often like to ask people, "What do you think keeps your CEO/president/executive director up at night?" The answers don't have to explicitly be about DEI, but a powerful DEI plan can certainly address those concerns and give your organization's leaders a good night's sleep.

4. **Draft your DEI mission and vision statement.**

Borrowing as much language as possible from your organization's overarching mission and vision statements, draft a new mission (what we do) and vision (where we are going) specific to DEI that will drive every goal/objective of your plan.

5. **Identify organizational values that align with DEI.**

Take some time to identify which of your organization's core values can be leveraged to support your DEI plan.

6. **Identify areas of focus.**

Based on the work you've done thus far, decide on what your DEI plan needs to focus on specifically. Sample areas of focus can include the following:

- Hiring and recruiting
- Board development
- Mentoring and coaching

- Outreach and external partnerships

- Volunteer recruitment and leadership

- Policy review

- Learning and innovation

- Customer experience (for example, health disparities, academic performance)

- Product/process design

- Customer/stakeholder accessibility

- Programming and resources

- Marketing and branding

Lean heavily on your SWOT analysis from Step 3 to decide on these areas, and keep them to a manageable number. What are the three to seven most important areas of focus for the near term?

REMEMBER

Although the leader of the DEI efforts may not own each of these areas, they should be in partnership with whoever does. For example, if the company has a learning and development director, the DEI officer doesn't need to own the training courses but should partner with the L and D director to embed DEI learning and to determine ways to roll out new DEI offerings.

7. Draft action steps.

Craft goals and objectives for each of the areas you identified in Step 6. Decide what you'll get done in the next year and what will perhaps take longer. Identify follow-on activities. Remember that training can be very valuable when attached to a larger plan; don't forget to give managers, leaders, and all employees access to necessary knowledge before implementing new policies and processes.

After you've drafted your initial goals, see whether you can identify some low-hanging fruit among your ideas — steps that will be relatively easy to achieve within a short period of time (zero to six months) but will have high impact and visibility throughout the organization. Plan to implement these objectives first to increase enthusiasm about your plan throughout the organization.

8. Create milestones with deadlines.

Be both realistic and ambitious when doing this work; you don't want to set yourself up to fail, but you also want to feel as though you've really accomplished something year over year.

9. **Create a communication plan.**

   Don't leave your work without first determining how you'll communicate your plan to the entire organization. As I discuss in the following section, a dynamic DEI plan isn't worth much if no one knows about it. Your plan should include information about not only the plan's existence but also what's expected from every employee (and volunteers, if applicable) to make the plan a success.

Communicating the DEI Plan across the organization

Everyone in the organization needs to know the overall strategy of your organization and what specific DEI behaviors are necessary for that strategy to succeed. When I first began this work over 25 years ago, I was surprised by organizations that touted their amazing DEI initiatives but didn't tell their employees what they were doing. The only people who seemed to be able to articulate the mission, vision, and values and commitment to DEI were in HR. Line staff and operations weren't included in the message.

Fortunately, that has changed in many organizations as more leaders recognize the need to embed DEI in the organization's business DNA as I discuss earlier in the chapter. However, too many times employees never hear about diversity, equity, and inclusion outside of a random or isolated DEI training or event that isn't tied to the organization's strategic plan. In these cases, employees can't contribute to DEI efforts, and the organization doesn't undergo any kid of long-term, sustainable culture change.

I always say that you must do three things with any new initiative or change:

1. Communicate.
2. Communicate again.
3. Overcommunicate.

One email blast to the entire company announcing your DEI plan with an attachment for people to read is just the beginning of your communication strategy.

REMEMBER

When you don't share enough information with staff members, they fill in the blanks. In other words, you leave too much room for interpretation and rumors, only to have to manage and correct misinformation later. So overcommunicate in the first place.

Yes, some people in your organization will certainly be eager to read how you'll operationalize your commitment to DEI over the next three years. Others will be resistant to your message, and many more simply don't read company-wide emails as a rule and will be likely to let this one languish in their mailboxes, untouched.

Involving leadership

If you've done a good job aligning your DEI plan to your organization's core business needs, your CEO is likely excited about the plan and the opportunities it brings. If so (or even if it takes a little convincing), get your senior leadership involved at the very beginning of your communication plan. An all-hands meeting and/or roadshow — whether in-person or virtual — where the organization's most senior leaders have the ability to speak directly to all employees is a great way to reveal your plan to the entire company.

An interactive webinar (or better yet, a series of interactive webinars) can be a useful follow-up, where people can hear about the particular focus areas, goals, and objectives and ask questions about the plan.

TIP

I recommend this communication process be a partnership between the CEO/president and the chief diversity, equity, and inclusion officer. Showing this kind of visible camaraderie goes a long way with building the staff's trust and belief that there's commitment and buy-in.

Making it relevant

When communicating about your DEI plan, you may be motivated to speak mostly on your commitment to diversity, equity, and inclusion and how this commitment makes your organization a place where people can feel proud to work. That message will resonate for some of your audience, but most will be far more interested in how the plan will affect their day-to-day lives — both in terms of the changes that will be made and, more importantly, what will be expected of them.

Therefore, take the time to focus on the observable behaviors that leaders, managers, and all staff will be expected to exhibit and how the organization will hold them accountable for these actions. Focusing on behaviors, not feelings, is vital; mandating that all employees value DEI is impractical, and holding people accountable to values separated from actions is impossible. (For example, most people will already claim to value DEI regardless of whether their behavior aligns with their words.) Formal training is a good place to communicate these behaviors and, if possible, practice them in a safe setting.

Keeping the Plan Alive

The DEI Plan must remain a living document and priority in the organization so keep it the following practices in mind.

» Continue to communicate it to the organization so everyone knows what progress is being made.

» Include the observable behaviors and business results you expect with that commitment.

» Involve leadership in the roll-out. Communicate to your managers what you want from them and provide the tools, support, and education to help them achieve objectives.

» Remember that when you think you're done, you're probably about halfway there.

» Ask staff about the plan in formal surveys to gauge their current level of understanding and the extent of how the culture is changing to be more inclusive, respectful, and equitable.

» Use these performance goals to implement your strategic plan to create a culture of DEI.

» Keep in mind that no goal stands alone. Most of these are concurrent and not consecutive, although they may build on each other as you accomplish them.

» Align general performance evaluations, compensation, and rewards to those DEI performance success metrics.

3

Implementing and Operationalizing DEI Across the Organization

Set up a recruitment strategy that attracts a more diverse talent pool.

Discover how to provide growth and development opportunities with an equity and inclusion mindset.

Maximize the benefits of a diverse team.

Establish metrics for DEI success.

Find out where and how to embed DEI in every part of the organization. Enhance your supply chain with diverse vendors and suppliers.

Create employee resource groups that contribute to the organization's DEI goals.

» **Knowing where to find diverse candidates**

» **Making your job descriptions inclusive**

» **Weeding bias out of the selection process**

» **Prioritizing diversity on your interview panel**

» **Recognizing what kinds of interview questions you can't ask**

Chapter **9**

Finding and Recruiting Diverse Talent

Finding and hiring a diverse workforce is critical if organizations want to remain relevant in today's competitive and changing environment. With the demographics changing and reflecting a new generation of talent, you need to ensure that you're opening up new seats at the table. That includes starting with reviewing your existing recruitment strategies and implementing new and innovative processes that increase your candidate pipeline. It also means writing more inclusive job descriptions, adopting more inclusive language, acknowledging and interrupting your own biases in the interviewing process, and ensuring that you're asking the right questions.

Attracting, recruiting, and retaining diverse talent can be a daunting task for many organizations. As a former head of recruiting and also the lead for diversity recruiting, I can't tell you the many conversations I've had with hiring managers trying to convince them why sourcing and hiring more diverse talent was important. Consistently, they'd meet me with the proverbial responses of "we can't find any" and "we're only seeking the most qualified/the best and the brightest." It was as though diverse talent was lost or hiding somewhere and couldn't be found or the standards and qualifications would have to be lowered if a company had to hire diverse talent. In all my years in human resources, neither of these was the case.

Finding great talent wasn't the hard part. The real challenge was twofold: getting leaders to understand why they needed to focus on it and convincing diverse talent that the job, company culture, geographic location, opportunities, and pay were the best fit for them. So companies have their work cut out for them if they want to find and recruit diverse talent. It means having a recruitment strategy that's broad reaching, innovative, less biased, and more inclusive. This chapter reveals how to build those elements into your recruitment strategy.

Reviewing Your Recruitment Strategy

To attract, recruit, and retain top diverse professionals, you should start by thoroughly assessing where your organization stands with respect to its understanding of and its commitment to diversity. A strong recruiting plan consists of specific action steps taken in response to issues identified after this kind of analysis.

If your company wants to remain competitive in the war for talent and to be viewed as an "employer of choice" and a "great place to work," it needs a short-term and long-term strategy for both. I break down these strategies in the following sections.

REMEMBER

Finding and recruiting diverse talent isn't solely the responsibility of human resources. Contributing to this effort is every leader's responsibility and every staff member's expectation. So communicating your short and long-term goals to all leaders and staff and ensuring that everyone is aware of their role in achieving them is important.

Shoring up your short-term recruitment strategy

Short-term goals include setting targets for how you want to increase your pipeline and with which diverse groups — the groups that are most underrepresented in your organization or in certain divisions, departments, and levels. It also means:

>> Outlining your employer brand strategy and the candidate experience.

>> Updating your website with messaging that explains your commitment to diversity.

>> Identifying a diverse slate of interviewers.

>> Training your leaders on how to best represent your company during the recruitment process. That training can include behavioral interviewing, unconscious bias in decision making, and what constitutes appropriate and inappropriate interview questions as a start. I talk about interview questions later in this chapter.

TIP

You should determine which job boards and social media sites to use and how often to post positions in your short-term goals.

Looking at recruitment with an eye on long-term goals

Long-term goals include workforce planning to identify the kinds of skills, knowledge, and expertise your company will need in the future as it grows, innovates, and responds to the changing demands. This process also means doing some competitive intelligence to see how you stack up against your competition and to assess how attractive and appealing your brand is in the marketplace.

Long-term goals should also include how leaders will be held accountable for accomplishing the recruitment goals. They can include how leaders live the values; contribute to hiring, developing, and promoting more diverse talent; and to what extent they foster a culture of respect, trust, transparency, and inclusion where all talent can thrive. These can be measured on the annual staff engagement and inclusion surveys.

A thorough review of what works and what doesn't in current processes is crucial. As part of this assessment, be sure to review job descriptions to ensure that the language doesn't inadvertently exclude certain groups of individuals. Be sure that what you've listed as job requirements and qualifications are indeed required and that descriptions aren't written so specifically that they unintentionally favor a certain kind of person. I talk more about this topic in the later section "Writing More Inclusive Job Descriptions."

Long-term goals should include investing in relationship-building inside and outside your organization. That means determining which and how many partnerships and alliances to build, which and how many events to attend and sponsor, and how much of your time and money to allocate. You've heard the saying that it takes money to make money? Well, if you want to find and hire top diverse talent, it takes money, time, and effort to make that goal happen, too.

When I led recruiting, an entire team (not just recruiters, but hiring managers and the general staff as well) was necessary to participate in the number of career fairs, conferences, and community events and the employee referral program that were required to find and hire diverse talent. It was competitive and it was time-consuming, but we knew that it was necessary if we wanted to find and hire the best.

Boosting your diversity recruitment strategy

As you review your recruitment strategy, consider a few of these methods and resources to enhance your ability to attract more diverse talent:

>> Scholarships

>> Internships

>> University/graduate schools

>> Search firms

>> Diversity-focused job fairs

>> Employee referrals

>> Diversity-focused employment portals

>> Word of mouth

>> Diversity- or special-interest-focused job websites

>> Recruiters dedicated to or tasked with a focus on diverse talent

In addition, here are some questions you can ask to ensure your recruitment process is more equitable and less biased:

>> Does your organization require that a diverse slate of candidates be provided for hiring managers to choose from?

>> Do you conduct calibration meetings with the interviewers and the recruiters to ensure they make the most objective selection decisions?

>> Are all candidates applying for a particular job asked the same questions in the same way?

>> Are interviewers aware of the biases they may bring to the hiring process, and are they working to minimize them?

>> Does your organization work with external search firms and require them to target a diverse slate of candidates?

TIP

Technology should also be a critical part of your recruitment strategy (whether short term in purchasing new software or training staff on it or long term in identifying, upgrading, or implementing a new applicant tracking system [ATS], a new human resources information system [HRIS], or artificial intelligence). Depending on local or regional laws and regulations, your ATS can collect candidate demographics for you to ensure compliance, and it can measure the diversity, or lack thereof, of the candidate pipeline you're attracting. If you find you're not attracting the types of candidates you're looking for, you can test out different recruiting techniques such as increasing diversity in your recruitment marketing. Additionally, AI-powered recruiting solutions can be trained to perform objective assessments of skills, competencies, and talents while ignoring demographic factors like gender, race, and age.

Casting a Wider Net to Build a Diverse Pipeline

To increase the diversity within your organization, you need to expand your efforts beyond the traditional employee referral program and the same places you've always sourced for talent. In other words, you need to build new relationships, establish new partnerships, and begin networking in new and different ways. Many external organizations exist that serve diverse individuals, working not only to increase representation in the workforce but also to provide support, development, and resources for succeeding in the workplace. These are organizations that you should get to know, get involved with, and leverage as viable new channels to source talent.

Building relationships and networking

When I led recruiting, one of the major aspects of my strategy was to build and nurture external partnerships and alliances with minority-centric groups, associations, and organizations. At one time, I managed 23 of these that fell into categories such as historically black colleges and universities (HBCUs) and other educational institutions that had a high percentage of diverse students and alumnae. I also fostered relationships with organizations that catered to the specific needs of women, BIPOC, the LGBTQ community, military service members, people with different abilities, and older workers, to name a few, and partnered with organizations that served a variety of industries and sectors such as engineering, accounting, architecture, real estate, manufacturing, sales, and construction. I came to discover that nearly all professions have a corresponding organization for minorities designed to help them in job searches, skill development, mentoring, and navigating in the workplace.

REMEMBER

Building the relationships isn't enough; you have to cultivate an inclusive external network. Simply put, this means getting involved. Here are several ways that you can participate in local minority organizations:

>> **Sponsor or contribute to a local or national event or organization.**

>> **Make employees available to speak at conferences.**

>> **Provide internships, apprenticeships, and scholarships for minority students at local colleges and universities.** Generally, all candidates will naturally be attracted to organizations that have a public reputation for promoting a culture of inclusion and respect and are known for valuing all their people. Candidates from underrepresented backgrounds may especially recognize and appreciate this kind of sincere effort that extends beyond the everyday recruiting process.

>> **Take advantage of opportunities to network with diverse professional organizations and campus diversity groups.**

>> **Encourage current employees to join diverse organizations and become actively engaged in identifying diverse talent.**

Non-diverse recruiters should also be comfortable networking with organizations that represent diverse populations. Be sure to include non-diverse employees in your diversity recruiting activities. Diverse candidates can sometimes be turned off when you send only your diverse professionals to diversity recruiting or networking events.

TIP

When everyone within your organization receives training on how to increase their awareness, cultural competence, and ability to articulate your organization's diversity and inclusion commitment, recruiters, hiring managers, partners, and other senior leadership become better equipped to recruit across diverse spectrums.

Communicating your commitment to DEI

I can't stress enough the importance of communicating your organization's commitment to and position on DEI and its benefits to the bottom line and the company's overall success. I've found in working with numerous clients that they don't do a good job of telling their stories about the great work and the progress they're making in their DEI efforts. Leaders within your organization need to share the value of diversity and inclusion in depth with both internal and external stakeholders.

Use all corporate communication channels, such as your website, intranet site, company newsletters, social media pages, and press releases, to highlight the accomplishments and advancements of your inclusive work environment.

TIP

Be active in drawing attention to how diverse employees are succeeding in your organization and to the opportunities available to qualified employees along all diversity dimensions. Where appropriate, consider publicly sharing your progress in achieving workforce demographics, or applying for one of the many available diversity awards.

Companies around the world tout the list of awards and recognition that they receive for their diversity efforts. Doing so aids in reinforcing your commitment to DEI and appeals to diverse candidates who want to be assured that your organization is serious about equity and inclusion. A few examples of those lists include the following:

>> Great Place to Work

>> *Fortune* magazine's 100 Best Companies to Work For

>> Glassdoor's Best Places to Work

>> DiversityInc's Top 50

>> *Working Mother* magazine's 100 Best Companies and Best Companies for Multicultural Women

>> Disability Matters Awards

>> Workplace Equality Index

>> Disability Equality Index

>> Forbes' America's Best Company for Diversity

Writing More Inclusive Job Descriptions

Recruiting diverse candidate pools is a top challenge and priority for most organizations. But many organizations fail to take some basic steps to set themselves up to attract candidates with diverse backgrounds and experiences, especially when it comes to job descriptions.

A *job description* outlines the responsibilities of the position and the desired knowledge, skills, experience, and abilities to perform a job effectively. A good first step in creating an inclusive description is to evaluate how any position the organization is recruiting for can advance the company's equity goals and how such expectations and responsibilities can be integrated into the job description.

REMEMBER

A job description is often a candidate's first exposure to both the job and the company's organizational culture and values. The way you write a position is written — the words you use to describe the ideal candidate and the information you do or don't include — can speak volumes to candidates.

Job descriptions that aren't inclusive may limit candidate interest and make attracting diverse candidates that much harder. But when they're inclusive, they enable a variety of talent to more easily see themselves in a role and decide to apply. Writing inclusive job descriptions may require recruiters and hiring managers to reexamine what the descriptions should look and sound like. What message are you sending to the candidate about your company culture?

REMEMBER

Don't just list job requirements; focus on how candidates will contribute to the bigger picture. The better the job description, the more candidates (of all backgrounds) will want to apply. Be sure the job description absolutely matches the job you're hiring for. Nothing is more frustrating for a candidate than finding out the job is different from the job description.

TIP

Here are some tips for writing more inclusive job descriptions:

>> **Avoid language that may signal to underrepresented workers that they won't feel welcomed, included, respected, or safe in your workplace.** This includes gendered wording (such as *businessman, chairman, competitive, aggressive, ambitious,* and *challenging*) and terms like *fast-moving* that older workers may take as a sign the job is for someone young.

>> **Provide key insights about your organizational culture.**

>> **Don't use company acronyms or jargon, such as *guru, ninja in technology, is a self-starter, thrives in entrepreneurial environment,* or *is a blue-sky thinker.***

>> **Make sure your job descriptions don't include extra or unnecessary requirements, especially regarding education.** For example, requiring a master's degree when one isn't even necessary to perform the essential functions of the job may unintentionally restrict the pool of available candidates. In other instances, job descriptions that emphasize specific types of experience when competencies gained from other experiences would be just as applicable or useful can push candidates way.

Minimizing Bias in the Selection Process

It is natural for us to make certain assumptions about other people who are different from us. We assume that people who are most like us are more qualified than those who are not. These assumptions and stereotypes — also referred to as *biases* — are based on the messages taught at a very young age and reinforced over time through family, communities, schools, places of worship, friends, experiences, and the media. When left unchecked, biases can undermine your organization's efforts to recruit, retain, and advance diverse talent.

Recognizing that everyone has biases

Unconscious bias is an opinion, positive or negative, we have about a group or person. We make spontaneous judgments about people or situations based on our past experiences, culture, background, and from what we learn from watching and listening to the media. These spontaneous judgments occur within 3 to 5 seconds of encountering a person. Biologically, we are hardwired to prefer people who look like us, think like us, and share our interests. The attitudes or stereotypes that develop early in life (as early as 1 to 6 years old) are reinforced over time, and they affect our understanding, actions, and decisions in an unconscious manner.

WARNING

These hidden biases can impact us in a variety of ways, especially when it comes to interviewing and hiring. As a former head of recruiting, I have seen hiring managers prefer people who attended their college/university, or who grew up in their community, or had other commonalities that they shared, so they gave them the benefit of the doubt and were willing to hire them over someone who had very little in common with them. I've also seen where they assumed a person was not a good fit simply because they had an accent, and the hiring manager didn't think they would be an effective communicator. Other examples I've seen include hiring managers making negative assumptions about candidates who didn't give a firm handshake or who had several noticeable tattoos or didn't come dressed in a suit.

The hiring managers assumed that the applicants were not confident, that they would not be taken seriously by customers, and that they were not professional. These are just a few examples of how biases play out in the selection process. Consider where you have biases that inform how you view applicants and candidates. Think about the last time you participated in the interview process. Which applicants did you prefer and why? Which did you immediately make negative assumptions about simply because of how different they were from you?

REMEMBER

Because of our biases we may make some inappropriate or even bad selection choices. It's been revealed in research, and it's been my experience that many hiring decisions are made within the first five to ten minutes of an interview. These decisions are not made on whether or not the person is qualified or capable of performing the job. These decisions are made on first impressions, which come from our biases. Referred to as *social categorization,* we routinely and quickly sort people into groups. The problem with this is that the categories we use to sort people are not necessarily logical or legal.

So if we have these hidden biases, what can we do about it? The good news is there are some processes you can put in place to counteract these biases.

First, ensure that all hiring managers and interviewers attend unconscious bias training and behavioral interviewing training so that they are aware of how theirs can inform and impact their selection decisions, as well as what questions are permissible and which are illegal/inappropriate. Be clear on what are the *required* versus *optional* skills needed to perform the job. Identify what knowledge, skills, competencies, and attitudes are needed and/or preferred for the job. And then create interview questions that will enable the interviewers to assess if the candidate meets the requirements of the job.

TIP

Behavioral-based interviewing can help you avoid making selections based on assumptions or intuitions or solely on credentials. It is based on the premise that one of the best predictors of a candidate's future job performance is their past job behavior. This can be explored by asking questions such as, "Describe a difficult work-related problem that required you to come up with a creative solution. Tell me the steps you took and why." Or, "Please give a specific example of when you collaborated with another individual. How would you evaluate or describe the results from that effort?" By gaining insight into a candidates past experiences, you'll develop a reliable indicator of how that individual most likely will perform in the future.

REMEMBER

When interviewing candidates be sure to ask each of the candidates the same set of questions in the same way. This will ensure that there is a level playing field, it helps to minimize biases, and it brings consistency in the recruitment process. Asking different questions of each candidate can lead to a biased assessment of the candidate. Keep in mind that you should only ask questions that relate to the job the person is being considered for. You should not ask any questions relating to age, family, marital status, pregnancy, gender, national origin and religion. The later section "Avoiding Illegal and Inappropriate Questions" has more information about questions not to ask.

You can also apply the tips for minimizing bias in the following sections across other aspects of diversity as well such as LGBTQ, personality, thinking style, language, socioeconomic status, and so on.

Replacing gender-coded words with gender-neutral ones

Hiring for a waitress, a salesman, a cameraman, or a foreman? Using gender-neutral titles — wait staff, salesperson, camera operator, or supervisor — will ensure the position appeals to a more diverse set of candidates. You may also consider using possessive pronouns, "they" or "their," in lieu of "he," "him," "she," or "her," when talking about the ideal applicant. Plus, studies show that words with masculine undertones like "ambitious" and "competitive" may deter women from applying for a job.

Research reveals that women typically apply for a job only if they meet 90 to 100 percent of the qualifications. Masculine or gender-coded language, including adjectives like "competitive" and "determined," results in women "perceiving that they would not belong in the work environment." Conversely, words like "collaborative" and "cooperative" tend to draw more women than men.

TIP

To avoid unconscious gender bias deterring women from applying to your jobs, consider eliminating requirements that are not essential. If the position is one where training can easily be provided, don't ask for experience in it. Generalize areas where transferable skills are okay, and clearly outline which qualifications are required and which are preferred.

Reducing racial bias

Like gender bias, racial bias can be implicit, and oftentimes is unknowingly perpetuated by recruitment professionals. But some careful attention to words and phrases used can help eliminate implicit and explicit bias. Here are some suggestions:

>> Avoid "Cultural Fit" and focus on "Value Alignment."

>> Limit employee referral hiring, and go beyond your network, especially if the staff population is less diverse.

- >> Don't divert from the qualifications for a select few (who tend to be mostly like you).

- >> Ask everyone the same set of interview questions in the same way.

- >> Avoid mentioning race or national origin and other attributes that may be protected by legislation or that have no bearing on a person's qualifications.

- >> Phrases like "strong English-language skills" may deter qualified non-native English speakers from applying.

- >> A "clean-shaven" requirement can exclude candidates whose faith requires them to maintain facial hair (it also indicates the position is for men only).

Curtailing bias against older workers

With more baby boomers working long past traditional retirement age, employers should keep ageism top of mind when writing job descriptions and when finding, interviewing, and onboarding new talent.

TIP

One way to avoid age discrimination is to make sure your employer branding reflects a wide age range of workers at your company.

Additionally, avoid phrasing like:

WARNING

- >> "Young and energetic"

- >> "Party atmosphere"

- >> "Work hard/play hard"

- >> "Tech-savvy"/digital native"

- >> "Calling all recent college grads!"

- >> "Athletic" or "athletically inclined"

- >> "Junior" or "senior" except as part of a job title

- >> "Supplement your retirement income!"

Diminishing bias against disabled (differently-abled) workers

Make sure your job postings are welcoming to workers of all abilities by advertising when a position has accommodations like flexible hours or telework policies that would appeal to disabled workers.

TIP

Let applicants know your workplace welcomes and values all candidates with phrasing like: "Ability to complete tasks with or without reasonable accommodations." Instead of writing "Access to you own vehicle isn't always necessary," try "Access to reliable transportation," which is more inclusive to people with disabilities.

Lessening bias against religious beliefs/spirituality/faith

In general, religious affiliation is easier to hide on a resume than gender and race. However, some recruiters and hiring managers may make assumptions about a candidate's religion on their name alone.

REMEMBER

Religious bias can be an issue for worshipers of all religions, but it especially affects Muslims. According to research, Muslim and Arab applicants are less likely to receive callbacks than applicants of different religious backgrounds. Avoid specifying preferences for candidates with certain religious beliefs. Additionally, many country's laws generally regard questions about an applicant's religious affiliation or beliefs as non-job-related and problematic.

Assembling a Diverse Interview Panel

Top candidates want to be able to see themselves represented in your company, and having a diverse interview panel sends the right message to them about the company's commitment to diversity, equity, and inclusion. But because everyone brings their personal biases into the selection process, assembling interviewers with a wide variety of diverse attributes who bring varying backgrounds, experiences, and perspectives to the process is a good practice. That way, qualities that may turn off some interviewers may be explained as cultural differences that have no impact on the candidate's ability to perform the job. But a diverse interview panel doesn't just help combat unconscious bias; it also helps uncover and fix any blind spots in the interviews and eradicates decisions made on "gut feeling."

I recall many post-interview panel meetings where one panelist would point out what they considered to be a weakness in a candidate and another panelist would see it as a strength. It was a great way to be more objective by calling out biases (and sometimes baseless assessments of candidates). Additionally, if one of your panel members connects with a candidate on a personal level, you still have others to balance the overall decision.

Here are some steps that you can take to assemble a diverse panel of interviewers and ensure a successful process:

>> Ensure that you have a fair mix of gender, race/ethnic and cultural diversity, age ranges, seniority, and experience, and so on.

>> Provide behavioral interviewing training to all panelists so that they understand what to ask, what not to ask, how to ask open-ended questions, and other best practices for successful interviews.

>> Ensure that each panelist has a standard questionnaire and rating sheet so they know which questions to ask and how to assess/score each candidate.

>> Come to some agreement about how the panel's input will be used and how the final selection will be made.

>> Use inclusive job descriptions (which I discuss in the earlier section "Writing More Inclusive Job Descriptions").

>> Conduct a calibration meeting following the interview.

This meeting allows each panelist to share their ratings/scores, discuss the candidate's strengths and weaknesses, and come to an agreement on the final candidates to move to the next step in the process or the final candidate to be offered the job.

Avoiding Illegal and Inappropriate Questions

Everyone wants to hire the best possible candidate for the job, and that means asking good questions to uncover the right information. However, HR and hiring managers need to be aware that some questions may be inappropriate and/or illegal. For example, in most countries, asking questions about a candidate's age, race, ancestry, religion, criminal record, disability, or gender is considered inappropriate. In some countries, it's even illegal and can expose a company to legal action. The intent of these questions may be to determine whether a candidate is a "good fit" for the job, but remember that you can ask about only information relevant to a candidate's ability to do the job.

Job requirements based on an employee's gender, national origin, religion, or age can be used in very limited circumstances. In the United States, for example, they're lawful only when an employer can demonstrate that they're *bona fide occupational qualifications* (BFOQs) that are reasonably necessary to the normal operation of a business. For example, being female is a bona fide occupational qualification for a modeling job with a women's clothing designer or for an acting job for a specific role. However, being a certain gender isn't a BFOQ for the vast majority of jobs. Hiring only men as managers or only women as teachers isn't a legal application of a BFOQ defense.

Understanding where to draw the line is important for employers to avoid accusations of unfair hiring practices or lawsuits. Here are some of the types of questions you should avoid asking in the interview:

>> Are you married?

>> Have you ever been divorced?

>> Are you pregnant?

>> How many kids do you have?

>> What religion do you practice?

>> What church do you attend?

>> What year did you graduate?

>> What arrangements are you able to make for childcare while you work?

>> How old are your children?

>> What does your wife/husband/partner do for a living?

>> Where did you live while you were growing up?

>> Have you ever been arrested?

>> Have you ever been treated for any mental health issues?

>> As a woman, can you manage a team of all men?

>> How long do you plan to work until you retire?

>> Have you experienced any serious illnesses in the past year?

>> What holidays do you celebrate?

Chapter **10**

Developing, Coaching, Promoting, and Retaining Diverse Talent

Being a woman, a person of color, a single mom, and a person very committed to my faith, I've had the unfortunate experiences of dealing with stereotypes, biases, prejudices, and discrimination. Each of these can impact decisions regarding selection, promotion, pay, performance ratings, coaching and feedback, delegation of special projects, and all other decisions regarding employment. And unfortunately, I've experienced this in every aspect of my career. I've been paid far less than my male counterpart for the same work. I've been denied opportunities for promotions that were given to others who were already preselected and been marginalized on performance reviews or surprised by ratings that had no justification. I've trained the person who'd become my supervisor. I've had my supervisor steal and take credit for my ideas. I've gotten certain roles due to tokenism and received offensive or insulting comments disguised as compliments — comments referring to me as "very articulate," "talking white," "even-tempered," "intelligent," and "not like those other Black women." I've even been mistaken for the secretary when taking my male direct reports with me to meet with clients.

I share these examples that happened to me throughout my career (even up to being a senior executive reporting to the CEO) because they still occur today. For example, when sharing these stories in my keynotes, audience participants often approach me to tell me that I'm sharing their story. Workers in my focus groups and inclusion and engagement surveys still report that they're experiencing these same kinds of biases, stereotypes, and prejudices in the areas of promotions, development, coaching, and retention.

With this in mind, this chapter outlines tips and strategies for how leaders can keep instances like these from occurring and how they can be more effective in developing, coaching, and retaining diverse top talent.

Developing Diverse Talent

Increasing representation in the organization is an important start because what people see in your leadership ranks, on your board of directors, on your website, and in your marketing efforts speaks volumes about your company's commitment. However, that's not enough. You need to adopt and implement strategies, policies, and practices to ensure that *all* talent has access to opportunities, is treated fairly, has a level playing field, and is set up for success.

I often ask leaders, "Can you have diversity and not have inclusion?" Some leaders respond with a resounding "yes," which, unfortunately, is the correct answer. And therein lies the problem. In my experience, far too many companies celebrate when they've hired one or a few people from underrepresented groups into key roles, and then they park there. I call this a "check-the-box approach." They don't focus on the work environment — creating a culture of inclusion, equity, and belonging. They don't invest in developing their diverse employees, utilizing their skills and bringing out their genius, and thus they don't promote, recognize, or celebrate them.

Employees who are from historically marginalized groups or who look, think, work, believe, and act in different ways from leadership may have a disadvantage in that many of them may not have had the coaching, mentoring, or guidance of navigating a workplace that's entrenched in dominant culture.

Leaders who have mostly worked with, hired, promoted, and recognized people like themselves often operate out of a "like-me" mindset. They're likely selecting, promoting, paying, and soliciting ideas from these same folks. But this practice leaves those who aren't like the leader feeling overlooked, undervalued, and excluded from opportunities.

Although employees from underrepresented groups can benefit greatly from development programs designed to meet their specific needs, leaders who are in the dominant group can also benefit from some development, such as being able to recognize their own biases, learning how to work effectively across differences, and increasing their level of cultural competence, crosscultural communication, and emotional intelligence.

What does your organization do to develop people based on their backgrounds and individual needs?

Coaching Diverse Talent

Coaching is about empowering others to maximize their personal and professional potential. Research studies have shown that effective coaching increases creativity, engagement, organizational performance, retention, and collaboration across departments. Building a culture of diversity and inclusion and building a strong coaching culture go hand in hand. As a certified coach and human resources professional, I can attest that as the workforce becomes more diverse, it's even more important that leaders develop the skills and competence to be able to coach diverse talent effectively. I see too many leaders who are uncomfortable and apprehensive in fully coaching their diverse employees because as leaders they haven't been trained, and they operate with assumptions and perceptions about those employees.

REMEMBER

Good leaders are good coaches. Inclusive leaders are also inclusive coaches. To be an inclusive coach, ask yourself the following:

>> Do I understand the specific issues and needs of employees who are different from me?

>> Am I clear about the specific strengths they bring to the organization?

>> Am I able to let go of one-size-fits-all coaching?

>> Have I taken the time to learn about the particular obstacles or paths they've had to take based on their cultural backgrounds, genders, races, ages, abilities, sexual orientations, and so on?

>> Am I able to listen closely, empathize, and see their needs as real?

>> Am I curious about differences and able to see the strengths employees' differences bring to the team and workplace?

>> Am I willing to admit that I don't know what I don't know and relearn or learn new skills and ways to help people on my team reach success?

>> Am I willing and ready to be coached by my employees on the best way to work with them?

The right coaching program is a key component to helping diverse talent succeed. When they're able to participate fully and contribute their genius, the whole organization profits. Following are a few points to keep in mind when implementing a coaching program:

>> **No one-size-fits-all coaching program exists for employees in a diverse workforce.**

>> **Consider employee demographics and what each person needs to grow.**

>> **Don't just use the same processes and the same people that have been in place for the last ten years.** Seek coaches who are experienced and knowledgeable about the cultures of the people you want to support but who also bring a fresh perspective and an open mind.

>> **Utilize a diverse group of coaches.** Coaches don't necessarily have to be from the same culture, gender, or race as the people they're coaching, but they need to have the experience and insight needed to develop them.

>> **If your program does not have a diverse group of coaches, you have a few options.** You can recruit some from across the organization by a call for volunteer coaches, or by nomination from senior leaders. If that still does not yield any diverse coaches, you should consider using an external coaching service. See additional tips later in this section for using coaching services.

>> **Coaches who are reluctant to address issues such race or gender when working with employees of color aren't the right coaches, and the coaching process fails.** Coaches who don't address issues of diversity, race, and so on and don't recognize historical barriers or bias in promotion and development systems have too often blamed the people they're coaching when objectives haven't been met.

>> **Provide managers with the skills they need to let go of biases, stereotypes, and assumptions that stop them from supporting employees who are different from them.** Managers and everyone in leadership need to be coached to be able to see beyond what's customary and comfortable to them.

TIP

If you use external coaches, you should ask the following questions:

>> What's the makeup of the group in terms or diversity?

>> What experience and understanding do they have about the issues of race, gender, sexual orientation, and so on?

>> How are they able to customize their coaching to ensure that underrepresented people gain the skills and strategies they need to navigate success routes in the organization?

Assessing Your Team's Needs

As a manager who supports a culture of diversity, equity, and inclusion, you want to recognize the differences and similarities of people on your team. The old mantra of "I treat everyone the same" is a good way to lose talent.

You should assess your team as a whole, as well as the individuals that make up the team — their attributes, experiences, potential, purposes, skill levels, career aspirations, and so on. If you don't understand the diversity of your team, you end up with ideas and participation from people who look like you. When everyone on the team looks and thinks the same, you get the same ideas that you've always gotten and lose the potential contributions and creativity and any benefit of a diverse team.

Here are some questions to ask yourself in assessing the needs of your team:

>> What's the team's purpose and vision?

>> What's the team's current state in terms of collaboration, trust, productivity, safety, and so on?

>> What do you need from the team in order to achieve the goals and objectives?

>> What are the team's strengths? Its challenges? What's missing?

Understanding the best ways to get your team's input

TIP

There's no one best way to leverage the brilliance on your team. To identify what each person on the team needs in order to be successful, feel included, and help others feel included, take the time to get to know them as individuals. The more time you spend doing that, the better you'll understand their individual needs, and the results will be a stronger team.

Consider the following:

>> How do they like to be recognized for their achievements?

>> Do they want to be recognized in front of the team or in private?

>> How do you encourage employees to share their ideas?

- Brainstorming

- One person at a time

- In written form

- One-on-one with you

- In pairs or small groups

REMEMBER

Though organizations commonly use brainstorming sessions, keep in mind that not everyone is comfortable shouting out their ideas. People who are introverted, have English as a second language, or tend to process internally may have a difficult time sharing their brilliance in a brainstorming session but give amazing input in writing. You may miss out on potential ideas, solutions, or product and service innovation if your only method of solicitation is brainstorming.

Even people who are comfortable speaking in front of a group may get quiet in brainstorm free-for-alls. Try doing round robins, where you go around the room and ask people for input. Allow people pass if they want. You can also try breaking people into pairs or small groups to talk with each other. This approach often allows people to build off each other's ideas and collaborate.

TIP

Asking people for input in a one-on-one conversation with you can also help you understand your team better and build stronger relationships.

If you want some practice, list the people on your team and try to answer the following questions:

>> What are their individual strengths?

>> What are their challenges? What keeps them up at night?

>> What obstacles are in the way of their doing their best work?

>> What biases may you have about who will be most successful

>> What changes if any do you need to make to your coaching process?

Mentoring across differences

Most successful people will tell you that they had a mentor to help them navigate their career trajectory. A key to developing a diverse workforce is creating mentorship programs that brings together an array of complementary differences among the mentees and the mentors. In my work setting up such programs, I've found specific best practices that make mentoring across differences successful:

>> **Cross-cultural mentorship programs need to be formal and structured.** That includes setting up a regular schedule with an agenda for each session.

>> **Mentors and mentees need to spend time getting to know each other and addressing any differences in culture, gender, and power dynamics.** This step allows mentor and mentee to work together, speak openly, and learn from each other more easily.

>> **Participants need to set up a process to deal with any disagreements or miscommunications that may occur.** Doing so ensures a more comfortable environment to work together.

All of these tips contribute to more successful mentorship for diverse talent. An additional benefit is that reverse mentoring occurs. In many of my mentoring relationships, I was usually partnered with an older, white male, and I remember how much two of my mentors told me they learned by me sharing my personal experiences as a woman of color. They were clueless prior to our mentoring relationship. It gave them a greater sense of how someone like me, who was listed as a high performer but not getting promoted as fast as my white counterparts, was treated and how it impacted my life. As a result, they were willing to question policies and processes and influence decisions that dealt with my performance.

REMEMBER

Being involved as a mentor or mentee across differences is an opportunity for people to learn from each other and actually be both mentor and mentee.

Customizing your leadership style to your team's diverse needs and talents

Different leadership styles work for different people and for different situations. Here are five common leadership styles. Identify the one that best models your style of leadership.

- » **Hierarchical:** *Hierarchical* leadership is top-down. The person in leadership makes the decisions and tells people what to do. This style can be most effective in a crisis when an action needs to be taken right away. Some people may be used to working within a hierarchy and need that kind of direction even outside of an emergency.

- » **Participatory:** A leader who uses a *participatory* style asks for input and feedback from team members but ultimately makes the final decision.

- » **Consensus or collaborative style:** Someone who leads by *consensus* allows their team to take the time to discuss objectives and decide together how to achieve those objectives.

- » **Task-oriented:** A *task-oriented* leader gets things done and gets to know their team by doing together. They don't take time to warm the group up. It's about getting down to business.

- » **Relationship-oriented:** A *relationship-oriented* leader first takes the time to get to know their team members, spending time talking with them and then getting the work done together.

Because a diverse team has different needs, talents, and strengths, no one leadership style works for everyone. None of these styles is wrong, but when you lead a diverse team, you need to be able to use all these styles depending on the needs of your employee and the situation. A good leader recognizes the need to adapt and customize their leadership style to those needs, strengths, and talents to help their employees do their best work.

REMEMBER

A number of books, research studies, and articles on leadership were written for a particular demographic — white heterosexual men. The workplace is a lot more diverse than when many of these items were published, and it will continue to become more diverse.

If you're able to adapt your style to different people and situations, your employees will feel like you see and hear them and be more motivated to do a good job. To adjust your leadership style to get results, adopt these three practices:

- » Listen to what people say (don't interrupt or trivialize their input).

- » Address what's important to them even if it's not important to you.

- » Let go of judgments about what should and shouldn't be important based on your perspective.

TIP

Be patient with yourself when you need to flex your leadership style. It's a learning process.

In addition to the tips shared earlier in this section, following are a few other best practices that I've seen leaders demonstrate who are committed to making the necessary adjustments to their leadership styles:

>> **Identify your own leadership style.** Be aware of when your default style is most effective and when it isn't. Be willing to adapt or flex your style.

>> **Recognize that sometimes using a single-decision or authoritative style is most appropriate, and other times getting input from people on your team is more effective.**

>> **Let go of the need to be right and focus on the results you want.** Ask yourself what's needed in order to get those results.

>> **If you're used to asking for the counsel of the same people, or those who look like you, all the time, be willing to seek out people you don't normally ask.** Adapting your style means changing your perspective, being more open, and allowing for disagreements. You'll get more engagement and full participation from your diverse team.

>> **Be willing to change direction, change tactics, or change the way a decision is made in order to hear from different people on your team.**

>> **Let go of any bias you may have that says your way of leading is the "right" way and every other way is "wrong."**

REMEMBER

Your team members aren't to blame if you don't take their leadership needs into account and then don't get the results you want.

Reviewing Performance with an Equitable and Inclusive Mindset

I wish all managers were fair and equitable in their assessment of performance for all their team members. But that's just not the case. In my 30-plus years of leading human resources — having experienced it firsthand — and now in my consulting work, I continue to see the inequities, lack of fairness, and discriminatory acts that still occur throughout the employee life cycle, especially in performance management. Much of this activity is because of the biases that people learn at an early age and carry into adulthood.

REMEMBER

It's not enough to just know what not to say. You have to be self-aware and conscious of your biases and how those biases impact your thinking about people who are different.

Combating microaggressions and bias

To provide performance reviews that focus on employee strengths, results, and areas that need improvement, leaders need to address issues of bias and microaggression that occur in the process. In Chapter 15, I spend a lot of time covering what bias is, how it's developed and reinforced, and how it plays out in everyday life and in the workplace. But for the sake of this topic, I want to highlight some of the most common types of microaggressions and biases that occur in assessing performance.

Microaggressions

Psychologist Derald Wing Sue, the author of two books on microaggressions, defines them as "the everyday slights, indignities, put downs, and insults that people of color, women, LGBTQ populations, or those who are marginalized experience in their day-to-day interactions with people."

WARNING

Here are a few examples of common microaggressions; as you read through the list, identify which you've used:

>> **Asking a nonwhite person, "What are you?" or "Where are you really from?".** Such questions assume that someone who's nonwhite must be from somewhere else and imply that only white people are "true" Americans.

>> **Saying, "I don't see you as a Black person. I see you as just like me," or "I'm colorblind; I don't see color.".** These statements imply that something is wrong with being nonwhite and erase who the person is.

>> **Asking a Black person whether you can touch their hair or whether it's their real hair.** That's not being curious. It's insulting and demeaning.

>> **Telling a person of color (usually a Black or brown person) how articulate they are.** These "compliments" indicate that you're surprised someone who isn't white can be intelligent and that most people who look like them aren't intelligent.

>> **Saying to someone who's LGBTQ, "You don't look gay.".** This comment is a signal that you have a stereotype of LGBTQ people, and this person in exception.

REMEMBER

To be an effective leader of a diverse team, being aware of some of the most common microaggressions and stereotypes that occur in the workplace is imperative so you can not only work to avoid using them but also intervene when you hear other people using them.

Biases

Here are common types of biases that show up in performance reviews. Do you recognize any from reviews you've given?

>> **Recency bias:** *Recency bias* ignores the employee's performance over the entire review period and instead homes in on more recent events.

>> **Primacy bias:** *Primacy bias* occurs when leaders allow their first/early impressions to affect how they view an employee.

>> **Affinity ("like-me") bias:** *Affinity bias* is the unconscious tendency to get along better with, give the benefit of the doubt to, or give higher ratings to people who are most like you.

>> **Power bias:** *Power bias* has you rating yourself higher than you do other people. As a person's power increases, so does their tendency for power bias.

>> **Implicit person theory/personal growth mindset:** If you don't believe people can change and therefore have a fixed idea of what their ratings should be, you're exhibiting this bias.

Many leaders haven't done the work to understand that they possess these biases, nor have they realized the impact that they can have on their workers. As a consequence, those directly impacted are left feeling undervalued, resentful, and unfairly treated, which affects their morale, productivity, engagement, and retention.

Providing feedback through an equitable lens

Reviewing how the organization has conducted performance reviews and assigned ratings in the past and then addressing the needs of today's workforce through an equitable and diverse lens helps ensure employees get the feedback and development they need to do their best work. Here are a few tips to keep in mind to ensure that you're reviewing performance with an equitable and inclusive lens:

>> Consider taking a more collaborative and holistic approach to performance management by using a 360-degree feedback process that involves soliciting other people's input in addition to yours.

>> **Separate the performance review, promotion, and compensation processes so that you can rely on external benchmarks and multiple inputs throughout the review process.** Be sure to hold managers accountable by having regular conversations with them and making sure they're making data-driven decisions when evaluating employee performance.

>> **Increase the frequency of performance reviews.** When an organization does reviews only once a year, it doesn't get a holistic view of employee accomplishments throughout the year, their areas of growth over time, or specific times they've shined. Yearly reviews tend to focus on the most recent performance or the biggest mistakes. My guidance to leaders is to conduct informal performance discussions at least quarterly and provide feedback/coaching on projects, tasks, and other assignments on a monthly basis. The reality is, everyone wants to know where they stand and how they can improve.

Applying Retention Strategies That Work

Your company works hard to source, recruit, and hire great diverse talent. The aim of every leader should be to make your company a place that not only attracts this talent but also creates an environment where those people stay and thrive.

An organization that focuses only on representation but not equity and inclusion doesn't reap the benefits that a diverse workforce brings. Likewise, it doesn't retain those employees if they don't feel valued and lack the opportunity to contribute to the organization. People don't stay if they don't feel included or enjoy a sense of belonging. They leave to work for your competition, retire in place, or become your competition. So here are some best practices for how to retain your diverse talent.

>> **Genuinely accept and value diversity.** Don't just do it because it's a mandate or because you don't want to look bad; do it because it aligns with your personal values.

>> **Learn about the cultural backgrounds, unique experiences, needs, and expectations of the individuals on your team and what's important to them.**

>> **Ensure that the onboarding and orientation process sets them up for success, creates community, and explains to them the unwritten rules of engagement (those that the dominant/majority group are often told).**

>> **Be intentional about seeking diverse ideas and perspectives, and be willing to use that input in your decision making.**

>> Become more aware of your own biases and do the work to develop greater cultural competence and emotional intelligence.

>> Involve new employees in crossfunctional innovation teams where they get to work with people who are different and use their unique talents and skills.

>> Provide access to information about promotion, new projects, or training that may benefit their careers.

>> Conduct stay interviews as a means of being proactive in identifying what they enjoy, need, and expect in order to remain committed, invested, and productive. You can hold these one-hour meetings between you and each of your team members at least twice a year as a means to identify and reinforce the positive reasons that keep each individual employee at the organization.

>> Create the kind of culture that makes them feel safe enough to bring their full and authentic selves to work, to speak up and share their opinions, and to do their best work and stay.

REMEMBER

A diverse workforce can improve your organization's innovation, productivity, and brand reputation. But it doesn't come with the snap of your fingers. Retaining diverse talent and diversity in the workplace is an ongoing effort and commitment from you.

Chapter **11**

Leading Diverse Teams for Maximum Performance

revious chapters outline the compelling business case for DEI, how to attract and hire more diverse talent, and how to enrich the employee experience. But I can't underscore enough the importance of homing in on the different ideas, experiences, and perspectives that come a diverse team. Much research has been done over the years proving that diverse teams are smarter and more creative and solve more complex problems. Moreover, companies with more diversity on their leadership teams, executive teams, and boards of directors report being more innovative and profitable and seeing higher returns on their investments.

But leading a diverse team to achieve this kind of performance isn't easy, and too many leaders are still lagging in their understanding of and effectiveness in doing so. This chapter provides some guidance, knowledge, and common practices for how to maximize the performance of a diverse team.

Assembling a Diverse Team

When I was asked to write this book, I knew how critical the task was. I knew that it was a first of its kind in the *For Dummies* book collection; that the world was reeling from a global pandemic; that there was an international outcry for greater equity, justice, and inclusion; and that everyone was living in uncertain, complex, and ever-changing times.

But I also knew I didn't want to write this book in a vacuum. Although I have nearly 30-plus years in the field of human resources and DEI, I still wanted to enlist the perspectives and experiences of other colleagues, both to provide more comprehensive and well-rounded points of view and to help offset the time commitment. I intentionally sought out a group of contributors who were diverse by race, gender, age, sexual orientation/identity, disability, geographic location, and personality styles; who were practitioners, researchers, consultants, and writers by trade; and who brought diverse perspectives, experiences, and ideas. By assembling this kind of team, and leveraging the benefits and talents its members all brought, I'm certain that this book came out a better product than it would've had I done it alone.

Similarly, I lead a diverse team in my global consulting firm. I have a mix of work experiences, ethnicities, ages, experiences, personalities, opinions, and skills. And I was deliberate about selecting my team and looking for what I didn't have. As a result, I've been able to grow my business and achieve sustained success for nearly a decade because of my learning how to utilize the unique gifts and talents of a diverse team.

How have you intentionally assembled a diverse team? What are some ways you're leveraging the unique skills, talents, and perspectives of each team member?

REMEMBER

Assembling a diverse team in an organization where it's not the norm requires intention, vision, and strategy. Here are five best practices that you can use to successfully assemble a diverse team:

>> **Hire differently:** If you keep hiring the same way, using the same recruiters, and recruiting from the same places, you'll get the same homogenous people in your organization. I discuss hiring and recruiting a diverse workforce in Chapter 9.

   Tip: Revisit the recruiters you've been using. If they aren't a diverse group or have no track record for bringing in a diverse candidate pool, you probably need to find another partner.

>> **Hire for the culture you want, not the culture you have:** Some organizations make the mistake of thinking they're demonstrating support for diversity

and inclusion by claiming to hire for "culture fit" as opposed to college or grade point average. That may not make a difference. If your goal is a diverse workforce and an inclusive culture, but everyone is the same, the culture will still be the same no matter how much everyone says they support diversity.

Tip: Develop a vision of diversity, equity, and inclusion for your organization. Think of all aspects of your business — culture, systems, and processes — and then take action to create that culture. Hire people who share those values. (For more about company culture, see Chapter 18.)

Get input from other people with the same passion for diversity, equity, and inclusion. Be willing to listen, let go of aspects of your culture that aren't inclusive, and begin taking steps to transform your present culture.

» **Be flexible:** Review your systems and processes, as well as the unwritten norms, and be willing to make changes to create an environment where everyone can thrive. Often, norms and habits are formed without malice or ill intent; they work for the people who created them, but they may not work for the diverse team you hope to build.

For example, a 40-person tech start-up made up of mostly single white people in their 20s gathered at the bar across the street every Friday to talk about the week and make plans for the next week. As the company expanded and hired more people who weren't all white, were in their 40s, and were from different cultures, leaders soon realized that this routine wouldn't work for people with families who couldn't stay late on Fridays or for people who didn't feel comfortable "hanging out in bars." They didn't totally stop the Friday night gatherings but limited them to once a month and set aside time during the workday to do their planning so that everyone had opportunities to contribute and help make decisions.

» **Be willing to let go of old ideas of who should be promoted, given opportunities to advance, or chosen for recognition:** Expand your criteria of what success looks like and what a successful person looks like. Focus on what the company needs, not what makes you the most comfortable. Resist making assumptions based on outdated stereotypes.

For example, a facilities services organization was concerned that women were reaching a certain level and then leaving. It wanted to be more inclusive. After meeting with the regional manager, leaders discovered that the vice-president wasn't promoting women because the job entailed sometimes working at night. He said that women had responsibilities at home and wouldn't stay after they got married. After the company stopped reacting to a harmful stereotype and gave women a chance to prove their work ethic, it became one of the top organizations for women to advance.

» **Check the language and imagery you use to describe your workplace and mission and identify how it can be more inclusive:** Here are some questions to ask as you determine how your current representation stacks up to your inclusivity goals:

- Is it too gender-specific?
- Do the posters and artwork reflect diversity, or do they have a bunch of the same people who look alike?
- Have you removed language that uses terms like "crush the competition" or that only uses sports or single culture metaphors?
- Do you recognize the holidays and rituals of different faiths, ethnicities, and cultures?
- What steps have you taken to make your organization attractive to people who aren't just like you?

Maximizing the Benefits of a Diverse Team

Taking time and effort to be deliberate about increasing diversity in the workplace (and on your team) can yield excellent business benefits, such as being considered an employer of choice or a great place to work, attracting top talent, and increasing employee engagement, productivity, and retention rates. For your teams, you enjoy better decision-making capabilities and better outcomes to complex problems. Even studies affirm that decisions made by diverse teams produce better results nearly 90 percent of the time and that these teams outperform more homogeneous teams.

This section covers six ways to maximize the benefits of a diverse team.

Creating opportunities for people to get to know each other

It's human nature for people to prefer to be with people who look like and think like them. When this tendency plays out in organizations, people tend to operate in demographic silos and not interact or support each other's success.

But when people who are different from each other take time to get to know each other beyond what they see, they're more comfortable asking each other for help, sharing ideas, and collaborating on projects. Leaders can help to facilitate the kind of environment that encourages relationship-building.

Often, people from different backgrounds don't know how to begin talking with each other. Use icebreakers, games, and other activities in your team meetings that get them started. This approach creates a path for people to get to know each other in a nonthreatening way and sparks more interaction and engagement. Here are some examples of topics that can get the ball rolling:

>> A passion or hobby outside of work

>> A hidden talent

>> A favorite vacation spot

>> Where they grew up

Embracing communication style differences

Keep in mind that one communication style doesn't fit all. Different cultures, age groups, and languages observe different business norms. Some may communicate with a more direct/assertive tone or with more hand gestures; some may allow superiors to speak first; some may prefer texting versus a phone call; and so on.

Learning how to relate to your team members in different ways and adjusting to various communication styles goes a long way with building trust and valuing their diversity.

Making your meetings no-judgment zones

A team of people who look and think differently is more likely to come up with creative ideas that lead to breakthrough products and services, but only if those people are motivated to bring those ideas forward. As a leader, you have the power to create meeting environments where people are comfortable presenting new ideas and solutions to problems without fear of ridicule or feeling trivialized or shut down.

To receive these ideas, you need to create team norms where people are rewarded for thinking differently. You set the example and encourage these ideas when people feel safe speaking without interruptions. Even a simple statement such as "I like the way you're thinking; keep it up!" can encourage innovative thought.

If a team leader listens actively, gives their team undivided attention, and follows up with objective questions, the rest of the team will do the same. Soon, everyone on your team will be more willing to take risks, participate, and share ideas that are away from the norm.

Focusing on the increase in market share and serving more diverse customers

People from different backgrounds, cultures, ages, and so on can be your best resource to understanding the needs of diverse customers and stakeholders. No matter how "informed" people are, they still tend to see the world from their own lenses. With a diverse team, you can implement strong marketing strategies and understand the perspectives of people from these communities instead of viewing different markets from your own single perspective. This shift helps grow your brand and increase your customer base.

TIP

When you're expanding into new markets, get feedback from a cross-section of people and especially people who are from your target market. You don't want to offend the groups whose business you want.

Addressing unconscious cultural bias

Recognize that everyone has biases that, if they go unchecked, can wreak havoc on the team. Provide education and skill building training to identify some of the prevalent biases that show in the team's decision making and problem solving, in their collaboration, and in how they treat each other. Make holding each other accountable when biases do show up a team effort and allow for mistakes and teachable moments.

To find out more about unconscious bias and how to evolve to inclusive leadership, check out Chapters 15 and 16.

REMEMBER

Talent comes in all shapes, sizes, colors, ages, backgrounds, abilities, and experiences, so expand your view on who are the "best and brightest." Often, that phrase ends up meaning "like us" or "who I'm most comfortable with."

A diverse talent pool gives you more choices and opportunities to hire people with new perspectives, experiences, and skills that can help your organization be more innovative, competitive, and relevant. Talented people have options for who they want to work for and where and how they want to work, and they're in great demand in the face of a skills shortage. (Flip to Chapter 2 for more on skills shortages.) When leaders work to intentionally recruit and hire more diversity on their teams, they're sending a message that they both value diversity and are committed to realizing its benefits.

Inviting Diversity of Thought to the Table

The world is more diverse than ever before, which means organizations can no longer afford to have the same table with the same seats; that's just not reflective of a more global society or of the workforce, clients, customers, or consumers. So leaders must welcome diversity, and by extension diversity of thought, to the table.

Diversity of thought has become a hot topic and a buzzword for the DEI world, but organizations realize that they need to embrace it in order to develop real inclusion and create companies where equity is the norm. The challenge is the way that many leaders view diversity of thought. Their views on this that can hinder DEI progress in general. The following section discusses the myth about diversity of thought, reveals the truth, and offers some tips for how to enlist more diverse perspectives.

Scrutinizing the myth about diversity of thought

Some people have the misconception that all an organization needs is people who think differently, even if all those people look the same, come from similar backgrounds, and have the same gender, sexual orientation, and so on.

Some organizations have used this logic to argue that they don't need to focus on dimensions of diversity such as culture, race, ethnicity, and gender because diversity of thought is more important. They say that this "diversity of thought" will result in enough creativity and new ideas.

This mindset is not only an inaccurate way to think about diversity but also a means of blocking efforts to transform the culture. Consider the following:

>> Diversity of identity is an important facet of diversity of thought. For example, a room full of white men may have different styles or personality traits, but none of them has real knowledge of the lived experience of women or people of color.

>> Visible diversity encourages a team to expand its thinking, listen to different points of view, and consider alternate strategies.

Therefore, without an emphasis on diversity of identity, the organization stays the same, and the ideas aren't that different.

Uncovering the truth about diversity of thought

You get real diversity of thought when you have people in your organization from different backgrounds, races, cultures, genders, sexual orientation, affiliations, experiences, and so on. Here are just five reasons:

>> You get to hear different perspectives of ideas and lived experiences.

>> You expand your market because you have employees that belong to your target market. They're your resources for establishing relationships and credibility in those markets. Plus, people like to do business with organizations that hire people who look like them. Get ready for more business.

>> Together, you can create a culture where everyone feels like they belong no matter what group or groups they're from. You discover what people from different groups need to do their best work.

>> Different backgrounds and experiences provide you with the diversity of thought you need to create revolutionary products and services for a diverse market.

>> You create a stronger community at work, and your employees take what they learn from each other to their own communities.

REMEMBER

In addition, a visibly diverse team makes your company more attractive for the new generation of diverse job applicants who report that they want and expect their employers to care about DEI and look more like them.

Mining diversity of thought at the table

You may have diverse teams in place, but how do you uncover and utilize the genius of diverse thinking? Having diverse voices at the table isn't enough if you can't capture their brilliance.

Not everyone communicates, contributes their ideas, or participates the same way. As you get to know your team members, discover how they like to communicate with others and in what ways they like to express themselves.

Create an environment where people feel psychologically safe with their communication styles and their ways of interacting and expressing their views — where people listen to each other without interrupting, attacking ideas, or voicing disapproval if they disagree. Get input from the team to create meeting and discussion norms. What makes people feel heard? How do they like to be shown respect? Decide what works and what doesn't for the group.

When people are used to being around the same people in the same function from similar backgrounds, they fall into habits of thinking and acting alike. New people and diversity of thought, perspectives, and experiences can be like a shot of creativity.

Put people in cross-functional problem solving and innovation groups. You can even have people from one function or department provide suggestions for another department or function; sometimes that's what coming up with fresh ideas takes. Bring people together to share those ideas.

When you've decided on your meeting and discussion norms, communicate them explicitly — in writing. You may not be able to create norms that meet the preferences of everyone in a diverse group, but putting them in writing allows everyone to know what's acceptable and what's expected of them.

Facilitating Relationship-Building and Cultivating Trust and Belonging

Relationship-building and cultivating trust and belonging among the team starts with you. You must be the lead relationship builder. If you're aloof and unapproachable when people are together, your team will take that as the norm.

I always say that leaders are the thermostat in any organization. They set the tone and create the atmosphere their team members have to work in. That atmosphere can be one of trust, respect, belonging, inclusion, open idea sharing, and appreciation. Or it can be one that's toxic — lacking trust, respect, and psychological safety and retaliating, blaming, and devaluing each other. If you don't spend time getting to know the people on your team and making them comfortable with you, you're setting the wrong temperature.

Consider where your team would rate you on these attributes of culture, and how much of it you could change by using a different leadership approach. I cover leadership styles in Chapter 10.

Building relationships

Your team needs to see you expressing interest in everyone. That means you may have to leave your comfort zone of socializing with the people you know best or who look like you.

The following are some ways to set the example:

>> **Spend time with people on your team:** Especially consider those on your team you spend the least time with and those who are least like you. Ask yourself why you don't spend as much time with them. Be intentional about building relationships across identities such as race, gender, sexual orientation, religion, ability, background, and diversity of thought.

>> **Develop a mindset of curiosity and ask people questions:** Look for commonalities and be interested to learn more about the differences. Practice being more curious by asking those team members questions such as these:

- What do you like to do when you're not at work?

- What brought you to this organization?

- What did you do to keep busy during the COVID-19 pandemic?

- What are your hopes for the future?

- What do you like best about working here?

- What can the organization do to make your work easier or more efficient?

- What's your favorite movie [or TV show, book, music, whatever]?

REMEMBER

Relationships and trust are a two-way street. You need to provide the answers to every question you ask. You build trust by sharing information about yourself and current issues in the organization.

Building trust

Trust increases when people know each other and they know each other's capabilities and strengths. When they know and trust each other, they become willing to collaborate, solve problems, and support each other's work. They're more likely to share resources and not duplicate efforts or compete in negative ways.

Trust in diverse teams and diverse organizations is a process that takes time. The sooner you set the example, the sooner people follow that example.

WARNING

Beware the following obstacles to trust:

>> Withholding information or sharing information with a select few

>> Not giving everyone opportunities to be leaders in different capacities but favoring the same people over and over

>> Not being willing to look at your own bias

>> Criticizing team members in public

>> Always asking for help from the same people (who probably look like you)

>> Taking the credit and giving the blame

>> Never apologizing or admitting you were wrong or you don't know the answer

>> Sharing with others confidential conversations without obtaining permission

>> Inattentive listening

TIP

Come up with ways for people to interact with each other in different environments and situations, both formally and informally. Take time for people to engage in small talk before meetings. Use icebreakers (such as those in the earlier section "Creating opportunities for people to get to know each other") to get people to talk with each other and find ways to laugh together.

Avoiding the Common Pitfalls of Leading a Diverse Team

I must admit that, in my many years of working for leaders at all levels and in many types of industries, I worked for more ineffective leaders than effective ones. Those who were ineffective at leading were even worse in leading diverse teams. And because I was a woman, a person of color, a person committed to my faith, and a single mom, I felt the effects of working for those leaders who minimized, trivialized, and marginalized my efforts, results, and aspirations. But they taught me what *not* to do when I had the opportunity to lead diverse teams.

The following pitfalls of leading diverse teams aren't ones only I've experienced; they're shared by the thousands of workers I've coached and consulted with and that my firm has heard in focus groups, employee surveys, and listening sessions.

>> **Lacking vision and goals:** Leaders who don't provide a compelling vision for others to follow will struggle with keeping employees focused and committed.

>> **Treating everyone the same:** Inclusive leaders understand that not everyone is motivated the same way. Instead of practicing the golden rule, they practice the platinum rule: Treat others the way they want to be treated.

>> **Showing favoritism:** Do you have someone on your team that you consider your go-to person? The problem is that when you single someone out as your favorite, you're excluding or overlooking others. When leaders avoid showing

favoritism and provide a sense of belonging and equity, they can establish a level playing field and a sense of trust.

>> **Being inflexible:** When leaders are rigid and unwilling to consider new ideas or new ways of doing things, they squelch innovation. Leaders must welcome diverse perspectives and create an environment where collaboration and creativity can thrive.

>> **Failing to recognize or reward equitably:** Everyone wants to feel valued and appreciated. When leaders take the time to recognize all employees' achievements, they see improved morale and performance, and team members feel valued.

>> **Failing to provide feedback:** All team members need feedback on how they're doing (positive and corrective), and they need it consistently. Effective leaders are willing to develop this skill and make it a consistent practice. They also encourage team members to share feedback with each other.

REMEMBER

Diversity alone doesn't cause a team to begin performing with maximum efficiency or peak innovation. In fact, without a strong leader, greater diversity may lead to greater conflict and segregation. To get to where you want to be, you need to ensure that every member of your team is included and able to access their brilliance and contribute new and innovative ideas without fear of retribution. Not every creative idea will be put into practice, but without the synergy required to access those viewpoints, you'll never access the imagination needed to bring your company to the next level.

Chapter **12**

Tracking, Measuring, and Reporting the Progress of DEI Efforts

O ne of the most common questions I receive from leaders is "How do you measure the success of DEI initiatives?" In the United States, companies that embark on implementing DEI strategies often track the conventional measurements of representation and rely on counting the number of people who belong to certain categories, such as BIPOC (that is, Black, indigenous, and other people of color — Hispanic, Asian, Native American); women; and sometimes age groups, people with disabilities, and veterans. They're mainly tracked in recruitment, promotions, and turnover.

But many other metrics can help an organization gain a sense of how effective its DEI efforts are and how all employees, especially those who are among the marginalized groups, are experiencing the workplace every day.

As a leader, you have to be intentional about the metrics you use. In other words, you need to measure what matters. That what I cover in this chapter: what DEI metrics to track and how to measure and report them.

Measuring What Matters

The major objective of measurement is to assess your progress along your journey. For example, measuring how fast a runner completes a 100-meter dash is irrelevant if that runner's event is actually a marathon, which requires much more endurance for running at a set pace for an extended distance. So a more appropriate metric for a marathon runner is pace per mile for a certain number of miles; that stat is a better predictor of that runner's ability to successfully complete a marathon.

And so it is with DEI efforts. You have to appropriately measure what matters — not just organizational performance, employee engagement, and a host of human resource practices but also marketing efforts, consumer behavior, and profits.

REMEMBER

Measurement is the outcome or quantification of a process. As an organizational manager and leader, you're seeking information to optimize the performance and profitability of your company. In order to do that, you have to methodically measure what matters. Diversity, equity, and inclusion matter.

Understanding what makes a metric good

What makes a metric good? First, think about how you use metrics: as a basis to make decisions. Take, for instance, your commute to work. Which is fastest or most efficient: driving your own vehicle, taking a rideshare or taxi, or using public transport? To answer that question, you have to consider the distance, the time and financial cost for each mode of transportation, and then how long you plan to work. Better yet, do you work in area that provides all these transportation options? If not, you have use different metrics.

Establishing and collecting good metrics is a strategic advantage to the overall health of your organization. Good metrics and the appropriate technology to collect, support, and track them are essential to data reporting that produces useful knowledge, such as value and return on investment, on specific initiatives such as DEI practices.

Considering common areas to measure

Each organization's DEI metrics are specific to that organization. However, the following are common areas to measure for DEI practices:

>> **Recruitment:** To have an organization that's diverse, equitable, and inclusive, you need to source and recruit members from underrepresented and often

marginalized groups. Identify barriers in the recruitment process, especially biases. If you're not sourcing enough diverse talent, you may be relying too much on referrals or a core group of not-very-diverse schools. If you have diverse candidate pools but aren't hiring a diverse staff, recruiter bias may be the problem. These are two very different problems with two very different sets of solutions. Especially in industries that are typically homogeneous, consider who is receiving applications and interview requests, what type(s) of candidates make it to the final round of interviews, and who is finally hired.

>> **Retention:** Organizations normally track their retention rates. However, collecting the demographic data of employees at every level in an organization helps identify trends among certain underrepresented groups and in business units/departments (if there are any). Next, when conducting exit interviews, consider collecting qualitative data, such as asking an open ended question to discover why an employee is leaving the organization. This approach provides insight into the organization's retention rate.

>> **Compensation:** For an organization to be truly equitable, it needs to assess salary levels to ensure that employees within the same role earn the same base salaries and that it calculates their annual performance bonuses equitably. That is, do the formulas to determine bonuses contain biases against certain work groups? You can also conduct industry compensation surveys to allow you to make more informed business decisions based on your industry, company size, and closest competitors for talent. They allow you to understand and manage the market for talent instead of being dictated to by the market. Additionally, you can survey your employees to assess their perception of pay equity among genders, various races and ethnicities, and age within the same roles.

>> **Employee engagement and satisfaction:** In Chapter 4, I discuss the importance of employee engagement and how it relates to employees' investment in an organization's performance. Measuring employee engagement and satisfaction lets leaders see whether their DEI efforts are positively impacting the workplace.

You can track this metric through employee engagement surveys and the number of complaints to human resources regarding negative retaliation, microaggressions, race-related conflict, and LGBTQ harassment. You can also monitor the number of C-suite leaders and employees who attend DEI trainings and programs and capture qualitative feedback through post-activity surveys and exit interviews.

>> **Feedback:** Employee feedback provides insight into how your workforce perceives and experiences organizational DEI programs and practices.

TIP

Note the perceptions and feelings of underrepresented groups, and use that information to make the DEI programs better and more effective.

To create impactful and meaningful change from the get-go, include employees from underrepresented groups in the creation and implementation of the DEI programs.

>> **Supplier diversity:** *Supplier diversity* is an aspect of DEI external efforts that reflects ethical actions and social responsibility. When an organization promotes and supports diversity within its supply chain, it demonstrates its commitment to inclusivity. It also builds trust and communicates to employees that the organization mirrors its internal actions with suppliers. I go into more detail about supplier diversity in Chapter 13.

Avoiding common metrics mistakes

One of the most difficult aspects of the DEI work is that leaders don't understand what to measure. It is often assumed that DEI work is in the "soft skills" category and has little or no impact to the bottom line. But research reveals the compelling business case for how DEI impacts organizational success, which I detail in Chapter 4. So there is much to be measured in DEI; you just have to do it the right way. Here are some common measurement mistakes to avoid.

>> Measuring components that aren't aligned with company goals, strategy, and business needs

>> Measuring just to measure and producing too many metrics with no actions

>> Failing to follow up

>> Using flawed methodology

>> Lacking *benchmarking* — not having data to compare from external sources or industry standards

>> Not trusting the data

Identifying the Problems with Tracking DEI

As mentioned, a major problem with tracking DEI practices is that many companies don't have the appropriate data to report their standings. Investors, community stakeholders, and future employees want to know an organization's standing with DEI. The issue is that it may not have much to report or a history of data to track. For example, companies may be able to report on gender diversity or racial diversity but not the other components of diversity such as sexual orientation/identity/preference, disability, religion, and so on. And even in reporting on gender and racial diversity, the company has to be careful not to make assumptions based on a person's physical attribute.

Often, companies rely on employee self-reporting, but workers may be reluctant to participate. That's why companies need to explain why they need the data — so they have a better idea of where they should dedicate resources — and how they're going to collect it. For example, AT&T explains that it has a "value proposition" for describing the importance of self-identification to its employees. At Mastercard, such reporting led to a 16-week gender-neutral parental leave program. To ensure anonymity, AT&T requires a minimum number of responses and takes the data as a whole.

Currently, there is not an established global standard specific to *DEI disclosures* (what companies should report or not); however, global benchmarks and standards of practice are available for DEI. I discuss them later in this section under "Developing a DEI Scorecard."

Another problem with tracking DEI is that metrics will vary from company to company and from country to country. Every company that I have been employed with as head of DEI were all at different stages and phases, and the metrics that were tracked varied. Additionally, having worked in over 30 countries, I've learned that programs must be consistent with the laws of the country in which the company is operating.

REMEMBER

This point is especially important when utilizing DEI metrics. For example, in the United States, the Equal Employment Opportunity Commission oversees employment legal practices with regard to civil rights laws and discrimination policies. In Canada, the Minister of Labour enforces their Labour Code by investigating incidents and complaints concerning health and safety in the workplace. Australia has the Fair Work Act, which has two regulatory agencies that oversee the correct adherence to the Act in workplaces around Australia. They include the Fair Work Commission and the Fair Work Ombudsman. Together, these agencies administer, govern, and cooperate fair work within Australia. These and all other countries will have laws with different requirements; therefore, the metrics may vary as well.

Developing a DEI Scorecard

Creating a DEI scorecard enables your organization to use metrics to identify areas of risk, prioritize actions, establish goals and accountability measures, and weigh the impact of the DEI practices. A *balanced scorecard* contains four perspectives: customer, internal process, learning and growth, and financial.

The balanced scorecard links performance measures and provides a clear view into each perspective, allowing for a true big picture of performance across an organization:

>> **Customer perspective:** How do customers view and experience our services/products?

>> **Internal perspective:** What do departments/divisions/regions need in order to excel?

>> **Learning and growth/innovation:** How can we continue to improve and add value?

>> **Financial perspective:** How well are we performing against our stated goals? How do we maximize our dollars to invest back into the company?

Examining these measures all together provides a road map to see which areas need improvement and at what expense to other areas.

To develop a scorecard, you need a set of measurements of various components or categories of DEI. The Centre for Global Inclusion engaged 112 experts from around the world to create the Global Diversity, Equity, and Inclusion Benchmarks (GDEIB) for organizations to use as standards for their DEI practices. I'm honored to be one of those experts and have been using this tool for years to assist clients in benchmarking and measuring their progress in DEI. Not only is it a free resource, but they offer a plethora of tools, checklists, and suggestions for usage on their website at https://centreforglobalinclusion.org/.

The GDEIB developed 15 actions needed for "world-class DEI work." The 15 actions are within 4 groups, from which 275 benchmarks can be established.

>> **Drive the Strategy**

1. Develop a strong rationale for DEI vision, mission, and strategy and align it to organizational goals.

2. Hold leaders accountable for implementing the organization's DEI vision, setting goals, achieving results, and being role models.

3. Provide vision, dedicated support and structure with authority, and budget to effectively implement DEI.

>> **Attract and Retain People**

4. Ensure that attraction, sourcing, and recruitment is done through the lens of DEI.

5. Ensure that DEI is integrated into talent development, performance management, advancement, and retention strategies.

6. Ensure that job design and classification are evaluated for bias and that compensation is equitable across key dimensions of diversity.

7. Achieve work-life integration, flexibility, and equitable benefits. Flexible work options are widely available and accessible.

» Align and Connect

8. Ensure that assessments, measurements, and research include a DEI lens.

9. Make communication clear, simple to understand, and a crucial force in achieving the organization's DEI goals.

10. Educate all to achieve a level of DEI competence and confidence needed to create a diverse, equitable, and inclusive organization.

11. Connect the organization's DEI and sustainability initiatives to increase the effectiveness of both.

» Listen to and Serve Society

12. Be proactive in working with community, public and private partnerships, government, and society at large, and through philanthropy.

13. Embed DEI in services and products development to serve diverse customers and clients.

14. Integrate DEI into marketing and customer service.

15. Practice responsible and ethical sourcing. Develop and nurture underrepresented suppliers.

As you think about your own organization, consider the following reflection questions:

» How does your organization currently measure DEI practices?

» What categories do you measure? Do they align with the categories and actions in the GDEIB?

» Can you already identify areas for growth and improvement based on these benchmarks? If so, think and plan ways that you can measure up.

Reporting the Data to Key Leaders

Data is information you can use. So when reporting data to key leaders in your organization, be clear and honest. The initial data may not be pretty, and that's okay; just ensure it's accurate.

One thing I've discovered in my years of facilitating DEI trainings is that many product-driven companies are in tune with their market and consumer base when it comes to diversity in advertising and the like. However, these same companies that have good external diversity practices don't reflect that internally. One way to look at this issue is to ask yourself whether your organization's employee diversity reflects its consumer base diversity and why that should matter.

Consider the balanced scorecard in the preceding section through a DEI perspective. Use the data to establish your base and now ask the following:

1. How can we continue to grow and create value without DEI? Imagine the possibilities with diverse talent.

2. How do our shareholders and stakeholders see us?

3. How do we look to our customers and consumers?

4. What areas need to excel??

REMEMBER

The measures you take help drive you and your organization forward. Metrics provide you an opportunity to see your success so you can know how you're winning. They can also show you where you're failing and what isn't working. Let the data tell the story; let the metrics be your guide toward a path forward full of progress and resilience.

Putting it all together

When developing a comprehensive DEI report for organizational leaders, utilize the following guidelines:

>> **Develop your narrative:** The narrative is where you tell the organization's DEI story and provide context and important historical and current information.

>> **Determine key data points to share:** Do so in a way that you can easily replicate over time so that future scorecards can show either progress or stagnation.

>> **Draw the big picture:** Use graphics and charts to depict the data. Everyone learns differently, and that means the methods you use to inform and instruct should vary.

>> **Describe in detail:** Take a note from this book and utilize concise, descriptive writing. Use bullet points to highlight key findings and predictions.

>> **Double-check the details:** Make sure the info you present is a correct and accurate reflection of the metrics. Your report should be in PDF form so that it's readily available for professional printing and other digital publishing. Research other reputable organizations that publish data reports and benchmark how they produce and present their reports.

Making sure leaders use the data presented

One thing to consider when reporting data to key organizational leaders is that they use that data to present information to the public. The CEO of one large financial institution publicly spoke about the lack of diversity in the C-suite due to a lack of qualified applicants within the organization. The institution's employees responded with a public outcry to the opposite effect. It was later discovered that layers of discrimination were occurring within the company's promotion pipeline. The backlash for the institution and the CEO was quite heavy. And of course, diversity training and recruiting were noted as solutions to this problem.

While watching this unfortunate incident unfold, my question was "Did someone provide this CEO with inaccurate data? Or, in the absence of data, did the CEO make a dangerous assumption?" Either way, the controversy didn't serve the CEO, the organization, or its people well.

Chapter **13**

Embedding DEI in Other Key Areas of the Organization

D iversity, equity, and inclusion initiatives can't be an isolated effort or the work of one person, nor can they be an exercise in recruiting more talent to fill representation goals and conducting some training on DEI. Rather, you have to fully integrate DEI into all your organization's processes and systems. This chapter offers a number of ways you can embed and integrate DEI programs and practices into the broader scope of the organization.

Incorporating DEI Messaging into Marketing and Branding Initiatives

A *brand* is a product, service, or concept that's publicly distinguished from other products, services, or concepts so that it can be easily communicated and usually marketed. A *brand name* is the name of the distinctive product, service, or concept.

For example, Coca-Cola and Nike are two of the most highly recognizable brands across the globe. For Coke you may be familiar with Smartwater, Sprite, and Dasani water as a few of their products. For Nike you may be familiar with Air Jordon, Converse, and Cole Haan. The messaging behind the brand requires strategically planned communications for both internal and external purposes. This section focuses on brand communications that are external to the organization.

Mattel is a leading global toy company and owner of one of the strongest catalogs of children's and family entertainment franchises in the world. Through a relationship that I developed with a colleague at Mattel, I was placed on the company's yearly mailing list of holiday gifts. Each year for nearly seven years, I received the most beautiful dolls of color. This act was important to me as a mom and a woman of color because I could show my daughter that toys she could play with that looked like her were available. We kept every doll, and today they're on display in a curio cabinet in my home. This personal story matters because Mattel has me as a customer for life because it demonstrated a commitment to DEI by developing products that reflected a multicultural marketplace.

And this multiculturalism isn't new to the brand. Even though Mattel has been around since 1959, it didn't release the first black and Hispanic dolls named Barbie until 1980. Many diverse dolls were previously available, but they were always only friends of Barbie. Over the past few years, Barbie has introduced more than 170 new looks, including body diversity, dolls reflecting permanent disabilities, and more skin tones and hair colors and textures.

Today, Mattel remains committed to DEI and continues to embed it into its new toy product development. For example, in 2021 it released a Play with Pride deck for the card game UNO that celebrates the LGBTQ community and includes a donation to the It Gets Better Project in honor of Pride Month. Additionally, Mattel integrates DEI into its marketing, branding, supply chain, recruitment, promotion, and philanthropic initiatives. In its 2021 progress update, it touted that it had achieved its prior year goals of 100 percent pay equity for all employees performing similar work in the United States and achieved 100 percent pay equity for all employees performing similar work globally. Women also accounted for 58 percent of all promotions the year before, and 50 percent of new hires at the VP level and higher were women.

Target, a U.S. retailer, is an example of a company that has expanded its DEI messaging into brilliant marketing and branding initiatives. It invites and collaborates with underrepresented and diverse suppliers to offer their products in its stores. They also provide a roster of diverse suppliers that are at least 51 percent owned, controlled, and operated by women, BIPOC, LGBTQ, veterans, or persons with disabilities. Additionally, they release new products and marketing campaigns in celebration of various diversity months throughout the year (such as Pride Month, Women's History Month, and Black History Month).

Now that you have a better idea of the important role that DEI plays in reaching more diverse consumers, customers, and communities through branding and marketing, consider what ways your organization currently does this and how effective their efforts are. What else can be done to embed DEI messaging into your organization's products and services?

In the next section, I go deeper into how inclusion can work as an advantage to your organization's brand and marketing efforts. I also provide some of the marketing faux paus that can damage your organization's brand.

Practicing inclusive marketing

REMEMBER

Branding is more than a logo and an image. It requires developing diverse and inclusive content reflective of your organization's DEI practices. You want the kind of content that resonates with your workplace and consumer base. This inclusive marketing involves consumer research, marketing team structure, a consistent style guide, and the consumer/customer experience.

Inclusive marketing is creating thoughtful and respectful content that reflects the diverse communities a company serves by elevating diverse voices and reducing cultural bias. Keep in mind that if the demographics of your organization are different from those of your customer base and customers feel unseen, they'll soon no longer be customers.

INCLUSIVITY AND MARKETING (THE GOOD AND THE BAD)

If you want to reach a broader, more diverse customer, you must consider how inclusive is the message, the meaning, and the medium you use. Companies who are thoughtful and intentional about these three considerations yield positive results, but companies who ignore them pay a significant price.

- **Good:** A software company imbedded inclusive marketing language into its online learning system for developers learning to code. The company puts the responsibility on its marketers to create and promote inclusive messaging.

- **Bad:** A global luxury designer and retailer introduced a turtleneck design that resembled blackface when pulled up to the wearer's face. The design house also sold Sikh-like turbans as "Indy Full Turban." These were two huge cultural mistakes that the company had to apologize and atone for. If the company had had an inclusive team of people of color and from various religions/faiths, or even knowledge of various faiths' religious symbols, it could've avoided these mistakes.

As I discuss in Chapter 1, diversity in the workplace focuses on the "who" is represented in demographics such as gender, race/ethnicity, sexual orientation, veteran status, and ability status. Inclusivity is the environment in which diversity grows and thrives. Inclusion recognizes and values everyone and their contributions.

Does your organization's content marketing demonstrate that your brand reflects diversity and embraces inclusion?

Avoiding cultural appropriation and other missteps

Inclusivity can help prevent cultural mistakes. At the basic level, a team should be sensitized and trained to ask thoughtful diversity and inclusion questions, as well as be encouraged to consult with communities where a possible problem or misunderstanding may come up.

WARNING

When offering and promoting products, be very sure not to commit *cultural appropriation* (taking something from another culture without showing knowledge of or respect for that culture). Through the years, myriad companies have learned the hard way — through marketing/messaging faux pas — how significant cultural appropriation is. Table 13-1 details a few ways marketing can go sideways, including an example of cultural appropriation.

TABLE 13-1   **Marketing and Branding Faux Pas**

Mistake	Description	Example
Minimizing oppression	Responding to social movements in a way that makes light of them or benefits the brand at the expense of a marginalized group	In a soft drink commercial responding to Black Lives Matter protests against police brutality, the protest looked more like a celebratory block party. A supermodel handed a police officer a can of soda as a "solution" to the divide. The ad was deeply offensive to racial justice activists and was immediately pulled.
Translation mishaps	Designing global marketing campaigns without expert translation services, to odd or harmful results	An English marketing slogan for a ballpoint pen was "It won't leak in your pocket and embarrass you." The Mexican version mistakenly used the verb *embarazar,* and the resulting copy read, "It won't leak in your pocket and impregnate you."
Offensive tropes	Employing outdated and offensive stereotypes, even unwittingly	A soap ad displayed a number of women removing their tops to show another woman underneath. The first woman to remove a brown top revealed a white woman in a white top. This portion of the ad was converted to a three-second GIF and went viral on social media, harkening back to a long-standing racist trope in soap advertising of turning Black people white, as if the melanin in their skin was equivalent to dirt.

Mistake	Description	Example
Misguided attempts at humor	Making jokes designed to appeal to a "mainstream" audience that come at the expense of a marginalized group	A candy bar ad showed two male auto mechanics eating a candy bar from opposite ends and accidentally kissing, to their mutual horror. One proposed ending to the ad showed the two men attacking each other to assert their masculinity. LGBT groups found the ad offensive, and it was pulled.
Cultural appropriation	Taking something from another culture without showing knowledge of or respect for that culture	A quick Internet search for "spirit animal t-shirt" reveals several garments being marketed to non-Native populations, including one that reads, "Wine is my spirit animal." Totems, commonly referred to as spirit animals, are an important part of many Native American religious traditions.
Erasure	Using overly homogenous campaigns that communicate that marginalized groups have been rendered invisible, or at least aren't important customers to your brand	A property management company posted a large window ad in one of its downtown buildings that read, "See Detroit like we do." The ad featured many faces but no prominent Black faces, even though Detroit's population is 85 percent Black/African American. The company apologized and canceled the campaign.

Reflect on some ways your organization has made some of these same mistakes. What was the impact? How did you recover? What did you learn from it for your next product/service launch?

Companies need to consistently consider their consumer bases and the market when introducing new products or even advertising flagship products. Accenture conducted a study of consumer behavior after the COVID-19 pandemic that found consumers won't support companies that don't support their values and will pay more for products from companies who do.

Can you think of ways to reimagine how you provide customer service and product offerings? In what ways can you and your organization create the necessary human connections that produce loyal customers?

Integrating DEI into Company Communications and Messaging

Many organizations need a change in perspective because they often see improving DEI programs and practices as a problem rather than an opportunity to learn and grow. Authentic, empathetic, and transparent communications are the foundation of a positive employee experience when based on a culture of equity, respect, and belonging. Internal communications serve a critical role in creating this environment.

REMEMBER

Regardless of how large or small, new or advanced your DEI programs and practices are, internal communications should be the authentic, outspoken voice and ally for every single employee.

Following are some tips for integrating DEI into internal company communications and messaging:

>> **Communicate the value of DEI to the business and the workplace:** Senior leaders should consistently communicate their commitment to DEI and reinforce that DEI is every person's responsibility.

>> **Ensure the messages and language are inclusive:** The same guidelines I cover in the earlier section "Incorporating DEI Messaging into Marketing and Branding Initiatives" also apply to internal communications.

>> **Lead conversations about the vision, mission, and goals of DEI:** Policies and practices should support the DEI programs and be communicated across the organization. The DEI goals should be aligned with the overall business goals, mission, vision, and strategy (see Chapter 8).

>> **Ask, listen, and act:** Leaders should be transparent and ready to have the crucial and difficult conversations surrounding the sensitive areas involving DEI. Establish a dialogue between leaders and employees that can include one-on-one meetings, listening sessions, town hall/all-staff meetings, and so on. After you've listened, actions must follow if you want to foster trust and build credibility. The fastest way to undermine both of these is to ask for employees' input and hear their concerns but not do anything to address them.

>> **Hold staff accountable for living the values and demonstrating inclusive behaviors:** Make sure employees understand their responsibility in creating an inclusive and respectful culture.

Connecting DEI to Environmental Social Governance and Corporate Responsibility

Strong community relations and philanthropy should be an integral part of an organization's strategic plan and should continuously adapt to the needs of society. More and more workers, and even customers, report that they want to work for and patronize companies that are committed to making their communities, the environment, and the world a better place. Today, corporate social responsibility (CSR) has evolved beyond compliance to include how a company earns and spends its revenues and what it stands for (socially, economically, environmentally, and in some cases politically). This facet has come to encompass environmental and social governance (ESG) as well. A November 2019 McKinsey & Company article defines ESG by its three elements:

>> **Environmental:** Environmental criteria include the energy your company takes in, the waste it discharges, the resources it needs, and the consequences for living beings as a result. It also encompasses carbon emissions and climate change. Every company uses energy and resources; every company affects, and is affected by, the environment.

>> **Social:** Social criteria addresses the relationships your company has and the reputation it fosters with people and institutions in the communities where you do business. It includes labor relations and diversity and inclusion. Every company operates within a broader, diverse society.

>> **Governance:** Governance is the internal system of practices, controls, and procedures your company adopts to govern itself, make effective decisions, comply with the law, and meet the needs of external stakeholders. Every company, which is itself a legal creation, requires governance.

As the world faced the deadly COVID-19 pandemic and was confronted with international protests against systemic social and racial injustices and cries for greater equity and inclusion, the importance of incorporating ESG into all business and investment decisions was clear and compelling. The number of organizations that responded by putting out public statements of their values and beliefs, and that made financial commitments for and against these and other social issues, was astounding. My firm was flooded with requests from CEOs; presidents; CHROs; chief diversity, equity, and inclusion officers; and even board members seeking guidance and expertise for how to address these issues both short and long term. Not just because they wanted to do the right thing, but because they wanted to position their companies for business success.

REMEMBER

The message throughout this book is that DEI is not only the right thing to do for an organization but also a predictor of organizational success, profitability, and innovation. CSR and ESG initiatives tend to focus on external communities while DEI initiatives focus on internal communities, but integrating these efforts as shared priorities so they mutually reinforce each other is important.

Consider some of the following common ESG and CSR initiatives and reflect on how you can/should align your DEI efforts:

» Racial justice, equity (across all marginalized and underrepresented groups), and inclusion

» Carbon emissions and carbon footprint

» Climate change and greenhouse gas (GHG) emissions

» Energy efficiency

» Renewable energy

» Green products and infrastructure

» Water conservation

» Socially responsive company policies

» Ethical and diverse supply chains

» Transparency in reporting

» Data privacy and data integrity

» Health and safety

» Executive compensation and golden parachutes

» Independence of the board of directors and management team

» Diversity of the board and its management team

» Ethical behavior and anti-corruption

» Fair trade agreements

Surveying Supplier Diversity Programs

Supplier diversity programs are a tangible way to demonstrate an organization's commitment to maintain ethical standards and generate economic opportunity.

A *diverse supplier* is a business that's at least 51 percent owned and operated by an individual or group that's part of a traditionally underrepresented or underserved

192   PART 3 Implementing and Operationalizing DEI Across the Organization

group. The classifications for these are based on the U.S. Small Business Administration:

» Small-Business Enterprises (SBEs)

» Minority-Owned Enterprises (MBEs)

» Woman-Owned Enterprises (WBEs)

» Veteran-Owned Enterprises

» LBGTQ Enterprises

» Proprietors with Disabilities

Many companies spend millions and even billions of dollars a year on goods and services. Yet historically, businesses owned by women and people from marginalized groups (including the ones I list earlier) have been left behind in terms of securing supplier contracts with large corporations. Additionally, government and nonprofit groups are increasing their efforts to monitor the percentage of contracts awarded to these enterprises.

Understanding the benefits of supplier diversity programs

Supplier diversity programs aren't just considered the right thing to do; they're also good for economy and the community. Here are a few examples from companies who publish their supplier diversity reports:

» As of 2019, Target spent $1.4 billion on goods and services from first-tier suppliers (those who Target directly buys from) and influenced their first-tier suppliers to buy $800,000 from second-tier suppliers (those who Tier-one suppliers use to purchase products or services).

» Coca-Cola has spent over $800 million annually on diverse suppliers, with goals to surpass $1 billion.

» UPS spends $6.2 billion annually with over 6,000 small and diverse suppliers.

Additionally, the National Minority Supplier Diversity Council reports that MBEs generate $400 billion in economic output that preserves 2.2 million jobs and $49 billion in revenue for the local, state, and federal tax authorities.

The benefits aren't just economic. Supplier diversity programs also include education, training, and entrepreneurship efforts. For example, institutes exist that provide education to disadvantaged groups on how to start businesses. Entrepreneurship trainings and mentorship opportunities are available for women.

A BRIEF HISTORY OF SUPPLIER DIVERSITY AROUND THE WORLD

Supplier diversity is an outcome of the United States civil rights movement of the 1950s and 1960s. General Motors established one of the first supplier diversity programs, and the rest of the American auto industry followed its lead. At the same time, IBM established a supplier diversity program in the electronics industry. U.S. federal law then established a program encouraging companies with government contracts to include minority-owned businesses in their supply chains.

In an article titled "How Supplier Diversity Is Going Global" published on the website of supplier.io (blog.cvmsolutions.com/how-supplier-diversity-is-going-global), Molly Larsen details the history of supplier diversity around the world. She writes:

Supplier diversity in the rest of the world is a 21st-century movement, arising from decades of progress in the U.S. The U.K. was the first non-U.S. country to pass legislative action addressing business equality. The Local Government Act of 2000 outlined the responsibility that local authorities have to promote the social, economic, and environmental well-being of their communities through diverse procurement practices. France followed suit in 2006 with socially responsible public procurement best practices, and soon other European countries were joining the movement to ensure equality throughout the supply chain.

Canada has had a formal minority supplier organization — the Canadian Aboriginal and Minority Supplier Council (CAMSC) — since 2004, but it was only in 2018 that the Canadian government had announced a new social procurement initiative that will provide greater transparency into federal procurement practices, and more opportunities for underrepresented populations to participate in the supply chain.

Although the Canadian government does not require that companies have a supplier diversity program to be eligible for government contracts (yet), the initiative mentioned above includes a significant effort to educate the public on the benefits of supplier diversity. As a result, supplier diversity is part of the public conversation and a key social and economic issue for Canadian voters.

Currently, the only other country to connect supplier diversity to federal contracts is Australia. The Indigenous Procurement Policy requires government suppliers to demonstrate engagement with Indigenous business owners. Supply Nation, modeled after the National Minority Supplier Development Council (NMSDC), certifies minority-owned businesses in Australia. So far, Supply Nation has certified nearly 500 businesses owned by Aboriginal and Torres Strait Islander individuals since the organization was founded in 2009.

In South Africa, supplier diversity is being built on the foundation of the Broad-Based Black Economic Empowerment Amendment (B-BBEE) Act. Following decades of apartheid, the B-BBEE was passed in 2013 to address South Africa's incredible level of economic inequality. This is one case in which supplier diversity is designed to allow the *majority* of citizens to participate equally in the nation's economy. A majority of South African citizens are Black, but decades of systematic exclusion resulted in a severe imbalance in every sector — in entrepreneurship, workforce inclusion, economic and social equality, government representation, and educational opportunity, among others. The B-BBEE is part of a multipronged effort to restore economic balance in South Africa.

China is another country that is still in the infancy of supplier diversity. With no government support, the task of establishing and developing a supplier diversity program is even more challenging. Supplier diversity in China is a grassroots effort supported by corporations that are interested in tapping into the potential of minorities in that country. MSD China, the largest supplier diversity organization in China, launched in 2008 and has so far certified about 100 minority-owned businesses.

Supplier diversity is emerging in other countries, such as Mexico and India. As supplier diversity in the U.S. matures, multinational companies are taking a global view and exploring opportunities to support the initiative elsewhere.

Some research has found that individuals want to work for an employer with a supplier diversity and inclusion program, so these programs can be a selling point to attract talent.

Other benefits of inclusive procurement strategies include the following:

>> Broadens the talent pool of potential suppliers

>> Promotes competition in the supply base, which can improve quality and drive down costs

>> Makes supply chains more resilient and agile

>> Provides access to a new network

Establishing and nurturing relationships with diverse vendors and suppliers

Getting the most out of a supplier diversity program means having strong relationships with suppliers. Supplier diversity organizations facilitate relationships between suppliers and those in need of their products and services. They often have vendor fairs and matchmaking to connect vendors and suppliers. The following is a listing (in no particular order) of supplier diversity organizations:

>> National Minority Supplier Development Council

>> CVM Solutions

>> WEConnect International

>> National LGBT Chamber of Commerce

>> National Veteran Business Development Council

>> United States Hispanic Chamber of Commerce

>> DiversityInc

>> Supply Nation (Australia's leading database of verified Indigenous businesses)

>> Bank Policy Institute

>> U.S. Pan Asian American Chamber of Commerce

>> Ralph G. Moore & Associates (RGMA)

>> Billion Dollar Roundtable

Partnering with organizations like these enables companies to build relationships with diverse suppliers. A company must have a planned and strategic effort in place in order to establish and optimize relationships with diverse suppliers. These efforts can include workshops and professional matchmaking at supplier diversity conferences.

Exploring best practices for supplier diversity programs

Each year, DiversityInc publishes their lists of top companies for diversity in a number of categories, including supplier diversity. The following are highlights of the best practices from the winning companies in the area of supplier diversity:

>> Integrating supplier diversity into corporate goals

>> Having the CEO sign off on supplier diversity results

>> Auditing supplier diversity numbers

>> Ensuring suppliers are certified

>> Linking procurement-management compensation to supplier diversity goals

Here are few more in-depth examples of companies' best practices and approaches for supplier diversity. As you can see, each company has a dedicated team to focus on supplier diversity strategy and execution, measurable goals, accountability, and detailed deliverables.

An Energy Company's Best Practices and Approach to Supplier Diversity:

Supplier Diversity Team: Monthly updates to executive leadership. Alignment with the DEI office and Employee Resource Groups. Quarterly engagement with suppliers. Strategy team of senior decision makers.

Connecting with Community Groups: Small business advocacy groups. Industry organizations. Connect with the energy company's economic development team.

Supplier Engagement and Touchpoints: Relationship building with supply chain and business unit teams. Prime contractors to diverse business engagement. B2B engagement.

Supplier Development and Capacity Building: Internal mentoring programs with senior decision makers as mentors. Collaborate with the small business development center and other advocacy groups. Business development programs.

Fortune 500 Financial Institution Best Practices and Approach to Supplier Diversity:

Diverse Spend Growth: Support strategic thinking and align with businesses around strategic opportunities that include diverse suppliers in competitive sourcing and procurement opportunities.

Supplier Development: Invest in building capacity and expertise for high potential diverse suppliers.

Outreach: Partner with internal and external stakeholders to deliver information to the diverse supplier community.

Global Communications Company (Fortune 100) Best Practices for Supplier Diversity:

Start at the Top: Chairman commitment. Accountability to metrics established. Resources through the supplier diversity leadership and team.

Understand Your Why: Brand enhancement. Community impact. Customer loyalty. Better business solutions.

Ensure the Supplier Diversity Program Is Meaningful (Impacts Communities) and Measurable: Diverse supplier spend and utilization. Diverse job creation and force impact. Diverse business fostering and advocacy.

Devote Proper Resources to a Supplier Diversity Program with Intentional Focus: Leadership and strategic direction. Advocacy. Stakeholder management. Business processes.

Create a Supplier-centric Approach: Development, advocacy, opportunity, and outreach.

Develop a Program to Recognize and Reward Those Most Aligned with the Supplier Diversity Program (There Is Something in It for Everyone): Supplier Awards. Employee, Executive, and Partnership Awards.

What can you implement from the best practices in this section to enhance your organization's commitment to DEI both internally and externally?

Measuring the success of a supplier diversity program

Evaluating a supplier diversity program normally begins with the dollars spent with diverse suppliers and ends with the impact on the community through corporate social responsibility efforts. The most common factors companies use to track supplier diversity programs are

» What is your organization's annual spend on diverse suppliers and vendors

» How many diverse suppliers your organization contracts with annually

» How many diverse suppliers your organization contracts within a given period

But measurement is unique to the company and the type of supplier diversity relationship. Business to business companies are mainly focused on meeting their customers' and government contracts' supplier diversity requirements. Business to consumer companies focus on the market value supplier diversity provides, such as

» More entry in diverse markets

» Creating social and economic benefits in diverse communities

» Enhancing the company's image

Some of the specific metrics gathered from the best practice examples in the preceding section include the following:

» Tracking of the number of opportunities with small and diverse suppliers within the supply chain

» Business to business joint ventures

» Spend growth across the company

» Number of new suppliers added to the pipeline

» Industry growth — winning new contracts with small and diverse suppliers and expanding the footprint with key industry partners

» Diverse supplier spend and utilization

» Job creation and workforce impact

» Development of business relationships

» Amount of advocacy effort

Can you identify your organization's supplier diversity strategy and goals? Can you name your diverse spend and diverse count?

REMEMBER

The reporting of diverse spend as a percentage of an organization's total spend is essential to the authenticity of a company's supplier diversity program.

IN THIS CHAPTER

Employee Resource Groups as separate but related units

» Understanding why having an executive sponsor is so important

» Creating DEI councils and Employee Resource Groups

Chapter **14**

Launching DEI Councils and Employee Resource Groups

D EI councils and Employee Resource Groups (ERGs) aren't new. They're decades old and continue to evolve. In recent years they've taken on new meaning and new roles as companies focus on building more inclusive workplace cultures and expanding their brands and reputations with customers and communities. This chapter describes diversity councils and ERGs and how they differ and complement each other. It also offers a step-by-step guide for establishing both for your organization and includes some best practices for how companies are utilizing them for business success.

REMEMBER

DEI councils originally were (and sometimes still are) called "diversity councils" because the focus was mainly on diversity. However, as diversity initiatives have evolved to include equity and inclusion, the term *DEI councils* has become more commonplace. I use both terms in this chapter.

Differentiating Between DEI Councils and Employee Resource Groups

DEI councils and Employee Resource Groups are often mentioned interchangeably. However, they're two distinct entities, although they work best when in collaboration and support of each other. Today, most organizations have some form of a DEI council or ERG or are in the process of establishing one.

A *DEI council* is usually the governing entity that provides the strategic direction; establishes the DEI vision, goals, and objectives for the organization; and provides oversight for the DEI activities. It also serves as a sounding board that organizational leaders can engage to accelerate the DEI initiatives. An organization that has a DEI strategic plan or wants to develop one should consider forming a diversity council.

The diversity council should be a reflection of employees from across the organization who represent the breadth of diversity (that is, age, tenure, location, level, race, experience, title, gender, sexual orientation, and so on). Large organizations usually appoint a Chief Diversity, Equity, and Inclusion Officer to drive the DEI initiatives. Where companies have no one to lead the DEI efforts, a member of HR or the senior leadership team (including the CEO) usually leads the charge.

Employee resource groups found their beginning as a result of the civil rights movement of the 1960s in the United States. They were also initially described as affinity groups. Today, *affinity groups* have evolved to be a type of ERG, BRG (business resource group), or DRG (diversity resource group) and are employer-recognized workplace groups voluntarily led by employees. These groups allow employees with shared interests, causes, experiences, and hobbies to meet, support each other, and help improve the business and their job satisfaction. They also give employees the opportunity to build community, have discussions about meaningful topics, and share resources.

Here are examples of the most common ERGs:

>> Women's network (and even more focused subsets, such as women leaders, women in technology, and so on)

>> Network for people of color, plus additional groups for specific marginalized groups such as Black employees, Hispanic/Latinx employees, Asian employees, and Native American and Indigenous employees

>> LGBTQ network

>> Working parents support group

>> Veterans support group

>> Network for people with disabilities

>> Mental health advocacy group

>> Mentorship group

>> Young professionals network

>> Community impact and volunteerism committee

ERGs are the outcome of efforts to become an inclusive culture and support DEI initiatives. Being involved with ERGs can help employees develop their leadership skills, increase engagement across the organization and also expand the company's market reach.

REMEMBER

There's no one exact and correct way to structure DEI councils and ERGs. Each organization has to consider its own organizational culture, structure, business functions, community stakeholders, and the like.

Understanding how diversity councils can support ERGs

A DEI council can support ERGs by doing the following:

>> Providing assistance and guidance to employees who want to start an ERG

>> Providing oversight and direction to the ERG executive sponsor and chairperson (head to the later section "Ensuring Engagement at the Top: The Importance of the Executive Sponsor" for more on this role)

>> Allocating budgetary support

>> Sharing best practices and industry insight

>> Helping with developing ERG mission and strategy

>> Driving awareness of and education about the ERGs

REMEMBER

DEI councils need to take special consideration to gain the insight needed to understand the dimensions, perspectives, and barriers to DEI and how to properly address them. In order to be effective, ERGs must be aligned with the organizational mission.

THE FIRST ERGs

The first ERG was founded by Joseph Wilson, former CEO of Xerox. The company had established a progressive hiring program for Blacks, but the Black employees were experiencing discrimination in the workplace after they were hired. As a result, Wilson joined with the Black employees of Xerox to form the National Black Employees Caucus so that employees could share their experiences and collectively advocate for racial equity within their organization. About ten years later, Xerox formed the Black Women's Leadership Caucus. Fortune 500 Companies such as HP and AT&T were trailblazers in the 1970s and 1980s with forming ERGs for LGBTQ communities.

Therefore, consider what you're more focused on: community service? Creating a more diverse workforce? Providing greater access for your population? Making sure ERGs are securely founded on the organizational mission and business goals?

Looking at what diversity councils and ERGs can accomplish together

Research suggests that DEI councils and ERGs can help organizations address the following questions:

>> How can we do a better job leading, managing, and funding DEI efforts to improve impact?

>> How can we integrate the values of DEI at all levels of the organization?

>> How can we understand the progress we make with DEI and determine next steps?

>> How can we motivate leaders and employees to make themselves accountable to creating and sustaining a culture of inclusive excellence?

Building an inclusive culture of excellence that truly supports diversity and equity takes an entire organization. DEI councils provide the governance. ERGs provide mobilization and opportunities for employees to engage and rally around shared interests. ERGs are specific to an organization's needs and interest, so the possibilities are endless as long as they're in line with organizational values.

Drilling down into the importance of ERGs

Individuals from marginalized groups are still underrepresented in the corporate workplace. For example, Asian, Latina, and African American women combined make up less than 4 percent of executive and senior level positions in the S&P 500. Individuals from underrepresented groups need a way of gathering with people like them to dispel isolation and increase engagement. Almost 85 percent of employees between 18 and 35 report that ERGs have a positive impact on their engagement at work.

These groups are essential to employer branding strategy because they offer alternative pathways for career advancement, development, and support. The ERGs provide a community and space for people to gather and address points of interest through a cultural or gender lens.

With that said, intersectionality and the multidimensionality of the workplace will only increase. Understanding this dynamic helps you manage DEI issues and the perspectives that launch innovative and effective ERGs. One of the best practices of ERGs is to offer multiple points of entry for employees who aren't a part of the same affinity group or specific demographic to get involved and learn.

REMEMBER

ERGs are designed for commonalities but should be open to all. For one thing, legal considerations often come into play when organizations fund groups that are exclusionary. More importantly, though, this approach prevents employees from feeling left out and promotes cross-collaboration.

TIP

Cross-collaboration between employee resource groups is an additional vehicle to create a more inclusive environment and address the points of intersectionality. For example, young professional and generational professional ERGs have a place for people of different genders, sexual orientations, races, and ethnicities to come together and navigate through intersectionality. Several years ago, I had the opportunity to serve on a young professional's advisory board for the largest non-profit serving agency in a large metropolitan area. We were selected to serve through a competitive process. However, we all shared the same mission of serving our community for the greater good. That particular group was comprised of many different races, genders, and professionals from various industries. We came to serve and ultimately became colleagues and friends.

Ensuring Engagement from the Top: The Importance of the Executive Sponsor

One thing the many areas of focus for ERGs all have in common is an *executive sponsor.* These sponsors are tasked with leveraging their influence as senior leaders to push the DEI initiatives and engage more senior leadership in conversation. Sometimes the executive sponsor is from a different demographic than the group, depending on the demographics of senior leadership. In these cases, executive sponsorship is an opportunity for a senior leader to learn about and empathize with an identity group other than their own, and it can have a strong impact on how they lead. Executive sponsorship is one powerful tactic for engaging the dominant-group members of the organization.

Though engaging white men as allies and champions of DEI can be difficult, it's also important and crucial. Currently, white heterosexual men hold the majority of the decision making power in the corporate workplace. Leaving them out of the DEI conversation is a grave mistake. DEI needs the senior leaders to influence the systemic culture change of an organization.

TIP

Here are a few things that I've done and that you can do to engage white men in DEI conversations and efforts:

1. **Define DEI in its broadest sense (both the visible and invisible traits of diversity) so that they see that they're diverse, too.**

   I usually make the statement upfront that diversity is about all of us because it's about people.

2. **Involve them in the discussions and allow them to share their stories and challenges (or fears of diversity).**

   Use that sharing as teaching moments to ease anxieties, to encourage more dialogue and learning, and to dispel myths (such as the ideas that hiring diversity means lowering standards, that the company can't find diverse talent, and that DEI involves reverse discrimination). I bust some of these myths in Chapter 19.

3. **Find allies and champions who are supportive of DEI and use them to bring their peers along and to advocate for funding, change, and resources.**

4. **Educate them on the basic DEI terminology, the importance of building more inclusive workplace cultures, and the business benefits.**

   I break down some key DEI terms in Chapter 1. Important concepts here are the difference between diversity and inclusion and between equity and equality; microaggressions; unconscious biases; prejudices; power; and privilege.

5. **Invite them to be executive sponsors, mentors, coaches, trainers, and ambassadors.**

6. **Hold them accountable for taking a leadership role in driving DEI initiatives.**

All these strategies have been successful in making white men feel like active and engaged partners in DEI versus feeling alienated, targeted, and accused of being the "bad guys." Remember, though, that every person and organization is different, and the approach you need to take may vary.

Establishing an Effective DEI Council

From my years of launching DEI councils and consulting with companies on establishing them, here are some best practices that I've seen work well and add tremendous value to the company's business objectives.

>> Set up a charter that outlines the council's mission, vision, objectives, goals, roles and responsibilities, and measures of success. Some even establish guiding principles and core values (often those of the organization), as well as a scorecard. You can read more about creating a charter in the later section "Developing a DEI council charter."

>> Seek out and invite diversity of all types from across the organization.

>> Work hand in hand with the office of DEI, HR, executive offices, and the board (if applicable).

>> Meet frequently and establish agendas for each meeting.

>> Establish ways that you'll hold the council accountable for meeting the goals/ objectives and how you'll communicate them.

The following sections break down some tactical steps for how to establish DEI councils.

Knowing your company and finding a champion

One of the first things you should consider when creating a diversity council in your organization is the history of that company. Ask yourself the following:

>> What are the historical and current demographics of the workplace?

>> Is the workplace racially homogenous?

>> What are the gender and cultural ratios?

>> What about the number of differently abled individuals in the workforce?

>> What's the most common way potential candidates are hired into the workplace — referrals, job postings, live recruitment activities?

When you have the answers to these questions, consider who can be your champion for the DEI initiatives. You definitely need to have a champion at the executive level, preferably the CEO or equivalent. The champion may also be considered the executive sponsor (they are both used interchangeably in many companies). From there, identify the other key influential leaders within the organization who have the potential to make up a dynamic, effective diversity council. Remember, you want a council made up of employees from across the organization, across departments and levels.

REMEMBER

Support and buy-in from the following parties is essential for the council:

>> Human resources

>> Legal

>> Finance

Particularly, make sure these departments are aware as you secure your budget from the CEO.

REMEMBER

You need to have not only have gender and racial diversity on the council but also participation from white men. I cover some ways to bring them into the fold in the earlier section "Ensuring Engagement at the Top: The Importance of the Executive Sponsor."

Even though executive and key influencer support if vital, make sure the council is led by key employees. Your messaging regarding the council needs to convey that it's led by interested and invested employees with program and financial support from executive leadership. This combination indicates to employees that the initiative is valuable not just in word but in action.

Establishing your mission, vision, and strategic areas of focus

This action requires input from the council and will most likely go through several versions before you settle on your final mission. This process is normal and simply means that the council wants to put its best foot forward when communicating the mission to the entire organization.

Consider the following as a sample of potential focus areas:

- ➤➤ Talent recruitment

- ➤➤ Onboarding and orientation

- ➤➤ Talent engagement and retention

- ➤➤ Metrics

- ➤➤ Messaging

- ➤➤ Training and education

- ➤➤ Social justice

- ➤➤ Community outreach

- ➤➤ Inclusion activities

- ➤➤ Equitable practices (promotion and performance review process)

Setting goals and establishing roles and responsibilities

The following are some sample of action items based on the focus areas in the preceding section:

- ➤➤ Conduct a diversity and inclusion survey.

- ➤➤ Analyze, present, and communicate the data.

- ➤➤ Create a communication platform, such as a newsletter, an app, or an intranet webpage, that serves as a virtual home for all things DEI in your organization.

- ➤➤ Publicize your goals on the virtual platform and track your progress. This transparency fosters trust and confidence in the council's efforts.

- ➤➤ Celebrate diversity through awareness campaigns and celebrations (some countries have heritage and Pride celebration months).

- ➤➤ Establish a speakers series on topics selected by the council and derived from the diversity survey data.

- ➤➤ Hold workshops.

- ➤➤ Establish Employee Resource Groups (see the section "Offering Employee Resource Groups to Support DEI Initiatives" in this chapter).

- ➤➤ Encourage community partnership and volunteerism. Offer PTO for volunteering.

>> Do the following in conjunction with HR and the Talent Recruitment team:

- Establish or publicize the recruiting goals for underrepresented groups in the company.

- Utilize tools for sourcing and recruiting underrepresented talent.

- Maintain your country's equivalent to Equal Employment Opportunity reporting.

- Identify and mitigate bias that impacts hiring, as I discuss in Chapter 9.

- Target recruiting strategies with universities and industries.

Recruiting and securing DEI council members

The steps I outline for recruiting diverse employees are the same ones you should use to recruit DEI council members. If the organization doesn't readily reflect the dimensions of diversity that are visible to the eye, your search has to deepen to the many other dimensions of diversity I discuss throughout the book.

TIP

When establishing a diversity council in an organization, have a company-wide town hall or team meeting so the CEO can introduce the council and its goals. Then the council chairperson should make call for more members and interested participants to further the work of the council's initiatives. You may be surprised at the number of employees who are interested in participating in a number of the ERGs and action items.

Here are a few out-of-the-box ideas for recruiting DEI council members:

>> Recruit a DEI expert who can provide their expertise as a consultant to the group or bring a customer's perspective.

>> Engage a cross-section of thought leaders that bring a full breadth of functional expertise.

Developing a DEI council charter

After you've selected the members of your DEI council (see the preceding section), you're ready to draft a charter to follow. The following list contains essential core elements to include in a DEI charter:

- >> **Vision (the why):** The long term objective of the council.

- >> **Mission (the how):** The purpose and an explanatory statement of how you'll fulfill the purpose.

- >> **Objectives (the what and when):** The measurable goals and intentions of the council. This part is where you list what you want to accomplish.

- >> **Leadership assignments (the who):** Reporting structures and individual roles.

- >> **Membership criteria:** Requirements for participation.

- >> **Responsibilities:** Clear definitions of the duties for the roles.

- >> **Operational procedures:** How you conduct business as a nonrevenue-generating business unit.

Keep in mind that the DEI council that you form or that's already in existence is specific to your organization. The councils come in many forms and structures but generally fall into one of two main types:

- >> **Executive:** *Executive diversity councils* are led by the chairman, CEO, or Chief Diversity Officer and comprised of senior leaders (vice presidents and business unit heads) from the company's business functions or core businesses. These councils normally develop the comprehensive DEI strategy that aligns with the company's best practices, strategies, goals, and objectives. In addition, they monitor the progress of the council's efforts toward the established goals and objectives.

- >> **Advisory or regional:** *Advisory* or *regional diversity councils* are designed to be broader in scope and reflect the diversity of the organization's workforce. They're often larger than executive councils. The advisory council may also implement the policies and strategies the executive council develops. They tend to be responsible for advising organizational leadership on the company's DEI needs and the progress of the DEI initiatives.

Offering Employee Resource Groups to Support DEI Initiatives

Employee Resource Groups support DEI initiatives, often working in tandem with a DEI council. ERGs not only integrate DEI practices to core business units but also help foster an inclusive culture. Some organizations refer to these groups as business resource groups (BRGs) to remind people that they ultimately exist to help the business by improving the culture and sometimes by expanding the customer or stakeholder base.

ERGs also exist as another avenue for employees to develop personally and professionally and interact with other employees across the company. Because ERGs are geared toward supporting underrepresented talent, so they're a way for companies to eliminate inequities. ERG functions include, but aren't limited to, these:

>> Providing a platform for group members to share questions and concerns

>> Connecting group members with mentors and organizational support

>> Increasing cultural competence (see Chapter 17)

>> Advocating for improvements within the organization

>> Reviewing products, marketing materials, and so on to ensure cultural relevance

>> Exploring intersectionality in the workplace

>> Demonstrating acceptance and value to employees

>> Contributing to increased employee engagement and job satisfaction

>> Providing opportunities for employees to demonstrate leadership potential

>> Providing opportunities for leadership to demonstrate commitment to DEI

>> Connecting new and existing employees

>> Creating additional professional development opportunities

A NOTE ABOUT RELIGIOUS ERGs

If a religious group in your company asks to start a related ERG, check with your legal department. In some countries, people may see ERGs created to support a particular religious group as proselytizing, which may be against the law. In many Christian-dominated countries, a Christian ERG may be proposed immediately after groups for Muslims, Jews, or the LGBTQIA+ communities have been approved.

I suggest being prepared for these requests before they emerge and deciding in advance whether your organization will allow religious ERGs. If so, consider how they'll need to function in order to best support your company's DEI goals.

TIP

Let ERGs form organically through a process that allows people to pitch their ideas for new groups to the DEI council. This approach ensures that a fledgling ERG has committed and enthusiastic leadership.

Realizing the benefits of the ERGs for employees and the organization

ERGs provide an opportunity for employees to build community around shared interests and topics and also share resources. Some of the benefits of ERGs that impact both employees and the organization are

>> Branding and marketing efforts

>> Training and development

>> Employee retention

>> Unique perspectives that grow business

>> Additional work toward the company's overall mission

ERGs contribute to the individual well-being of employees and the overall business. Supporting ERGs in your organization is another positive outcome of an inclusive culture that fosters diversity and equity.

Identifying the various types of employee resource groups

Following are four common types of ERGs:

>> **Diversity resource groups:** *Diversity resource groups* are designed for employees from the underrepresented communities within the workplace. The various commonalities normally fall along racial, cultural, and gender identities. The diversity group provides a safe space where people can share thoughts, ideas, and challenges. Diversity groups also help employers address cultural challenges. As I mention earlier in the chapter, these groups should be open to allies within the organization, especially if they're to receive financial sponsorship.

>> **Volunteer groups:** *Volunteer resource groups* provide an opportunity for employees to gather to give back to the community and support various causes. These groups increase awareness of matters from health to social

justice and environmental issues and. help employees from various backgrounds find common ground over a shared value or passion.

Creating volunteer groups also lets an organization channel its employees' altruism toward corporate social responsibility (CSR) efforts that are strategically important to the organization. Organizations commonly sponsor various charity events or provide matching donations or resources for events.

>> **Affinity groups:** *Affinity groups* (sometimes called *affinity clubs*) exist so that employees with similar hobbies can come together and socialize. These groups bring together employees who share a love for a specific interest (such as wine, cycling, or reading) and help employee get to know one another. Creating connections outside of the workplace helps improve the organization's climate, employee communication, engagement, and teamwork.

TIP

Affinity groups focused on the arts (books, theatre, museums, and so on) create an excellent opportunity for your DEI team to influence the group to improve their cultural competence by focusing on works by marginalized groups.

>> **Professional development groups:** *Professional development groups* provide the space to connect employees of all levels and departments. They allow for knowledge sharing, garnering support for those wanting to advance their leadership and other professional skills. For example, a public speaking/ Toastmasters session or a coding group would qualify as a professional development group.

Deciding when to launch ERGs and which to launch first

To determine which ERG to launch first and when, you must start by assessing the company's DEI goals and the data from the DEI research and surveys collected from within the organization.

1. **Consider what the abundant needs are and which groups of underrepresented people need help with retention and promotion.**

   Remember, each ERG needs a purpose based on the overall company and DEI strategy goals and objectives.

2. **Secure an executive sponsor from the DEI council or from the executive leadership team.**

   Having a senior leadership member supporting the implementation of the group is essential. I talk more about executive sponsors in the earlier section "Ensuring Engagement at the Top: The Importance of the Executive Sponsor."

3. **Start small and grow.**

   Allow space for the ERGs to grow over time while assessing progress.

4. **Spread awareness about the ERGs and promote through the various communication channels.**

TIP

Make sure part of the ERG proposal process includes data that indicates that a targeted community is behind the idea. Doing so helps set a new ERG up for success.

Recruiting ERG members and executive sponsors

Here are some tips for getting the people you need into your ERG:

>> Utilize members of the DEI council to serve as executives sponsors.

>> Take advantage of the DEI council's span and reach to recruit ERG members.

>> Just ask!

>> Make information easily and frequently accessible through digital platforms and other communication channels. Make sure information about the ERGs is readily available during the onboarding process.

Establishing an ERG charter and measures of success

Creating an ERG charter is similar to the process I detail for creating a DEI council charter in the earlier section "Developing a DEI council charter."

The ERG charter should be aligned with the DEI council's strategy and goals. What's unique about the charter is that it will represent the needs of the specific underrepresented group. These needs are usually identified from staff surveys, focus groups, exit interviews, documented complaints, or past/pending legal actions. The charter serves as the roadmap for how the group will work together, what goals it will achieve by when, and its expected impact to the organization. I've also seen them include committees that the ERG will establish such as Communication, Marketing, Programming, and so on, and external partnerships and activities that it will engage in.

>> As you define your purpose and goals, you can define how you'll measure success.

>> Check out the diversity metrics in Chapter 12 for some ideas on measuring your success.

4

Sustaining DEI in Your Organization

» Seeing how bias shows up in everyday life

» Getting a handle on different types of biases

» Looking at ways bias can affect decisions in the workplace

» Discovering how to make less-biased decisions

Chapter **15**

Understanding Implicit Bias and Its Impact in the Workplace

In my business, I travel nearly 80 percent of the time delivering presentations all over the world. When traveling within North America one of my preferred airlines is Southwest, which doesn't assign seats. It assigns passengers to zones with a numbered position. Most of the time I remember to check in within the 24-hour window to get in zone A or B. But a few times I've been late checking in online and ended up in zone C, in the last position. You can imagine where most people who are in zones A and B sit: in the front of the plane, in the aisle seats, and in the window seats. So what's left? The middle seats. And this is where my biases kick in.

Imagine boarding the plane and having two to three seconds to decide which middle seat to take. I begin scanning the aisles and the passengers who are already seated to determine who I want to sit beside and who I prefer not to sit beside.

Those preferences may include avoiding the parents traveling with babies, the oversized passenger, the one who's eating food, or the one who's talking too much. It may even be the person who's coughing or showing signs of illness. By going through this quick decision making process, I exercise my biases to make the determination. These biases are based on previous, unpleasant experiences (that is, sitting beside an infant that cried for an entire six-hour flight, feeling squished by the man whose body covers my armrest and part of my seat, or sitting beside someone that coughed and sneezed my way).

When in that same situation, who would you decide not to sit beside? Why? This kind of scenario is how biases play out in everyday interactions (more about this later in this chapter).

When most people hear the word *bias,* their minds quickly go to something nega-tive. Words like *discrimination, prejudice,* and *bigotry* typically spring to mind. Here's a little thought experiment. Say you've just tuned in to the local news, and the headline at the bottom of your screen reads, "Evidence of bias at City Hall." What do you think this story is about? Chances are, it doesn't reflect well on your city government.

But bias isn't evidence of a deficit in character; rather, it's simply one way that the brain makes decisions. It's not the only way, and it's not always a bad way to reach a conclusion. If you step off the curb and into the street and immediately hear the loud, screeching brakes of a bus, you're liable to jump back onto the sidewalk in a matter of seconds. That decision to jump back probably didn't feel like a *decision*; it happened too quickly and felt too automatic. But if you run the scene again in slow motion, the sound you heard was a piece of data, one that part of your brain quickly flagged as a possible source of danger and another part verified in less than a second. Your body made the decision to jump back subconsciously, and you had already responded physically before the conscious parts of your brain knew what had happened. That decision was a *bias,* and it may have saved your life.

So why does bias have such a bad reputation? Mostly because these ancient sec-tions of your brain are constantly trying to help you out, even when you're making complex decisions that are far above their pay grade. When your health and safety (or the health and safety of others) is truly at risk, and you absolutely must decide in a matter of seconds, biases can be very helpful. Most workplace decisions don't fit these criteria, though, and biases can easily do more harm than good in these situations.

In this chapter, I go into more detail about the many types of biases that exist and the fact that all of us have biases because it's a natural part of our brain function. I also provide examples of how it shows up in our everyday lives. Lastly, this chapter provides examples of how bias informs our decision making and our interactions in the workplace.

An Important Word on Bias

Managing and mitigating bias is an enormous challenge for individuals and organizations to take on, mostly because of its invisible nature. If people can't even detect biases within themselves, they can be difficult to stop before real damage is done. However, by approaching the topic with humility and curiosity, leaders can not only make their environments more welcoming for people like and unlike them but also learn about themselves in the process. That kind of self-awareness is invaluable for a leader who hopes to effect great change, both in themselves and in others.

Tracing the Origins of Biases and How They're Reinforced

Where do biases come from? The short answer is that they come from the brain. The human brain is actually a complex machine with many parts and pieces, each with a specific function. As a manager or leader, you don't need to have an encyclopedic knowledge of the human brain, so in this section and the rest of the chapter, I discuss it in terms of what Nobel-prize winner Daniel Kahneman refers to as the Fast Brain and Slow Brain (System One and System Two).

System One, or what Kahneman sometimes calls the *Fast Brain,* is where biases originate. It consists of the following parts:

>> The amygdala (your brain's "threat response center")

>> The hippocampus (a memory function)

>> The hypothalamus (a gatekeeper of sorts; among other things, the hypothalamus determines which data in your environment are important and which can be ignored)

True to its name, the Fast Brain processes data (mostly emotional data), arrives at conclusions extremely quickly, and largely operates outside of your conscious awareness. It's designed to make split-second decisions when health, safety, and lives depend on it.

By contrast, *System Two,* or what Kahneman sometimes calls the *Slow Brain,* is where you can, if you choose to, mitigate your biases. The Slow Brain mostly processes logical or analytical data; contrary to its name, processes information quickly — just nowhere near as quickly as your Fast Brain. Your Slow Brain also houses your values.

Table 15-1 offers a quick breakdown of the two systems.

TABLE 15-1   **Fast Brain versus Slow Brain**

Fast Brain (System One)	Slow Brain (System Two)
Automatic thinking below the level of consciousness	Deliberate, conscious thinking
Based primarily on emotion and memory	Based primarily on logical, analytical thought
Incredibly fast and efficient	Fast, but slower than the Fast Brain; requires more glucose and oxygen to function
Driven to keep you safe, healthy, and alive	Responsible for other core values (equity, respect, integrity)
Where bias originates	Where the ability to disrupt or mitigate bias is

Truly, the Fast Brain has one value: to keep you safe and alive. Of course, this aim isn't a bad thing, but you probably have other values that are important to you, such as integrity, respect, a desire for excellence, equity, or inclusion. And if you're going to weigh a decision against this set of values, you must do it with your Slow Brain.

It's estimated that 95 percent of your thinking takes place in the Fast Brain, meaning that your biases are influencing your view of the world and your behavior all the time. You simply have no way to function without bias. Indeed, you wouldn't want to; simple, repeatable tasks like tying your shoes or making the coffee would require so much thought that you'd never be able to handle complex tasks like planning a budget or crafting a presentation.

REMEMBER

The goal, therefore, isn't to rid yourself of bias but to identify the values-based decisions you make that require deliberate thought, and to make those decisions more conscientiously by using your Slow Brain. At work, these decisions include the following:

>> Sourcing, hiring, and interviewing candidates

>> Assigning work

>> Giving feedback

>> Writing performance appraisals and assigning ratings

>> Assessing employee potential

>> Promoting staff

>> Handing down progressive discipline

>> Deciding on terminations

Automatic, emotional thinking can negatively impact every one of these decisions. A member of your team who went to your alma mater and laughs at your jokes may be a more tempting candidate for promotion than the more qualified colleague who speaks with a heavy accent and doesn't always maintain eye contact. Assigning a challenging task to the most experienced and knowledgeable member of your team without stopping to consider their current workload or who else may be ready for a stretch assignment can be difficult. Choosing to take the team member you believe will make a good first impression to the senior leadership team meeting is tempting. Delivering feedback in a way that's constructive and not completely demoralizing is important, even when the mistake made is costly. When writing performance appraisals, recalling the three deliverables an employee completed last month is easy, even though this important process happens only once annually and is supposed to contain all relevant performance indicators for the past year.

In each of these cases, employing your Slow Brain thinking is crucial, despite biases that appear much faster. Doing so requires planning in advance, plus keeping a watchful eye for any biases that may appear as you're completing these tasks.

Identifying Ways Biases Show Up in Everyday Life

The most harmful belief about biases is that they're inextricably tied to morality. The truth is that the world has both good and bad people and that *both* kinds of people are influenced by bias. After all, both kinds of people have the same brain anatomy, and therefore both can make instant decisions using their Fast Brains. I discuss the Fast Brain and its counterpart, the Slow Brain, in the preceding section.

Biases are created by the patterns you're familiar with and are often exacerbated by any emotional reactions you're experiencing at the time. These patterns can take root based on your life experiences, observations, media representations, or awareness of stereotypes in society. They can range from the reliable to the benign to the stereotypical to the downright dangerous:

>> **Reliable:** The sound of a bus braking directly to your right may mean you risk being struck. Even if not, better safe than sorry, right?

>> **Benign:** Someone with white hair who walks very slowly with a cane is probably elderly.

>> **Stereotypical:** Women with children are less committed to career growth. A Latino who speaks Spanish is less educated that a white man who speaks English. People who wear glasses are smarter. Women are more emotional than men. Asian people are hard workers who avoid the spotlight.

>> **Dangerous:** Black people are more apt to engage in criminal behavior. Atheists are essentially amoral. Gay men are sexually attracted to minors.

WARNING

What's especially insidious about bias is that you don't need to believe these patterns for them to affect the decisions your Fast Brain makes. Simply being aware of the stereotype is enough. Consider the now-classic study by the University of Chicago and the Massachusetts Institute of Technology (MIT) on the impact of names on resumes. Researchers Marianne Bertrand and Sendhil Mullainathan sent fictitious resumes in response to employment ads in Boston and Chicago, each with either "white-sounding" names (like Emily or Greg) or "Black-sounding" names (like Lakisha or Jamal). The candidates who were perceived to be white received 50 percent more responses than those who were perceived to be Black, even though the resumes were identical. This discrepancy happened even when companies had expressly touted their commitment to diversity. When the resumes were updated to contain more or better experience, those tagged as "white" were called back 30 percent more, but this increase was much smaller for those tagged as "Black."

Some of the individuals who were sorting through these resumes may well have been consciously and unapologetically racist. But most likely were simply trying to pare an enormous number of responses down to a manageable number without taking enough time to mitigate their racial biases. Even if their Slow Brains believed in racial equity and equal opportunities for all, their Fast Brains were all too aware of a stereotype that assigns intelligence and cultural savvy to white people and links anyone named Lakisha or Jamal to run-down schools, an inability to adapt to corporate culture, and a sense of "otherness."

Distinguishing among the Various Biases

Various types of automatic thinking are grouped into the kinds of decisions labeled "bias." Table 15-2 includes the 11 biases that I think are most prevalent and worthy of attention in the workplace. As you peruse the list, think of times that you may have been impacted by these patterns or times you've observed them in others.

TABLE 15-2

Eleven Common Biases

Name	Definition	Example
Affinity bias	A tendency to be drawn to people who remind you of yourself	Jake, a father of two, finds it much easier to make small talk in the break room with Mary, who has children close to the same age as Jake's, by asking about her kids' activities. He finds it much more difficult to connect with Julian, a single gay man with no kids who just moved to a hip neighborhood downtown.
Anchoring bias	An inclination to rely too heavily on one piece of information	Melanie is working on performance appraisals for three of her team members. This is a fast-paced office filled with ambitious, hard-working people. Like nearly everyone else on her team, Philip and Samir usually log an average of 60 hours a week on their time cards, while Janice rarely logs more than 45 and never more than 50. Even though Janice always works a full-time schedule or more, Melanie wonders whether she's pulling her weight.
Attribution bias	Giving dominant identities (such white, male, straight, and able-bodied) more credit for their accomplishments and less blame for their mistakes	Karen works on a project team with all males. When she shares her ideas with excitement or she shares her disagreement in a passionate way, she is told by her male peers to stop being so emotional. When her male counterparts share the same excitement or vehemently disagree about an approach taken on a project, nothing is said. When it came time for performance reviews, that same feedback showed up on her review.
Confirmation bias	Favoring data that supports a pre-existing conclusion over data that invalidates that conclusion	Sehr usually hires people from Ivy League schools but, under pressure from her boss, took a chance on Adam, who graduated from a state university nearby. Adam has done great work during the past 12 months, and most of his clients really like him. But when one client complained that his work sometimes lacked the polish of his peers, Sehr declined to give Adam the promotion that most new employees receive after their first year.
Negativity bias	The tendency to pay more attention to negative data than positive data	Donald is finishing up Victoria's performance appraisal for the past 12 months. Victoria's projects throughout the year were consistently on time, well under budget, and executed with high quality. But Donald can't stop thinking about her poor choice of words when speaking to a journalist six months ago, which earned the company some bad press in an industry journal. Under the category of "Excellence," Donald rates Victoria as "Fair."
Performance bias	Judging people from dominant groups (for example, white, male, heterosexual, or able-bodied) based on potential, while judging others solely based on accomplishments	During a calibration meeting, Marceline starts to notice that all the young men who are up for promotion are described with aspirational phrases like "I think he'd be really good at that" or general descriptors like "very bright" or "solid work ethic." However, when it's time to evaluate a young woman's performance, questions arise, such as "Has she done this kind of work before?" Often, the women's promotions are put off for another year until they can prove themselves worthy.

(continued)

TABLE 15-2 *(continued)*

Name	Definition	Example
Priming effect	Altering your reaction to current stimuli based on exposure to previous stimuli	Before a presentation on the company's performance the prior year, Monica overhears a vice president say that the company "only exceeded our target by 5 percent" in a resigned tone. Meanwhile, Jourdain is told by another senior executive that "not only did we meet our goals, but we exceeded them by an incredible 5 percent margin!" When sitting together in the presentation and the data is revealed, Jourdain wonders why Monica isn't more excited by the good news.
Recency bias	The ability to recall events in the recent past more readily than those that took place some time ago	Rashid tends to procrastinate when filling out performance appraisals, a task he dislikes. His report on Shilpa, a member of his team, is due tomorrow. He quickly fills out the Summary section, noting the three most recent projects she has worked on. He neglects to review the self-appraisal she has submitted, which outlines in detail an enormous success that she orchestrated nine months ago, a project that doesn't appear in Rashid's finished report.
Stereotype threat	The tendency to typecast yourself based on common beliefs about your group identities	Sonya is the only woman in her team of five. Whenever her boss, Roger, asks for a volunteer to take notes during meetings, all eyes turn to Sonya. She knows that the stereotype women are expected to exhibit is supportive, nurturing, and communal teammates as opposed to strong, dynamic, assertive leaders. Because of this, she doesn't want to be pigeonholed as the note-taker and, like the others, remains silent. But when Roger asks her directly, she fears that refusing to take notes will give the impression that she isn't a good team player. After a long silence, she says, "Sure, no problem."
Urgency bias	The inclination to focus on work with high short-term impact even at the expense of more meaningful work, with long-term consequences	Grace, who leads the events team for a large association known for its annual conference each year, has just received some upsetting news. Tameka, her deputy conference manager, has been urged by her doctor to apply for long-term disability effective immediately, and the conference is happening in two weeks. No one else on the team can fill Tameka's shoes in that time. Grace begs her HR director to skip some of the steps in the typical recruiting process. "You don't understand," she says. "I need another Tameka, and I need her yesterday."

Name	Definition	Example
Warmth bias and competence bias	When meeting people, especially for the first time, immediately seeking data to answer the questions "Do I trust you?" and "Do I respect you?"	Ben is about to present his team's research findings to senior leadership and has been asked to invite one other member of the team to co-present. Renée, who conducted most of the research, is an obvious choice. She's an African American woman who wears her hair in locks. Ben knows her to be very intelligent but wonders whether she has the polish to impress the senior executives. Shabina was another principal researcher. A practicing Muslim, she wears a headscarf and typically speaks in short, clipped sentences, particularly when addressing authority figures. Ben wonders whether he should ask Stephen, who did far less work on the project but is an amiable young man with an easy smile and confident demeanor. (**Note:** Women often find that they must choose between being perceived as either warm or competent, whereas men can often choose both.)

Describing the Ways Biases Affect Decision Making in the Workplace

So many of the decisions that managers and leaders make revolve around people, and whenever you think about people, bias is likely to show up. Whatever patterns you're aware of around categories of people (race, gender, and so on) may present themselves, as may memories of important figures in your life that your colleagues and team members may remind you of.

I often describe the job interview as a petri dish for biases. Deciding who to hire for an open position often comes with a great deal of short-term time pressure (for example, "We need to fill this seat as soon as possible"), but is also one with a great deal of long-term impact. After all, the person you hire this week may still be with your organization in 20 years (urgency bias; see Table 15-2 for details on this and the other biases I cover in this section).

At the beginning of that interview, you're meeting someone, usually for the first time, and the weight of that first impression is heavy as you determine whether you like this person (warmth bias), whether you respect this person (competence bias), whether you believe what this person says to you as they advocate for themselves to be hired, and how this person will work with your existing team.

During the interview, anything you know — or know that others believe — about the candidate's racial group and those of their perceived gender (attribution bias, performance bias) is fighting for space in your brain with the information that's listed on their resume and the substantive answers they provide to your questions. If they're tall, you may be prone to believe that they're a good leader; if they display confidence, you may be inclined to believe that they're intelligent. If you make no effort to mitigate your biases, they'll likely have more input in your final decision than anything you learned during your conversation. If you're aware of bias and make every good attempt to separate what's valid and relevant from what's not, even hearing what your candidate is saying can be difficult.

And when the interviews are over, you're left with a decision. Who, among all the candidates you saw, will be the best addition to your team? Who will be pleasant to work with? Who will be ready to work independently the quickest? Who has the skills you need today and the potential to become the leader you'll need in five years? Who's the least likely to leave for greener pastures before they're fully onboarded? Who offers a skill or perspective that your current team currently lacks? Who will it be: the candidate who left your office five minutes ago whose resume was so impressive (priming effect) or the one who went to the same university you did (affinity bias) who, because of scheduling difficulties, you last saw more than a week ago (recency bias)?

It's a lot to sort through, and although understanding all the ways that your biases may be impacting your decisions is important, all that knowledge comes with its own set of challenges.

As I mention earlier in the chapter, bias impacts your decision making at every step of the talent management lifecycle. Biases can impact performance reviews, promotions, pay, who gets a seat at the table, who gets listened to and why/why not, and who gets mentored/sponsored and who doesn't.

TIP

In addition, certain dynamics can make your bias-creating Fast Brain even more powerful than it already is! (I cover the Fast and Slow Brains in the earlier section "Tracing the Origins of Biases and How They're Reinforced.")

>> **If you're hungry or tired, you're more prone to bias.** This is because your Fast Brain requires significantly less glucose and oxygen to function than your Slow Brain does. So if you've skipped breakfast or failed to get adequate sleep the night before meeting with potential vendors (or any other day when you'll try to make clear-headed decisions about people), your biases may have even more influence over your decisions than usual.

>> **If you're rushed or stressed, making your decisions quickly (your Fast Brain's specialty) is very tempting.** Say you've just finished your vendor meetings at noon on Friday, your senior leader wants your final recommendation by 2 p.m., and you still have lots of work to do before the holiday weekend (which you promised your spouse you'd be fully present for and not distracted by work). How tempting is simply recommending the vendor you

had the best *feeling* about? The one who seemed the most comfortable and therefore made *you* the most comfortable, as you traded stories about common experiences you'd had and laughed at each other's jokes?

Summoning those feelings takes not only very little energy but also very little time — and honestly, in that situation, I'd advise you to call your senior leader immediately to tell them that you'll have an answer sometime next week, after you've had a chance to calmly and deliberately review your notes and compare them to the contract being filled.

Reprogramming Your Brain to Make Less Biased Decisions

Because bias is so invisible, so taken for granted, and so outside your awareness, intention, or control, it can be difficult to address. It can be a fascinating topic to explore, but it's also frustrating for people who are primarily solution oriented. "Okay, okay, I have bias," you may be saying, "but what do I do about it?"

I'm sorry to say I can't give you a quick and easy fix. Mitigating bias is a continual process that takes consistent effort. But you can implement some proven tactics that can lead to better, more values-driven decision making. To simplify, in the following sections I separate them into two categories: mitigating bias as an individual and managing bias within a system.

Mitigating bias as an individual

Because bias is necessary for survival, doing without it is both impossible and unwise. There's simply no such thing as a healthy, functioning human without bias. However, take heart: There can be such a thing as an unbiased decision. Ironically, the first thing you must do to make an unbiased decision is to honestly and courageously look for bias. Then, if you identify any biases, you have to source them, test them, and validate them as I outline in Table 15-3. You can read more about the Fast and Slow Brains in "Tracing the Origins of Biases and How They're Reinforced" earlier in the chapter.

Bias is a part of our human make up. We all have biases, and we learn them at early age and reinforce them over time. Biases can also be mitigated, minimized, and even eliminated. But it takes work, time, and commitment. It requires that we develop new habits, evaluate our network and establish broader relationships, and take a deeper perspective.

TABLE 15-3   ## Sourcing, Testing, and Validating Biases

Source	Test	Validate
What pattern am I seeing?	Is this bias based on a real link or an unfair/potentially untrue stereotype?	Is there any truth in what my Fast Brain is telling me?
Where did this bias come from?	Is this information relevant?	Are there other sources of data I should examine to get a more complete picture?
Does this person or situation remind me of something from my past?	How would another person without my unique life experience or intersection of identities see this?	Should I incorporate this data into my decision or set it to the side?
Am I being influenced by one of my group identities?	What else may be true?	

Habits

One of the reasons bias is so powerful is that it's borne out of habit. You can use that to your advantage when attempting to mitigate your own biases in your day-to-day work. I've noticed, in my personal attempts to manage my biases, that every time I become annoyed with someone in either my personal or professional life, I immediately ask myself, "What else can be true?" Then I begin listing all the ways in which I could see the behavior more generously. It's become such a routine that it happens automatically at this point, but it does have a profound impact on what I do next. I'm much more likely to begin my next conversation with relevant questions as opposed to accusations built from a single point of view — my bias. And even when my initial biases are correct, those questions have enabled me to strengthen relationships by moderating my reactions.

Social networks

Another way to mitigate personal biases is to examine your own social network. Researcher Kristi Lemm conducted a study by interviewing test subjects (all self-identified heterosexuals) to determine how many relationships they had with LGBTQ people and how close those relationships were. She asked them about their feelings about the gay community and movement for gay rights. Then, she asked them to view a series of images, some featuring opposite-sex couples and others featuring male same-sex couples, and monitored their reactions for signs of anti-LGBT bias. Not surprisingly, when she compared her data, she found that those "who reported having more relationships and closer relationships with gay, lesbian, or bisexual people tended to exhibit more favorable attitudes toward gay men on implicit as well as explicit attitude measures." In other words, relationships with LGBTQ people reduced bias.

The same holds true for other identity groups. If you have deep relationships with people who are unlike you, you're less likely to act on biases that may result in discriminatory behavior. This finding doesn't mean that you need to cut ties with your current group of friends and make a whole lot of new ones. But it does mean that evaluating your social network would be wise. See who's there and who isn't. If a prominent group is missing from the circle of people you're closest too, take note and be extra mindful of bias the next time you encounter someone from that group at work. Also, take care to be honest with yourself about the closeness of your relationships. Research has shown that many white people, eager to avoid the label of "racist," exaggerate the depth of their friendships with Black people, most of whom would be better described as "acquaintances."

Perspective-taking (empathy)

One of the key activities for any individual to mitigate bias, especially when the goal is to create a more diverse and inclusive organization or team, is empathy, or *perspective-taking.* The ability to take another's perspective, and to treat that perspective as equally valid to your own, is imperative to reducing the impacts of bias at work.

Take a moment right now to imagine that your CEO has gathered their five most senior leaders and trusted advisors into their office. Who's in the room? Can you picture them? How do you feel when you imagine those individuals speaking around a table? Now, how would a straight white man see those same people? Now put yourself in the shoes of a Black man, and now a Latina woman. Do those people see themselves reflected in that senior group? Does that change their perspective? What about someone from the LGBT community? A Muslim? A person with a disability? Do they have the same level of trust in your organization's leadership that you do? Do they have more confidence, or less? What would have to change for the organization to be more equitable in this regard?

Now imagine yourself pulling together a panel to present at an upcoming conference. Thinking only of the people in your network that you personally regard as experts, you immediately create a list of five individuals with lots of valuable things to say. But before you write to each of them and ask them to take part, you notice that all of them are white, and all but one are men. To the best of your knowledge, all are heterosexual, none have a visible disability, and none are below the age of 50.

Now consider the perspective of your audience. Is it a diverse group? If so, how likely are they to be excited about the panel you've pulled together? Who may be inclined to skip the panel altogether, doubting that anything it may say will be relevant to what they need to know about the topic? If your initial reaction is to get defensive, or to dismiss these concerns, remember that you only considered people you were acquainted with. Could you construct a more diverse panel, with diverse viewpoints and inclusive of a diverse audience, by approaching the task in a different way?

Managing bias within a system

Mitigating biases at an individual level as I discuss in the preceding sections can have a profound impact on the quality of your decisions and therefore on the diversity and inclusion experienced by your direct reports in the workplace. But to truly transform an organization's culture requires system-level interventions. When policies, processes, and the unwritten (cultural) rules that govern behavior in an organization allow people to make important decisions too quickly, without enough data or input from others, bias continues to keep you from reaching your diversity and inclusion goals.

The following sections cover some additional ways that your organization can facilitate accountability around minimizing bias. They can ensure that there is sufficient training on unconscious bias and consistency in processes as well as how they're administered. They can also ensure that they remove the obstacles and information used to make biased decisions and ensure a broad array of input when assessing performance.

Anti-bias training

Although attending workshops on bias is essentially a tool to help individuals mitigate their own personal biases, organizations that invest in these training programs can also see some system-level impact. Quite simply, when organizations spend their money in this way, people notice. If the training itself is engaging, challenging, and high quality, it sends the message that the work is real and important.

When introducing anti-bias training to your organization, having senior leaders take the training first is important, as is making sure the workshops they take are at least as long (preferably longer) than the training required of employees at lower levels. Another best practice is for leaders to welcome their employees to the training, explain its importance, and (if possible) tell a story about how they received value from the training when they experienced it. If a live introduction from a leader isn't possible for every session, then a group of senior leaders may consider making a video that's played at the beginning of every workshop that communicates these same messages.

Consistency

Sometimes, the lack of a defined process can heighten the impact of biases. For instance, if managers are simply told to onboard new team members by taking them out to lunch and getting to know them without any additional guidance, some will likely develop a list of topics to cover, while others will simply say, "So, tell me a little something about yourself," and let the conversation go where it will. In the latter case, those candidates who are similar to their new managers will surely benefit (affinity bias; see Table 15-2), regardless of how well qualified they are for their new job. In fact, the job they were hired for may not enter the conversation at all. Even in the former case, a list of topics that I cover may be very different from those of my peers, creating an unequal experience across teams.

A far better option would be for everyone in the organization to receive a basic template for a first meeting that all managers are asked to cover. Of course, managers would have the freedom to steer the conversation as they chose, and hopefully the new employees would be given time at the end of the meeting to ask questions of their own. These dynamics naturally create some difference among the lunches. However, a common list of topics would give all new employees a much more equitable place to start and allow those from historically disadvantaged groups to better integrate themselves into a new team. This would, in turn, benefit the organization by making it more likely to support talent that shows up in diverse or unexpected forms.

Consistency can also show up in the day-to-day work of existing employees. Women end up doing more "office housework" (planning off-site events, taking notes, arranging lunch) than men in all kinds of organizations. This phenomenon not only prevents women from focusing on their actual jobs and impairs their productivity but also is demeaning. When these administrative tasks need to be done and aren't part of anyone's official job descriptions, they fall to women — not because women are pleased to take on the extra work but because of deeply ingrained biases that expect women to take on these communal behaviors and the very real consequences to a woman's reputation of being less than a team player if she refuses.

TIP

Although many on your team (perhaps mostly men) see nothing wrong with asking for volunteers the next time notes need to be taken or lunch needs to be ordered, a more inclusive and equitable solution would be to create a process to ensure that all members of a team are doing their part. In this way, if you took notes at the last meeting, you aren't asked to do so again until every member of your team has done the same. On a large team that meets once a week, you likely won't take notes more than a few times a year.

Removing bias-inducing information

Sometimes, the best way to prevent bias is simply to shield people from the data that activates it. This is why most orchestras and symphonies throughout North America and Europe conduct blind auditions, where musicians simply play behind a screen and listeners simply judge the music without regard to the age, race, gender, or physical appearance of the player.

Earlier in this chapter, I discuss the study that found resumes with "Black-sounding" names to be rejected at a higher rate than those with "white-sounding" names. Although individual anti-bias training may help mitigate this issue, even people who believe in diversity and inclusion and enthusiastically attend training can find that their Fast Brains take over when completing rote, repetitive tasks like sorting through large piles of resumes.

In this case, a more effective and efficient approach would likely be to simply remove the names from the resumes before they were sorted. Without the data to move their biases in one way or the other, people would automatically judge identical resumes the same, without regard to race or gender. Some organizations may also find removing the name of the school a candidate attended beneficial, especially if that organization has a tendency to prefer candidates from Ivy League schools with lofty reputations.

360-degree processes

One clear way to manage bias at the systems level is to force people to take different perspectives when making decisions. The most frequently used version of this tactic is probably in performance assessment. Many organizations require those who write performance appraisals to receive input from a minimum number of sources, including the self-assessment of the employee under review. In this way, the author's biases have less of a chance of impacting the final product. Some organizations even give the task of writing performance appraisals to independent parties outside the reporting structure of the person being assessed, leading to an even more objective output. Although these systems usually spend much more time (and therefore money) on the assessment process, the assessments themselves are likely to be much less impacted by bias.

Other 360-degree processes can include receiving input from all members of a team, sometimes anonymously, when innovating new products or solutions. In this way, the contributions of junior staff members aren't discounted in favor of ideas that come from more senior sources.

IN THIS CHAPTER

» the bottom line

» **Identifying the qualities of inclusive leaders**

» **Watching out for major indicators of poor leadership**

» **Tracking microbehaviors that contribute to inclusivity**

Chapter **16**

Moving from Unconscious Bias to Inclusive Leadership

s the workforce becomes more global, diverse, multigenerational, and multicultural, and work gets done in different ways and from different locations, the need for more inclusive leadership is imperative. Becoming an inclusive leader isn't as easy as it sounds. It's much more than having a title, giving a hug, and being nice. It requires intentionality. It demands a paradigm shift and openness to different ways of thinking and doing things. It means leaning into some discomfort and demonstrating courage to embrace the unknown and the unfamiliar.

These requirements of 21st century leaders are driven by the needs and expectations of the new generation of workers who have changed the way the work gets done and the way that leaders lead. As a result, the ability for leaders to lead across differences are a key lever for attracting, engaging, and retaining top talent, new customers, clients, members, and donors.

In this chapter, I reveal the business benefits of inclusive leadership, guide you through a list of the key competencies workers say they want in their leaders, and identify a model called the six Cs of inclusive leadership. I also provide you some pitfalls that leaders should avoid and some microbehaviors that leaders can demonstrate to be inclusive every day.

Realizing the Benefits of Becoming an Inclusive Leader

A leader isn't simply someone with a title or a position or someone who creates followers. A leader is someone who builds more leaders through vision, inspiration, and inclusiveness.

One of my best bosses was this kind of leader. His motto for me was "Shirley, I don't care how fast you're going; just tell me *where* you're going, and I'll help you get there." In other words, he wanted me to "be me" and to "do me" in a way that I could be my authentic and unique self. It was under this inclusive leader that I thrived and did my best work.

As I detail in Chapter 2, numerous demographic disruptions have occurred over the past decade in the workforce, marketplace, and workplace and will continue into 2050. With all these differences working alongside each other at the same time, inclusive leadership is clearly required to fully maximize and capitalize on all the diversity in workplaces.

Inclusive leaders recognize that talent comes in all shapes, sizes, colors, ethnicities, personalities, cultures, and the like, and they embrace it as the new normal for achieving competitive advantage, high performance, and business success.

The workforce will continue to shift in dramatic ways well into the 2030s. The ability for leaders to lead amid these disruptive forces and across differences and create more inclusive work environments — in a wide variety of contexts, cultures, and complexities — will be a key lever for attracting, engaging, and retaining top talent.

Working in an inclusive work environment and for an inclusive leader can have tangible benefits for the company such as the following:

>> Driving financial performance

>> Enhancing employer brand that attracts top talent

» Increasing employee engagement and team performance

» Achieving greater innovation in products and services

The following sections cover each of these benefits in more detail.

Driving financial performance

Research shows a significant relationship between having a more diverse leadership team and better financial performance. Much of this correlation comes from receiving broader perspectives on product innovation (as I discuss later in the chapter) and in serving diverse customers and from identifying creative ways to solve business challenges. In 2015, 2018, and 2020, a McKinsey team of researchers delved into the leadership composition of over 1,000 companies in 15 countries and compared the makeup against their financial performance. They found that companies in the top quartile for gender diversity on executive teams were 25 percent more likely to have above-average profitability. Companies in the top quartile of racial/ethnic diversity were 36 percent more likely to have financial returns above their national industry median.

Similarly, the Boston Consulting Group and the Technical University of Munich conducted a survey of diversity managers, HR executives, and managing directors at 171 companies across Germany, Austria, and Switzerland. The study found that higher levels of diversity in management positions contributes to increased revenue from new products and services. The research also revealed that companies that establish favorable work conditions for employees have higher earnings before interest and taxes (EBIT) margins (17 percent) than those who don't (13 percent).

REMEMBER

Research can establish only correlations, not causations, between diversity and financial performance. It shouldn't be the only basis for building more inclusive workplaces and becoming a more inclusive leader. Other benefits, such as the ones I discuss in the following sections (including enhancing employer brand to attract diverse talent and driving greater innovation in products and services) should all be part of improving your company's culture.

Enhancing employer brand that attracts top talent

The reality in today's competitive job market is that top talent has options for what kinds of jobs they want, what types of leaders they want to work for, and in what kind of culture they thrive. If organizations want to set themselves apart from their competitors (who are after the same top talent), they must focus on building a strong employer brand and then tout it. Companies that do this well showcase their employer brands on their websites (through employee testimonials, videos, and photo highlights of company events), in their newsletters and publications, on job boards, on social media, and during the interview process. Leaders should be well versed in sharing what working at the company is like and selling themselves as great leaders.

As an HR professional who led recruiting for over ten years, I've observed that today's candidates, especially underrepresented talent, are doing background checks on your company as you're doing background checks on them:

>> They reach out to their connections on social media.

>> They visit websites such as Glassdoor.com to inquire about what employees report working at your company is like.

>> They view your company's website and annual reports to see whether anyone in leadership looks like them.

>> They ask bold questions about your culture in the interview.

>> They demand certain conditions and benefits in job negotiations.

Consider how your company's brand shows up in these areas and what you can do to enhance it so that it attracts top diverse talent.

Increasing employee engagement, satisfaction, and team performance

I've been one of those employees who became disengaged, disenfranchised, and dissatisfied. I couldn't stand working for my boss, I dreaded going to work, and the work environment was so toxic that it affected my creativity, my productivity, and my attitude. It happened because I was working for someone who wasn't inclusive — someone who marginalized my efforts and undermined my credibility yet took credit for my results. She provided me no feedback and no guidance; I was training her to do her job, yet she was my boss. It took my leaving that department to re-engage and become productive and happy again.

Unfortunately, my story isn't uncommon. Maybe you've been there, or you've been that kind of boss. More and more companies realize that they must focus on developing inclusive leaders because those leaders have a direct link to employee engagement, job satisfaction, and team performance, which have a direct impact to the bottom line.

Employee engagement

Employee engagement refers to the connection and commitment employees exhibit toward an organization, leading to higher levels of productive work behaviors.

What percent of the global workforce do you believe is "actively engaged" at work? *Actively engaged* means that employees want to work at your company, are productive and invested in your company, go above and beyond, and are ambassadors for the company both internally and externally.

According to a Gallup poll, globally, 67 percent of the workforce isn't engaged. In a company of 10,000 employees with an average salary of $50,000 each, the cost of that disengagement is $60.3 million annually. Productivity among highly engaged teams is 14 percent higher than that of teams with the lowest engagement, and employees who aren't engaged cost their companies the equivalent of 18 percent of their annual salaries.

As I conduct employee engagement surveys for clients and lead them through culture transformation strategies, I often remind them of these three realities:

>> Many of their employees quit a long time ago; they just didn't leave.

>> People don't leave bad jobs; they leave bad bosses and toxic workplace cultures.

>> If you're hiring right, you're hiring highly engaged workers (not disengaged workers). So if they've become disengaged, something most likely happened inside the organization to cause it. Most of the time, it's a leadership issue.

Other issues that drive employee engagement include offering challenging work, providing the opportunity to develop and learn new skills, having a sense of meaning and purpose that is tied to vision, allowing flexible work arrangements, paying a competitive salary, and fostering a sense of belonging.

REMEMBER

Having diversity of thought brings broader perspectives and experiences to the table that wouldn't be possible with groupthink. Successful organizations recognize that an inclusive workplace culture is a critical ingredient in increasing employee engagement, job satisfaction, and strong performance.

Job satisfaction

Job satisfaction refers to how employees feel about their compensation, work environment, career development, and relationship with management. What do companies such as Hilton, Amazon, Cisco, Salesforce, Apple, American Express, Netflix, and Wegman's have in common? They're consistently ranked among the most admired and/or best places to work by *Fortune* magazine and Great Place to Work Institute. They're known for fostering an environment where employees feel valued, are encouraged to contribute, and are achieving business success. Today's workers consider workplace culture as much as they consider salary and benefits when considering employment. In fact, a welcoming and inclusive company culture is almost expected along with other traditional benefits.

When employees feel they have a fair and level playing field to succeed, and when their supervisor is open to their ideas and their actions are aligned with what they say, employees have greater job satisfaction and higher engagement. This gets to the heart of inclusive leadership traits, which include valuing and leveraging different opinions and being adaptable, open, and trustworthy.

Team performance

Dozens of studies and decades of research have found that diverse teams are smarter than homogeneous teams. One significant study conducted by Catalyst included responses from 1,500 employees from Australia, China, Germany, India, Mexico, and the United States. It concluded that diverse teams outperformed homogeneous teams. It also showed that employees who feel included are more likely to go above and beyond the call of duty, suggest new product ideas, innovate new ways of getting work done, and be supportive of one another.

Additionally, according to Cloverpop's study *Hacking Diversity with Inclusive Decision Making,* inclusive decision-making drives better company performance and gives a decisive competitive advantage. Teams outperform individual decision makers 66 percent of the time, and decision making improves as team diversity increases. Inclusive decision making leads to better business decisions up to 87 percent of the time.

Achieving greater innovation in products and services

Today, companies have come to understand that reaching and meeting the needs of a diverse customer and consumer base, which has a large and important part of the total buying power, is critical to expanding their market share, exceeding customers' expectations, and outpacing their competitors. And one way to do that is to attract diverse talent that understands and can serve diverse market segments. (Of course, you also have to create the kind of work environment that invites diverse perspectives, values new ideas, and fosters innovative problem-solving.) DEI practitioners also call this *leveraging diversity of thought.*

Here are a few examples of companies who have reaped the benefits of inclusion and innovation by inviting diversity of thought:

>> **Reaching new markets and customers:** At 3M, diversity is a core corporate strategy implemented to generate new ideas, grow business units, and drive innovation. The company uses its diverse talent to reach out effectively to new markets and customers and to understand cultural differences.

>> **Solving local business needs:** DuPont has opened more than ten global Innovation Centers around the world to work together to solve local problems and industry needs through development and open innovation. Its goal is to partner on solutions that fuel local collaboration and application development and engage customers in inclusive innovation — wherever they are in the world.

>> **Developing new products:** At Campbell Soup Company, women employees successfully developed a new line of all-natural soups called Select Harvest for women consumers who were more health conscious. Listening to suggestions from its diverse employees, Frito-Lay, a division of PepsiCo, profitably creates new products and flavors and targets its marketing. When it asked its employee affinity groups to look at all the company's snack foods and combine them with something from their own background, the Hispanic affinity group came up with the guacamole chip, which ended up bringing in $100 million in revenues a year. (*Affinity groups* are employee-led special interest groups that are formed around common diverse identity groups, such as women, Black, and LGBTQ, and that support the organization's DEI goals.)

Increasingly, inclusive leaders recognize that the direct correlation between diversity of thought, inclusion, and innovation and that this correlation creates an economic impact.

Over the next 30 days, I challenge you to look for ways to be more inclusive of diverse opinions, perspectives, and ideas. Most likely, you'll find new and better solutions to tackling some of the complex business challenges that companies are facing today, and you'll establish new ways to reach your customers and clients.

Honing the Competencies and Key Traits of an Inclusive Leader

To meet the needs of the changing global workforce, leaders must be able to embrace the differences that workers represent and demonstrate behaviors that are inclusive and that foster an inclusive work environment. Unfortunately, I find in my work that too many organizations suffer from underdeveloped and ineffective leaders who still neither understand diversity nor demonstrate the key traits of inclusive leadership.

One of the most practical and useful global models I use was developed by Deloitte. It outlines six Cs of inclusive leadership, which you can read in Table 16-1. As you review them, reflect on your own level of effectiveness at each trait and give yourself a rating on a scale of 1 to 5 (5 being very effective, 1 being not effective at all).

Now look at your scores and consider what one thing you can do to increase your effectiveness in the next 90 days.

TABLE 16-1   **The Six Cs of Inclusive Leadership**

Trait	Description	Rating
Commitment	Highly inclusive leaders are committed to diversity and inclusion because these objectives align with their personal values. They know that by committing their time, energy, and support to investing in people, they engender inclusive workplaces. By demonstrating this level of commitment, they empower and inspire others to achieve their potential.	
Courage	Inclusive leaders challenge the status quo and aren't afraid to call out deeply held and ingrained beliefs, attitudes, and behaviors that foster homogeneity. They're willing to have the difficult conversations and lean into their discomfort.	
Cognizance of bias	Inclusive leaders understand that personal and organizational biases narrow their field of vision and prevent them from making objective decisions. They exert considerable effort to identify their own biases and learn ways to prevent them from influencing talent decisions. They also seek to implement policies, processes, and structures to prevent organizational biases from stifling diversity and inclusion.	
Curiosity	Inclusive leaders have an open mind-set and a hunger for other perspectives and new experiences to minimize their blind-spots and improve their decision-making. Additionally, their ability to engage in respectful questioning, active listening, and the synthesis of a range of ideas makes the people around them feel valued and respected and creates a sense of belonging. Inclusive leaders also refrain from making quick judgments, knowing snap decisions can stifle the flow of ideas on their teams and are frequently marked with bias.	
Cultural intelligence	Inclusive leaders have an ability to function effectively in different cultural settings. They also recognize how their own culture impacts their personal worldview, as well as how cultural stereotypes can influence their expectations of others. They know when and how to adapt while maintaining their own cultural authenticity.	
Collaboration	Inclusive leaders understand that collaboration is the key to team performance and success. As a result, they create a safe space in which all individuals feel empowered to express their opinions freely with the group without judgment or retribution. They also realize that diversity of thought is critical to effective collaboration; thus, they pay close attention to team composition and team processes.	

REMEMBER

These six traits represent a powerful capability highly aligned with diversity. Embodying these key traits lets leaders operate more effectively in leading teams within diverse markets and allows them to better connect with diverse customers, access a more diverse spectrum of ideas, and enable diverse individuals in the workforce to reach their full potential.

Avoiding the Pitfalls of Ineffective Leadership

Ever dreaded going to work because of a boss? Remember feeling stressed about your upcoming performance review? Have you ever worked for someone and rarely or never received feedback, or gone the extra mile to successfully complete a project only for it to go unrecognized? If you answer yes to any of these questions, chances are you were (or are) working under an ineffective leader.

WARNING

Based on my 25 years of experience, here are seven of the most common pitfalls inclusive leaders should avoid if they want to keep great talent and get the best work out of them. As I describe each pitfall, conduct your own personal assessment and write down those that you need to work on.

>> **Lacking vision and goals:** I always say that if you're a leader and no one is following you, you're just taking a walk. Leaders who don't provide a compelling vision for others to follow will struggle with keeping employees focused and committed. Great leaders see the untapped potential in others, and they seek to bring out the best in them.

>> **Treating everyone the same:** Inclusive leaders understand that not everyone is motivated the same way, so they take the time to know each person on their team individually and interact with them accordingly. Instead of practicing the golden rule, they practice the platinum rule: Treat others the way they want to be treated.

>> **Showing favoritism:** Do you have someone on your team that you consider your go-to person? You both think alike, you have the same personality type, and you share a lot of other things in common. The problem is that when you single someone out as your favorite, you're excluding or overlooking others. When leaders avoid showing favoritism and provide a sense of belonging and equity, they can establish a level playing field and a sense of trust.

>> **Being inflexible:** When leaders are rigid and unwilling to consider new ideas or new ways of doing things, they squelch innovation. They embrace the status quo: "We've always done it that way." Inclusive leaders welcome diverse

perspectives, and they create an environment where collaboration and creativity can thrive.

>> **Being a know-it-all:** Leaders who think they're never wrong or who won't admit that they don't know it all are sadly misguided. Employees today appreciate when leaders show some level of vulnerability and authenticity. Inclusive leaders surround themselves with people who are smarter than they are and who have strengths that they don't, and they aren't threatened by it.

>> **Not recognizing or rewarding:** Everyone wants to feel valued and appreciated. Yet so often, leaders acknowledge employees only when they make mistakes. When leaders take the time to recognize employees' achievements, the result is improved morale, performance, and loyalty.

>> **Failing to provide feedback:** All employees need (positive and corrective) feedback on how they're doing, and they need it consistently. This skill tends to be one of the most underdeveloped of most leaders. They avoid the tough conversations and don't provide the specificity that employees need to course-correct, especially when it's with a person who's very different from them. Inclusive leaders develop this skill and make it a consistent practice.

How did you do? How many pitfalls do you need to avoid?

Strong leadership is undeniably the strength of an organization, yet inclusive leaders are hard to find. By actively avoiding these pitfalls, you can work toward being the kind of leader that motivates, engages, includes, and celebrates your followers.

Being Inclusive Everyday: Microbehaviors Leaders Often Overlook

Microbehaviors are small things that we do or say that can impact how we make others feel. They are can be both verbal and nonverbal, very subtle, persistent, and influence by your biases.

WARNING

Negative microbehaviors can make people feel devalued, invisible, and singled out. Some examples that leaders often overlook include:

>> Ignoring a team member's comments or ideas made in a meeting (especially those who may be new to the team or a young professional)

>> Answering a call in the middle of conversation

- » Pronouncing a person's name incorrectly after being informed how to pronounce it

- » Interrupting someone before they finish their thought

- » Watching the clock while talking to someone

- » Correcting someone who speaks with an accent, not thanking someone for their contribution

TIP

Some microbehaviors (such as holding eye contact, using open gestures, and asking for others' opinions) help create an atmosphere in which all feel secure, valued, and engaged. Following is a list of 16 microbehaviors that people often overlook but that can go a long way in creating a more inclusive workplace:

- » Live your mission; walk to talk.

- » Listen to understand not to respond.

- » Don't focus on difference, find common ground.

- » Practice the Platinum Rule (treat others the way they want to be treated).

- » Assume positive intent first.

- » Second-guess your first impressions.

- » Engage with others who are different from you.

- » Smile.

- » Be flexible and adaptable.

- » Invite/value different opinions.

- » Demonstrate mutual respect

- » Be open-minded.

- » Communicate respectfully.

- » When in doubt, ask.

- » Don't ignore; speak to others.

- » Be a coach/mentor to new hires.

Chapter **17**

Enhancing Cultural Competence

C *ulture* is predictable behaviors and beliefs among a defined group of people, as I explain in Chapter 3. These groups can include examples like the following:

» Companies and organizations, defined by their employers

» Industries, defined by the kind of work they do

» Racial and ethnic groups, defined by origin or background as well as common experiences of privilege/oppression

» Religious groups, defined by their faith

» Other types of marginalized people (such as those in the LGBTQ community and people with disabilities), defined by common experience

» Nationalities, defined by citizenship

You may be part of four or more defined groups at once that exhibit predictable behaviors or rely on predictable beliefs!

REMEMBER

By the way, *predictable* doesn't mean that everyone in a defined group believes the exact same things or behaves in the exact same way. No group is monolithic; however, you can often predict that most people in that group share some common beliefs and behaviors.

For instance, you can reasonably predict that a Spanish funeral will feature some mourners openly weeping or beating their breasts, conveying emotion in a way that would be very out of place in a country like Japan, where mourners tend to be much quieter. In many deaf cultures, where people communicate through sign language, being candid and saying exactly what you mean is a virtue. People from hearing cultures often find these communications to be blunt or overly harsh. (On the flip side, deaf people can perceive hearing people as being indirect or inauthentic.) People who work in engineering or highly technical fields often want to see hard data to support a new way of doing things; for those who work in the arts or humanities, knowing that people are generally unhappy with the status quo is often enough.

Cultural competence can be a bit obscure for leaders who are still trying to understand the fundamentals of DEI. And quite frankly, it's a term that's gaining more traction and understanding even among those of us who have been practicing DEI for a long time. It's a personal learning journey that all of us should take if we want to be more effective in working and leading across differences.

Cultural competence isn't a destination; it's a process that involves constant learning. Most organizational leaders say they want to create a more inclusive workplace to truly leverage their diverse workforces in building productivity and innovation. Relatively few organizations truly achieve this goal, however. Being a culturally competent leader isn't easy; often, no one way of doing things makes everyone in a culturally diverse team happy. You'll make mistakes, but in today's changing workforce, the effort is absolutely necessary if you want to help the organization in achieving its key business objectives through diversity, equity, and inclusion.

In this chapter, I define what is cultural competence, and why as leaders it is important to develop and demonstrate in the workplace. I explain how our level of cultural competence affects the cultures that we create as well as the people whom we lead, serve, and work with. This chapter also reveals the corresponding behaviors of cultural competence, such as cultural humility and cultural intelligence, and provides a framework for assessing and mapping your cultural competence development journey.

Understanding What Cultural Competence Is (And What It Isn't)

Cultural competence, which is often used interchangeably with intercultural competence, is the ability to work effectively in a multicultural environment. In today's increasingly global workforce, people are working together on teams with colleagues who are literally on the other side of the world, from very different cultures. But even if your work teams and customers are completely domestic, they're increasingly diverse. Communities of color, the LGBTQ community, different faith communities, and communities based on ability each have different, but predictable, beliefs and behaviors that guide how they perceive the workplace and show up at work.

Cultural competence has three central components, each of which builds on the last:

>> Self-awareness around your own cultural background (the beliefs and behaviors that guide your perceptions and actions)

>> Knowledge of other cultures (especially those you interact with on a regular basis)

>> The ability to adapt, if necessary, to achieve harmony and maximum productivity in the workplace

Self-awareness

Author David Foster Wallace tells a comic parable about fish that perfectly describes the invisible nature of culture. In it, two young fish are swimming in the ocean when they happen by an older fish. "Morning, boys," the older fish says. "How's the water?" Only after the older fish has swum away does one of the younger fish look to his companion and ask, "What the hell is water?"

People often think about their culture the way fish probably think about water. Though it's omnipresent in their lives, it's also very easy to take for granted. And they typically don't have to think about it, because it's always just there. But, just like a fish, people can become very aware of their culture when it's taken away from them.

Therefore, being aware of your own culture takes a bit of work. Suppose you have a new client or customer who doesn't make eye contact. Depending on your culture, you may draw very different conclusions about this client's trustworthiness.

A wise leader frames this observation as an open question ("Should I trust this person?") as opposed to a declarative statement ("This person can't be trusted"). If you're a leader from a Western culture (for example, the United States or Canada) you may believe that the person isn't trustworthy without ever thinking about the data that led you to that decision (the lack of eye contact) or the belief that prompted your reaction (direct eye contact is both polite and sincere; those who avoid it have something to hide).

A self-aware leader responds to all interactions that strike them as wrong or bad and checks them against their own cultural background in a search for cultural misalignment.

Knowledge of other cultures

Although knowing about every culture in the world is practically impossible, a leader should be well versed in the cultures that they engage with on a regular basis. If you work in a country where Catholicism is the dominant religion, you're probably already aware of major Catholic holidays and don't question why many employees show up to work with ashes on their foreheads each year around February or March, for example. However, if you're about to welcome the first Muslim member of your team, you may not be aware of the holidays, traditions, and requirements of practicing Islam, and obtaining this information is your responsibility. The same holds true if you're welcoming someone raised in another country, a person with a different race or ethnicity, a member of the LGBTQ community, or a person with a disability.

How you get the information doesn't really matter as long as you don't make your new employee responsible for everything you need to know. (Internet search engines can be very helpful, but make a real effort to look at reliable sites for your research.) It will mean so much more to your new employee if their new leader has some basic knowledge about their culture on their first day. You should feel free, however, to let your new team member know that you're open to new information they may choose to provide about their community or themselves in general. Always remember that your new employee is both a member of a community as well as an individual and may not adhere to all traditions or taboos that are true for the culture at large.

The ability to adapt

Often, an unspoken rule dictates that members of minority cultures should *assimilate* to the larger culture they find themselves in — that is, to let the larger culture replace their own. Usually, this assimilation happens to at least a small extent.

However, the leader who is a true champion of DEI also strives to adapt their own behaviors when necessary.

For instance, if you have members on your team who were born and raised in India, they may be extremely uncomfortable disagreeing with you, their leader, in public. You may believe that dissent is a necessary part of innovation. You can ask these employees directly to act in direct opposition to their culture, but a better course of action is to keep your own opinions to yourself in large team meetings so that your Indian employees can speak authentically without worrying about contradicting you, and to thank the entire team for its robust contributions.

What cultural competence isn't

Understanding the aspects of cultural competence in the preceding sections is one thing. Know what cultural competence *doesn't* include is equally important.

Learning everything about every culture

Cultures are fluid and changeable. And if cultural competence were defined as knowing everything about every culture on earth, no one could be considered competent. There's simply too much to know.

Being able to unconsciously assimilate

As I note earlier in the chapter, assimilating to another culture means letting go of your own cultural identity so that another can replace it. Being culturally competent doesn't require you to lose any part of who you are, but the goal is to adapt.

Being above or without culture

Even you could be above or without culture (which is impossible), you probably wouldn't want to. Rather, you should experience cultural competence as a process, one that you must repeat at each interaction across difference.

Code switching

Code switching is often defined as freely moving between two languages or dialects, but the modern definition encompasses not only the words a person uses but also the tone of voice, physicality, and other culturally based behaviors. It sounds a lot like cultural competence, right? But the key difference is intention. Code switching usually isn't performed by leaders, or people with power, with the goal of being more inclusive of others. Rather, the people without power code switch so they can fit in with the larger power structure.

What I've learned is that code switching is a survival technique, a tool to help you fit into different social and professional settings — particularly when you're part of a marginalized community. As a woman of color and often the "only one" in the room with my male (mostly white) colleagues, I remember many occasions when I code switched to fit in. I'd tone down my voice when offering ideas or giving feedback so that I wouldn't be perceived as the aggressive or "angry Black woman." I'd listen to all of the buzzwords they were using and inject them into my speech when I could even when I didn't know what all of them meant; I pretended to know. I dressed the way they did to fit in and went out to the bars after work with them even though I don't like that scene and didn't drink. I had to pretend to like certain sports or other activities so that I'd be seen as "one of them." The point is, I didn't feel that I could be my true and authentic self and be accepted. The culture didn't give me a sense of belonging or safety to be myself.

Truthfully, everyone code switches to a certain degree. Even people who belong to nearly every dominant group behave differently at work with their colleagues than they do on the weekend with friends. But unlike cultural competence, repeated and necessary code switching involves a denial of self and can take an emotional and psychological toll.

REMEMBER

If you're adapting to cultural norms to create a more inclusive environment for staff, that's cultural competence. If you're shielding your own culture from view because it's unwelcome at work, that's code switching — and a sign that your organizational culture needs work.

Distinguishing between Cultural Humility and Cultural Intelligence

To be culturally competent, you first need to have cultural humility and cultural intelligence. Combining cultural humility with the cultural intelligence needed to work with your team gives you the tools to adapt so that everyone feels a sense of belonging and can be their most productive on the job.

Considering cultural humility

Most people have an innate belief that their culture is the very best one. It's an expected feeling because your culture is the one that naturally makes you the most comfortable. That feeling of ease when surrounded by your own culture is undeniable and shouldn't be a source of guilt.

At the same time, a culturally competent leader can't successfully adapt to another cultural way of being, even temporarily, if they persist in thinking that their culture is somehow superior. *Cultural humility* means recognizing that we don't know everything about every culture and never will, and thus we are open to learning, listening, and being respectful towards people from different cultures. It's about accepting our limitations and doing the work to increase our self-awareness.

If you come from a culture where people greet each other with a bow rather than a handshake, a belief that your culture is superior doesn't prevent you from shaking another person's hand, but it may create the impression that touching another person in this way makes you uncomfortable. Likewise, if you come from a culture that shakes hands, your bow is likely to be read as stiff or insincere. Even if you can convince others that you've authentically adapted to their way of being, doing so takes an enormous amount of mental energy that you could better spend focusing on the work.

Those who succeed in moving beyond the perceived superiority of their own culture find letting go of the behaviors they're so attached to — and truly adapting — easier.

Investigating cultural intelligence

Cultural intelligence is a cursory knowledge of both how culture works and the specific culture(s) you're interacting with.

How culture works

As I mention earlier in the chapter, culture is made up of beliefs and behaviors. Part of cultural intelligence is recognizing how closely tied these beliefs and behaviors are. Behaviors, of course, are external and can be observed. Beliefs are internal and can't be observed except when they manifest in — you guessed it — behavior.

Usually, belief drives behavior, although it can also work the other way. Your culture may have an intrinsic belief that a person's achievements should define their level of success (for more on this belief, see the later section "Achievement versus ascription"). In such cultures (the United States is one), various structures in most organizations, such as the job interview or the performance assessment, focus almost entirely on what the individual being appraised has achieved (or has the potential to achieve). Dynamics such as nepotism (favoring relatives, usually with jobs) certainly exist, but children who inherit entire companies from their parents are easy subjects of mockery until they can prove their rise was warranted.

Sometimes, however, behavior drives belief. If your organization practices 360-degree feedback for every performance appraisal, that process may drive a belief that cultivating good relationships throughout the organization is important. If, however, managers write your performance appraisals with no other input, the belief may be that you're successful as long as your direct manager is pleased with your performance.

Obviously, these two different beliefs can then be exhibited in a range of predictable behaviors. Those who join one kind of culture after years of being employed by the other may have some initial difficulty adapting to the new belief but typically adapt their behavior after a while without realizing it.

Therefore, adapting to a new culture isn't simply a matter of imitating different behaviors but of understanding how those behaviors serve the culture, or at least stem from a core belief.

Knowledge of specific cultures

The world simply has too many different cultural patterns for any one person to memorize them all. Luckily, an encyclopedic knowledge of every known culture isn't necessary to be culturally intelligent. You just need to be aware of the cultures you work with every day.

For example, say a U.S. leader surveys their team and notes the following cultural demographics:

>> Three people on the team were born and raised in the United Kingdom and work out of the organization's London office.

>> Another team member whose parents were born and raised in Mexico is a devout Catholic.

>> Two employees belong to the LGBTQ community.

>> One employee uses a wheelchair.

This leader has plenty of work to do right there. It may be helpful to know these points:

>> British culture tends to approach problems more pragmatically than the U.S. culture, which tends to be more optimistic. The British sense of humor tends to be very dry and shouldn't be taken too personally.

>> Being raised by Mexican parents may mean that one employee has a much more relaxed view of time than others on the team; the leader should take care to speak in terms of specific deadlines when they're important.

>> Mexican Catholics observe several holidays most American Catholics don't; the leader shouldn't be skeptical if these days are to be observed by taking a day off.

>> Many in the LGBTQ community appreciate the use of pronouns to support trans or nonbinary employees; the leader may consider adding their pronouns to their email signature line to model this behavior for the entire team.

>> Most people with disabilities dislike being overly fawned over. After ensuring that a person with a disability has every accommodation they require to perform the functions of their job, the should make it very clear that they're happy to assist their employee at any time at their request.

Of course, the individual team members may surprise their leader by not conforming exactly to most of the predictable beliefs and behaviors found in that culture. But they're likely to appreciate their leader being prepared for these cultural traits nonetheless. And even if their employee of Mexican decent doesn't take January 5 off, they may appreciate being wished "¡Feliz Día de Reyes!"

Knowing How Cultures Differ: Seven Dimensions of Culture

One of the most well-known and widely used models of culture is called the Seven Dimensions of Culture. Management consultants Fons Trompenaars and Charles Hampden-Turner spent ten years researching the preferences and values of people in dozens of cultures around the world. They sent questionnaires to more than 46,000 managers in 40 countries and then published this model in their 1997 book *Riding the Waves of Culture* (McGraw-Hill).

Their cultural model features seven different cultural dimensions that have been applied to nations around the world, each pointing to a set of predictable beliefs and behaviors. I describe them in the following sections. Feel free to use it to understand people from different cultural backgrounds better so that you can work with them more effectively and prevent misunderstandings.

REMEMBER

Be sensible in how you apply seven dimensions. Treat people as individuals and remember that many factors have a bearing on how you communicate and interact with other people.

Universalism versus particularism

This dimension examines the nature of rules in society. In a *universalist* culture, ideas and concepts are fixed and can be applied anywhere. An action that's morally wrong in one situation is therefore morally wrong in any situation. A *particularist* culture believes that relationships are more important. In a business context, establishing a trusted relationship with a person before entering into business with them is incredibly important because the rules naturally change as a result.

Universalist cultures: The United States, Germany, Canada

Particularist cultures: China, Venezuela, South Korea

Individualism versus communitarianism

This dimension refers to how people see themselves. In an *individualist* culture, people are encouraged to see themselves as individuals and therefore consider their needs and desires as primary. In a *communitarian* culture, people are encouraged to see themselves as a part of a group and to always consider how their actions will affect the group when making decisions. (Keep in mind that people in individualist cultures still tend to view others as groups; this dimension refers specifically to how someone defines themselves.)

Individualist cultures: The United States, Mexico

Communitarian cultures: China, France, Japan

Neutral versus emotional

As you may expect, neutral cultures are ones in which people are encouraged to keep their emotions in check. By contrast, emotional cultures are ones where people are encouraged to express their emotions freely. Even when emotions are not running high, people from emotional cultures are likely to keep eye contact or nod along with a speaker to constantly communicate that they're listening. The lack of eye contact or nonverbal reactions from someone from a neutral culture can often be misinterpreted.

Neutral cultures: The United Kingdom, Japan

Emotional cultures: Italy, Israel, The Netherlands

Specific versus diffuse

This cultural dimension explores privacy and formality. In a *specific* culture, how a person behaves (and is treated by others) depends on the specific nature of their role at that time. For example, when giving a speech in my area of expertise, I'm likely to be introduced as "Dr. Shirley Davis," and those asking questions from the audience are likely to address me as "Dr. Davis." But when I'm having a meeting at work with colleagues, they usually refer to me as "Shirley," and when I'm in public with my daughter, she simply calls me "Mom."

If I belonged to a more *diffuse* culture, my public persona would be "Dr. Shirley Davis" regardless of whether you were a person in the audience at one of my keynotes or a colleague I'd worked with for years. Believe it or not, even my daughter would refer to me as "Dr. Davis" when we were in public together; terms of endearment like "Mom" would be reserved for more private moments.

When working with people from a more diffuse culture, I could easily assume that someone was stuffy or aloof, and I should take care to remind myself that I'm only interacting with their public persona.

Specific cultures: The United States, Canada

Diffuse cultures: Germany, Japan

Achievement versus ascription

This cultural dimension explores status in a society and how it's attained. A *high-achievement* culture emphasizes an individual's accomplishments and proven competencies. In a *high-ascription* culture, people derive status from who they are. Considering attributes such as age, gender, or family connections when granting status to others is acceptable and even expected in high-ascription cultures. Therefore, an older person from a high-ascription culture may have a difficult time taking direction from a much younger person from a high-achievement culture. In fact, a younger person from a high-ascription culture would likely be just as uncomfortable in this situation.

High-achievement cultures: The United States, the United Kingdom, Switzerland

High-ascription cultures: China, Indonesia, Venezuela

Sequential time versus synchronic time

This dimension explores how a society views time. In a sequential culture, time is measured concretely and is generally viewed as a finite resource. Therefore, such cultures take a dim view of "wasting" time and place great value on "using time wisely." In a synchronic culture, time is more abstract. In these societies, time is an infinite resource, deadlines are more flexible, and multitasking is more prevalent. (Just take a moment to think about the word *deadline*; someone from a sequential culture surely came up with that one!)

Sequential cultures: The United Kingdom, South Africa, the United States

Synchronic cultures: Italy, Brazil, Argentina

Internal direction versus external direction

This cultural dimension defines how people see themselves in relationship to their environments. In *internal direction* cultures, people are encouraged to live in harmony with the outside world. By contrast, people from *external direction* cultures believe more often that the outside world can be controlled. Think about the different ways that highly external direction cultures responded to the global COVID-19 pandemic: Many people in the United States (also a highly individualist culture; see the earlier section "Individualism versus communitarianism") were reluctant to wear masks, socially distance themselves, or confine themselves to their homes, believing that such actions were an affront to their personal freedoms.

Internal direction cultures: China, Russia, Saudi Arabia

External direction cultures: The United States, the United Kingdom, Australia

Mapping Your Own Cultural Orientation

Dr. Milton Bennett outlined a path for developing intercultural competence called the Developmental Continuum for Intercultural Sensitivity (DMIS). This system identifies six worldviews classifying how people experience cultural difference based on their current understanding.

The first three categories indicate less-developed intercultural sensitivity. The second three stages reflect a deeper awareness of other cultures and their validity. To find out exactly where you fall on the continuum, you need to take the IDI assessment (discussed in the next section, "Assessing Your Cultural Competence — Tools You Can Use") yourself, but knowing about the different mindsets is still helpful:

>> **Denial:** People in the *denial* mindset miss difference entirely. They operate from the belief that all people are essentially the same, which may be well-intentioned but is quite naïve given the overwhelming evidence of how culture impacts behavior. Most people in the denial mindset probably haven't had much experience dealing with people of different cultures or traveling to places where they're in the minority (culturally speaking) and have been forced to communicate across this kind of difference.

Even while staying close to home, people in the denial mindset likely find themselves in multiple dominant groupings (for example, white, male, or able-bodied) within their own culture, because nondominant groups who engage with mainstream societies are often forced to grapple with cultural difference just to get through the day. When an organization has many people in the denial mindset, DEI efforts can often be stymied by lack of interest or support.

>> **Polarization:** The next mindset recognizes difference but judges it. It's more hostile to the idea of difference, seeing the world through the lens of "us versus them." People in this mindset either strike a posture of *defense* (believing that their culture is superior to all other cultures) or *reversal* (believing that other cultures are superior to theirs). People in the defense category often exhibit xenophobic behaviors, which can be very damaging to an organization's DEI efforts. People in the reverse posture are often eager to be allies to the DEI cause but typically operate with little understanding, which can be frustrating to those they claim to support. When many people in the polarization mindset exist in an organization, DEI initiatives are often beset by conflict.

>> **Minimization:** *Minimization,* the mindset at the midpoint of the continuum, de-emphasizes difference. People in the minimization mindset believe that different cultures exist but that they're just not that important. These people tend to avoid conversations around difference, preferring to solve problems by focusing on commonalities and basic, universal human needs.

Members of both dominant and nondominant groups can fall into this category. Typically, dominant groups' members (for example, whites, males, or heterosexual people) are driven by ignorance of cultural dynamics (they see different behaviors but don't understand the different belief structures of culture) or a desire to protect the more comfortable status quo. Nondominant group members are adept at code switching to fit in and find that doing so is both manageable and profitable. When many people in an organization have the minimization mindset, DEI initiatives are actively avoided.

WARNING

People in the minimization mindset can sound an awful lot like people in the denial mindset, so telling them apart can be difficult.

>> **Acceptance:** The *acceptance* mindset is one that understands difference at a deep level. This understanding extends to other cultures but includes knowledge about one's own culture as well. People in this mindset express curiosity when introduced to a new culture, about not only how different behaviors are exhibited but also how they work within the cultural context and what beliefs they may be tied to. But although they have the understanding, they don't have a consistent ability to adapt. They often also have difficulty when another culture's behavior contradicts with a deeply held moral or ethical belief from their own culture. An organization with many people in the acceptance mindset can have successful DEI initiatives, but these efforts often spend a great deal of time focused solely on learning and education.

>> **Adaptation:** Finally, the mindset most closely aligned with interculturalism, *adaptation,* is able to build a bridge between differences. People in this mindset are able not only to understand culture but also to apply that understanding to their own behaviors to interact successfully with people of different cultural groups. They can do so while being fully aware of their own culture and how it affects the way they see the workplace. The only drawback to the adaptation mindset is the impatience that some people here can feel toward others with different mindsets who may be working their way toward more cultural competence. When many people in the acceptance mindset exist in an organization, DEI initiatives can truly thrive.

Each person is at a particular place developmentally on this continuum based on many factors, including their self-awareness, life experiences, and their receptiveness to difference.

Assessing Your Cultural Competence — Tools You Can Use

When you have a basic understanding of cultural competence, you need to know how effective you are at working and leading across differences. Luckily, several tools are available to assess this. Here I recommend a few widely recognized options that my colleagues in DEI and I have used. I happen to know the designers of these tools and have a high regard for their expertise and thought leadership in DEI, but of course do your due diligence to determine which tools may work best for your organization.

The Global Diversity Survey (GDS), created by Dr. Alan Richter, helps you navigate through the diverse global landscape. It builds on the head, heart, and hands (H3) model, presenting information in three categories:

>> Insight (Head)

>> Inclusion (Heart)

>> Adaptation (Hands)

You administer and score it yourself, calculating scores for these three categories as well as for the areas of Self, Others, and the World. The materials then recommend developmental strategies depending on your results.

Another self-assessment and 360-degree assessment tool is the Inclusion Skills Measurement (ISM) Profile developed by Dr. Helen Turnbull. It helps you improve in seven categories related to embedding inclusion:

>> Diversity sensitivity

>> Integrity with difference

>> Interacting with difference

>> Valuing difference

>> Team inclusion

>> Managing conflict over difference

>> Embedding inclusion

A third tool is one of the oldest and most recognized assessments, the Intercultural Development Inventory (IDI). Since 1986, when it was first developed, hundreds of thousands of individuals and organizations have used it to build cultural competence. The developers, Dr. Mitch Hammer and Dr. Milton Bennett, are pioneers in the DEI field. In this tool, they use the term *intercultural competence* (often interchangeably with *cultural competence*), which they define as "the capability to shift cultural perspective and appropriately adapt behavior to cultural differences and commonalities." I've been using this tool since 2013 when I became a certified administrator.

Employing the Most Important Attributes of Cultural Competence

So how culturally competent are you? Here's a list of questions to consider as you chart your own development in this area.

>> Knowledge

- Can you define the specific beliefs that define the cultural groups you belong to?

- Can you tie those beliefs to predictable behaviors that are common in your cultural groups?

- Can you name the different cultural groups that your direct reports, managers, and peers belong to?

- Do you know how to find reliable sources of information about the different cultures you interact with?

- Do you know enough about these cultures to recognize which behaviors may be culturally based?

>> Humility and vulnerability

- Do any of the cultures in the earlier section "Knowing How Cultures Differ: Seven Continuums of Culture" sound better? More logical? More ethical?

- What mindsets of the DMIS in the preceding section resonate with you personally?

- Which if any elements of your own culture do you wish were different?

- If your words or actions make someone from another culture embarrassed or uneasy, are you prepared to take full accountability for your mistake?

>> Adaptation

- Are you willing to adapt your behaviors when necessary, even if doing so feels odd or uncomfortable?

- Are you adept at coaching others so they can also exhibit more cultural competence?

Chapter **18**

Cultivating a Culture of Inclusion, Equity, and Belonging

The topic of culture transformation has become a focus for many firms worldwide, as I discuss in Chapter 6. Culture consists of the norms, values, behaviors, and attitudes that a firm rewards or highly regards. It can also be illusive and invisible, yet its effect can be seen and felt.

But changing a culture isn't easy, nor is it a quick fix, which explains why most efforts either fail or stall. In this chapter, I explore the complexities of how culture is established and what the key characteristics of low versus high performing cultures are, including what toxic cultures look like. And you discover how to transform culture and how to measure the impact of diversity, equity, and inclusion.

REMEMBER

Moving your current culture to one of equity, inclusion, and belonging isn't something to focus on after you meet other, more pressing goals. Rather, it's one of the key pathways that helps you realize those goals: a place where people can't wait to get to work and an organization that continues to grow, thrive, and make its mark upon the world.

Understanding Company Culture and How It's Established

In Chapter 3, I define *culture* as "predictable behaviors and beliefs among a defined group of people." To add to this definition, culture is a combination of values, behaviors, and attitudes that are supported by strategies and structure. This simple definition can apply to teams, departments, organizations, regions, countries, ethnicities, religions, or other groups based on traits such as generation, sexual orientation, or disability. But unlike a country, ethnicity, or religion, a company has the unique ability to influence its own culture by clearly stating its norms and values; adhering to them through policy, practices, and processes; rewarding people who demonstrate the norms and values, and holding people accountable when they don't demonstrate them, up to and including terminating employment.

REMEMBER

Regional cultures are often slow to change, but company cultures can radically alter in a comparatively short amount of time when leaders are committed to the change and enforce it by who they employ, how they create policy, and how committed they are to enforcing their norms and values.

So if culture is predictable behaviors, then *company culture* is predictable behaviors within that company — how people interact, whether they defer to leadership, how and when the company gives rewards, the extent to which employees promote themselves in the system, and the extent to which different kinds of people are or aren't included.

Realizing every company has a culture

The most important thing to know upfront is that your organization has its unique beliefs and behaviors. Regardless of whether your culture has been thoughtfully constructed or has been left to chance, it exists. So unless you're founding your own company tomorrow, this conversation isn't so much about building a culture of inclusion, equity, and belonging. It's about culture transformation.

Of course, the first step to transforming a culture is knowing where you are now — specifically, how inclusive is your company and how equitable are your practices at this moment? You can use several pieces of data to answer these questions. I outline a few of them here; for more detailed information about culture/organizational assessments, refer to Chapter 6.

>> **Employee engagement survey responses:** Can be tracked by gender, age, race/ethnicity, location, tenure, and so on.

>> **Sourcing data:** Who/how many apply for each open position? What sourcing channels are used? What criteria is used for sourcing talent?

>> **Hiring data:** Who is hired (demographics); who declines and for what reasons? What's the makeup of the interviewers? Are your hiring numbers as diverse as your applicant pool?

>> **Performance assessment data:** How do the competence rankings compare across race/gender? What disparities appear in promotions? Pay equity?

>> **Retention data:** Who leaves willingly (by demographics), and why? Who is terminated (by demographics), and why? Who plans to stay two years and beyond, and why?

>> **Complaints/lawsuits/settlements:** What are the common themes? What are the demographics of the people who took this action?

TIP

Even if all this data is easily accessible and retrievable, consider hiring an outside firm to conduct the cultural audit, for several reasons:

>> You get a more objective and expert opinion.

>> Using an outside party can ease the concerns of staff who may not trust the internal process. Unfortunately, this situation is all too common in organizations worldwide. Employees report that they fear being identified and fear retaliation.

>> The data you get is generally much richer and authentic because those interviewed are less likely to hold back when speaking to someone from outside the organization who will feed the data back anonymously.

>> An outside firm includes not only a quantitative data analysis but also a qualitative look at your organization, which may include the following:

- Focus groups with a representative sample of staff

- Stakeholder interviews with select individuals, including senior leaders, board members, community leaders, partners, and customers

- Leadership assessments (personality, communication, cultural competence, emotional intelligence, and so on)

- Benchmarking studies that review best practices in your industry or among your top competitors

A full cultural audit by an outside party also comes with specific recommendations for moving your current culture to one of greater diversity, equity, inclusion, and belonging. This report can be a great starting point for your journey of culture change.

Understanding that company culture is an open culture

Almost every organizational culture is what I call an *open culture.* In other words, the boundaries between your organization and the outside world are porous. People leave work and go home. They participate in the culture outside your company walls. They may have a small effect on the culture around them, but the culture always greatly impacts them, and they bring those values and beliefs with them to work the next day.

If your company is situated in one specific locale, or even within the borders of one specific country or nation, the culture that surrounds it has an enormous impact on the current culture of your organization. For instance, if your organization is headquartered in Delhi and nearly all your employees born and raised in India, the culture of India will naturally leave an enormous imprint on your company culture. Any cultural change you attempt will need to happen within this very specific cultural context.

Alternatively, if your company is global across many national boundaries, you may find that your culture is similarly fractured. People from the United States who work in your U.S. offices, for instance, may behave very differently from the Korean people who work in your Korean offices. Colleagues from these two offices may have a hard time effectively working together unless a strong company culture guides their beliefs and behaviors toward successful collaboration. I cover strong and weak cultures in the following section.

Defining the beliefs that drive behavior

Nearly all cultural behaviors are driven by common beliefs. If you believe "If I make this choice, bad things will happen," then you're not likely to make that choice. When nearly everyone in an organization avoids that choice, it becomes a predictable behavior across the group and therefore a cultural dynamic.

A *value* is something you believe is important. Diversity, equity, and inclusion are all values that organizations possess (or don't) to some degree. Ensuring a common belief that these things are very important is crucial in encouraging behaviors that align with those values.

Does your organization have an explicitly stated list of core values? If so, can you clearly articulate them? If not, take a moment to look them up. Has your organization communicated these? When you look at the values and their definitions, are the behaviors expected of you on the job clear?

Creating a clear set of core values

Creating and defining your company's core values is an excellent first step to creating a culture of inclusion, equity, and belonging. Although you can use words such as *inclusion* and *equity* (or even *diversity, respect,* or *authenticity*), nowadays more companies are defining their values in terms of behaviors.

TIP

If you're in the process of creating core values for your company, I suggest the latter approach; it not only makes your values clear and laser-focused on the behaviors you want to see but also helps your company stand apart with values that are clearly unique. If your values are in the form of nouns as opposed to behaviors, I suggest creating action-oriented, behavioral definitions for each so that your employees know exactly what's expected of them.

The following are examples of core values from various global company websites. As you review them, identify where you can see an emphasis on inclusion, equity, and belonging. Which values are common to them all? Are these values strong enough in your opinion? How would you strengthen them?

Examples of Company Core Values

Apple is a multinational technology company that specializes in consumer electronics, computer software, and online services.

We believe that we're on the face of the Earth to make great products.

We believe in the simple, not the complex.

We believe that we need to own and control the primary technologies behind the products we make.

We participate only in markets where we can make a significant contribution.

We believe in saying no to thousands of projects so that we can really focus on the few that are truly important and meaningful to us.

We believe in deep collaboration and cross-pollination of our groups, which allow us to innovate in a way that others cannot.

We don't settle for anything less than excellence in every group in the company, and we have the self-honesty to admit when we're wrong and the courage to change.

Honda is a global manufacturer and seller of engine-powered vehicles, serving all 7 continents of the globe.

Respect for the Individual: **Initiative** (Initiative means not to be bound by preconceived ideas, but to think creatively and act on your own initiative and judgment, while understanding that you must take responsibility for the results of those actions); **Equality** (Equality means to recognize and respect individual differences in one another and treat each other fairly. Our company is committed to this principle and to creating equal opportunities for each individual. An individual's race, gender, age, religion, national origin, educational background, social or economic status has no bearing on the individual's opportunities); **Trust** (The relationship among associates at Honda should be based on mutual trust. Trust is created by recognizing each other as individuals, helping out where others are deficient, accepting help where we are deficient, sharing our knowledge, and making a sincere effort to fulfill our responsibilities.)

The Three Joys: **The Joy of Buying** (The joy of buying is achieved through providing products and services that exceed the needs and expectations of each customer); **The Joy of Selling** (The joy of selling occurs when those who are engaged in selling and servicing Honda products develop relationships with a customer based on mutual trust. Through this relationship, Honda associates, dealers and distributors experience pride and joy in satisfying the customer and in representing Honda to the customer.); **The Joy of Creating** (The joy of creating occurs when Honda associates and suppliers involved in the design, development, engineering and manufacturing of Honda products recognize a sense of joy in our customers and dealers. The joy of creating occurs when quality products exceed expectations and we experience pride in a job well done.)

McDonald's is one of the world's leading food service brands with more than 36,000 restaurants in more than 100 countries.

Serve: We put our customers and people first

Inclusion: We open our doors to everyone

Integrity: We do the right thing

Community: We are good neighbors

Family: We get better together

Verizon is a global leader delivering innovative communications and technology solutions.

Service: The company has work because its customers value its high-quality services.

Customer focus: Verizon focuses on customer needs rather than its own.

Teamwork: Verizon embraces diversity and personal development.

Integrity: The company adheres to sound business practices.

Performance: Bureaucracy is an enemy to a large company.

Values: Everything the company does is based on its values.

Obviously, a set of core values is about more than just setting expectations around diversity and inclusion. However, employees (and job seekers) will look to your core values to understand how your company expects people within the organization to treat each other. Therefore, including some clear language to this effect is important. Your people should not only know what behaviors align to your values but also easily be able to sense what kinds of behaviors aren't acceptable.

Putting core values into action

Of course, simply defining a set of core values and hanging them on a wall in the office isn't going to do much to change your culture. You have to put your values into action. You can do so by creating policies and norms/processes that directly align to those values. Here are some examples:

>> **Policies:** Forbidding discrimination based on identity markers, making it easy for people with disabilities to get the accommodations they need from a centralized fund that doesn't burden hiring managers, allowing medical leave for those seeking gender-affirming procedures, allowing holiday leave for those of different religious groups for whom important holidays coincide with work days

>> **Norms/processes:** Making team decisions in a way that captures the perspectives of both extroverts and introverts, placing pronouns in your email signature and asking your team to do the same

Some companies go as far as to include their core values in their performance assessment systems, while making it very clear that violating the organization's core values is a much more serious matter than falling short of a competency. This kind of violation may even involve the termination of employment. This is why crafting your values carefully and with precision is so important—because employees are held accountable for them in their performance reviews, and they can lose their jobs if they are not adhered to. Before finalizing your list of core values, ask yourself whether these beliefs are truly imperative or simply nice to have.

An organization's core values should be a barometer for every major decision a leader makes in an organization. Often, leaders make decisions in organizations without thinking through how they're either encouraging or discouraging specific behaviors or outcomes. For instance, many organizations have employee referral programs that benefit employees who circulate job openings to friends and former colleagues/classmates. Usually, such programs are implemented to cut down on costs associated with finding talented and qualified candidates, but an unintended consequence, especially for companies that aren't very diverse, is that applicants are even more homogenous than they were before, mirroring the population that already exists in the organization rather than expanding it.

If inclusion is a stated value, creating a program that makes your organization less diverse makes no sense. It only takes one instance of hypocrisy (conscious or not) to convince employees at every level that your core values are only there for show and not to be taken seriously.

Introducing the Culture Spectrum

In my work, I speak to many organizational leaders, whether I'm coaching them or helping them think through strategic decisions. Most of these leaders tell me that their company cultures are inclusive and high-performing. But when I speak to those at lower levels of the company, a distinct disconnect appears. The same culture isn't nearly as inclusive from their vantage point, and they see lots of room for improvement in terms of company performance. They talk about not feeling welcomed or about instances of unfairness that they've witnessed. This discrepancy is why consistently and accurately assessing your culture (as I describe in Chapter 6), and not taking for granted that your view from the corner office matches the view that others may see every day, is so important.

If you decide to embark on a journey of culture change, the change can begin at the top of the organization, among its leaders. Sometimes the change process starts more organically, outside of the C-suite. Either is fine; what's important is that after the change process is underway, it needs to include everyone. A change effort led solely by executives will likely result in something that looks like success from the boardroom but less so from outside of it. If the process itself isn't inclusive, the outcome likely won't be, either.

After the COVID-19 pandemic, a PricewaterhouseCoopers study found that 69 percent of leaders who successfully adapted to the new business environment said that their culture had been a source of their competitive advantage. A startling 85 percent of them revealed that culture was an "important item" on their leadership agenda. And yet, for all of this emphasis on culture, very few organizations succeed in transforming their cultures.

Peter Drucker, an Austrian American management consultant, explained this disconnect by saying, "Culture eats strategy for breakfast." I believe it eats strategy for lunch and dinner, too, but basically, what he was saying is that your culture tends to validate itself. Beliefs cause behaviors that lead to predictable outcomes and validate the original belief. If changing behavior is difficult, then changing belief is grueling, and changing the beliefs of many people at the same time can seem impossible. Not every strategy is up to the task.

If your organization is going to succeed in its effort to change its culture, you need to be exact — almost surgical — in your approach. You need to know what behaviors need to change, what beliefs those behaviors are rooted in, and what rewards, incentives, and consequences you need to provide to allow those beliefs to change.

In 2019, I commissioned researcher and analyst Matthew Walker to conduct an extensive qualitative study. The study reviewed a pool of 300 organizations from around the world, including private-sector companies, nonprofit organizations, and U.S. federal agencies.

The purpose of the research wasn't simply to rank these sample organizations in terms of cultural "proficiency" but rather to use these comparisons to identify the traits and behaviors that were most impactful in determining these rankings across the sample. We considered some key questions:

>> Why do some organizations thrive in the face of adversity where others struggle to keep team morale afloat?

>> Besides profitability, what determines whether an organization heroically earns the forgiveness or admiration of the public?

>> What failures have dragged other organizations down to appear as scarlet-lettered villains?

The research didn't interact with the employees or former staff of these organizations directly. It was focused on the public image and sentiment these organizations generated and how their actions (or inactions) have led to the challenges, victories, and failures that have come to be defining characteristics of their employer brand. We used three major criteria for determining the sample companies, given the breadth of experiences we aimed to capture:

>> **Financial performance:** The sample was largely composed of Fortune 500 companies and top-performing nonprofits, giving us a broad selection of some of the world's most well-known employer brands.

>> **Public prominence:** We included organizations that had been in the media spotlight in recent years, both for positive and negative press related to human resources, DEI, and culture issues.

>> **Best of the best/worst of the worst:** We used resources such as best/worst places to work rankings (such as Glassdoor, Great Place to Work, and DiversityInc,); employee engagement reports by Gallup, BlessingWhite, Willis Towers Watson, and others; and public sentiment research to identify best/worst performers. These sources also helped highlight the best/worst practices that drive movement along the Culture Spectrum (which I discuss in a moment). Each company was assigned a score that seeks to reveal the most likely path of development for each organization along a Culture Spectrum based on all publicly available data/reports.

My firm has been working with organizational leaders for nearly a decade on culture transformation, and we have developed a model and diagnostic tool that includes six key strengths of cultures that are high-performing and inclusive. Correspondingly, it identifies six deficits in organizations that are low-performing and potentially (or actually) toxic. This model is called the Culture Spectrum, and you can see it in Figure 18-1. It's meant to help leaders identify their organization's strengths and weaknesses during a culture transformation process. Companies that possess the six key strengths fall on the right side of the spectrum. Those whose cultures comprise most of the deficits fall on the left side of the spectrum. During the change process, which can be rocky (see Chapter 3), you need to lean on your organization's strengths while taking steps to correct the areas of your culture that are on the left side of the spectrum.

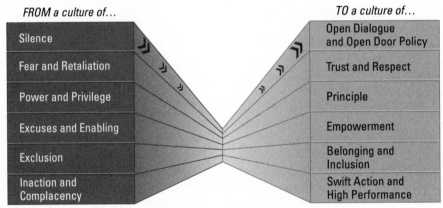

FIGURE 18-1: The Culture Spectrum.

FROM a culture of...

| Silence |
| Fear and Retaliation |
| Power and Privilege |
| Excuses and Enabling |
| Exclusion |
| Inaction and Complacency |

TO a culture of...

| Open Dialogue and Open Door Policy |
| Trust and Respect |
| Principle |
| Empowerment |
| Belonging and Inclusion |
| Swift Action and High Performance |

Courtesy of Dr. Shirley Davis

The left side of the spectrum

Six clear signs indicate that your culture is toxic and low-performing.

Silence

In organizations that put an emphasis on safety, open communication, or even trust, you hear the phrase "If you see something, say something" a lot. But in many toxic, low-performing organizations, a culture of silence pervades. In these environments, people have seen that speaking up is either dangerous or simply pointless because no one listens and no action is taken. They may notice that those who do speak out are seen as annoyances and are routinely passed over for promotion or advancement opportunities or even retaliated against (see the following section).

Fear and retaliation

In some organizations, employees know all too well the immediate negative consequences that come from speaking out or stepping "out of line" in any number of ways. These "infractions" can range from using innovative and creative ways of completing routine tasks to reporting unethical (perhaps even illegal) behavior to simply sharing an opposing opinion. People know these actions have limited or ended others' careers.

REMEMBER

In fact, when a company culture is laden with fear and retaliation, unethical behavior will surely follow because people can use it to get ahead without paying a price. Often, these environments are especially hostile to people of color, women, LGBTQ people, people with disabilities, and other underrepresented or marginalized groups. This culture can result in their being marginalized, discriminated against, and overlooked.

Power and privilege

What do the C-suite and board of directors look like in your organization? Are they overwhelmingly made up of a certain gender, ethnicity, age, and sexual orientation? Do they contain people who look, think, and act differently? How do their demographics compare to those of your mid-level line leaders or entry-level workers? If there's a noticeable lack of visibly diversity between the top levels of the organization and those they lead, how do you explain the discrepancy?

Unless you believe that race, gender, sexual orientation, gender identity, ability, or other identity markers are true indicators of talent and work ethic, this scenario has only one explanation: You're working in a culture of power and privilege, where the most talented people from underrepresented groups are either denied advancement or voluntarily leave your organization before you have the chance to stall their careers. Are people who look like your organization's leaders evaluated based on their perceived potential while everyone else must work to justify their place at the table? If so, this performance bias is likely a deficit in your culture that you need to address. You can read more about performance bias and other biases in Chapter 15.

Excuses and enabling

When people behave badly inside your organization, what do people — especially those with power — typically say about it? Do they honestly admit unethical behavior and take accountability for it? Or do they tend to make a lot of excuses about how much money the person brings in, how they were raised, how tough the industry is, and so on. When a culture lacks accountability and transparency and enables people to get away with bad behavior because they're "rainmakers" or have valuable connections with the majority/dominant group, it can be a toxic workplace, especially for those from underrepresented groups.

Exclusion

Exclusion doesn't just keep people out; it often keeps them from trying to get in in the first place. Studies have shown that the same regions of the brain that register physical pain also react to exclusion. Just like you probably won't put your hand back on a hot stove after you've been burned, you're probably not going to keep trying to get into a group that has excluded you repeatedly. You're far more likely to disengage. You may polish up your resume and look for another, more welcoming job, but you may interpret this lack of inclusion as proof that your ideas have little merit and simply withdraw. You may also do what I did early in my career: I internalized the rejection, and it affected my self-esteem and self-confidence.

Consider these questions as you determine whether your culture is one of exclusion:

>> How engaged are your employees? Who's most engaged and who's least engaged, demographically speaking?

>> Does everyone feel they can have equal access to opportunities or get a seat at the decision making table?

>> Which voices/ideas are heard loud and clear and which ones are drowned out or dismissed?

>> How much turnover do you experience, and how many dollars do you spend trying to fill the seats of people who have voluntarily separated from your organization? How do these numbers look demographically?

>> Are lively debates commonplace at your organization, or do most of your staff simply "go along to get along"?

>> What are you learning from conducting exit interviews when employees turn in their resignation? These interviews can yield valuable information about the company's culture, what works and what doesn't, and how the employee experienced it.

Inaction and complacency

When you discuss diversity, equity, and inclusion inside your organization, how do people typically respond? Does an authentic reckoning take place of how far you need to go and all the ways the organization hasn't lived up to its potential? Or do people just shrug their shoulders as if the work is too difficult to manage?

REMEMBER

The work of culture change is difficult, especially when your company is decades (or perhaps centuries) old. This kind of environment is called an *ingrained culture,* and that means that changing it will take a lot.

Most people don't like change, and when leaders live by the mantra "we've always done it this way" and work to preserve the existing culture rather than act to change it, things will remain the same. An unwillingness to try to do what's difficult not only means that diversity, equity, and inclusion will be hard to achieve but also points to a general lack of passion and drive that can only lead to mediocrity at best and a failing business at worst.

The right side of the spectrum

The six strengths that signal an inclusive, equitable, and high-performing culture are essentially the opposite of the six deficits I cover in the earlier section "The left side of the spectrum."

REMEMBER

Be honest about the current state of your organization. If you don't have high scores in every category of the right side of the Culture Spectrum, that's okay; very few organizations can honestly say they do. Rather, let these signposts serve as inspiration for your journey. Take a moment to imagine how powerful your company could be and what joy you'd experience at work almost every day if being on the right side of the Culture Spectrum were your reality. It can be if you do the work strategically and steadfastly.

Open dialogue and open door policy

A *safe-to-speak* culture talks about the issues and problems that are impacting the organization, its customers, communities, and the world. It both solicits and brings forth ideas from all levels of the organization; it doesn't act on every idea, but it does appreciate the act of bringing forth an idea and recognize and reward bold thinking. Contrast that with the culture in the earlier section "Silence."

Of course, you can't have every important conversation out in the open, but in this kind of culture, leaders have an open door policy where staff can schedule time with their manager or leader to discuss matters large and small: how their current project is going, their long-term career goals, elements of the organizational culture that are difficult to navigate or may be holding them back, and so on. Often, leaders see an abundance of these conversations as a sign of weakness, but they actually point to strength.

REMEMBER

As I discuss earlier in the chapter, your company culture is most likely an open culture; the issues that impact the communities and societies in which your workers live follow them into the office. The ability to address them and talk about them is an asset that every organization should strive to achieve.

Trust and respect

Unlike the organizations I describe in "Fear and retaliation" earlier in the chapter, high-performing companies have teams that work well together and manage conflict effectively. Workers have confidence in their leaders and what leaders tell them, they feel safe to share ideas, and they can engage in difficult conversations because they trust the organization not to react negatively. When an organization is dedicated to rooting out bad actors and toxic behaviors, it respects and appreciates those who report unethical behavior — which, by the way, is a rare occurrence among companies that are on the right side of the Culture Spectrum. In this kind of culture, ideas come from every corner of the company and are considered based on an inherent respect for every employee.

Principle

More and more companies have realized success by competing in the marketplace based on principle and purpose. They realize that products and services can easily be replicated, but customers and employees are increasingly drawn to what they stand for, not just what they sell. And workers report that they want to work for a company that has both — that does the right thing and that lives its values. They also want their employer to take a stand on important social and political issues that they care about. Leaders who operate based on principles are the same each day, each week, and each year (they're consistent), they call out unethical behavior that isn't aligned with the company's values, they treat others with respect and create an environment that promotes mutual trust, and they make decisions that are in the best interest of all versus a few.

Empowerment

The combination of open dialogue, trust, and a strong emphasis on people not only influences your employees away from shady behavior and toward ethical, morally sound choices but also enables them to take their own actions. This empowerment includes taking calculated risks in the name of doing the right thing. In this kind of organization, employees admit when they've made mistakes because they feel safe to learn and grow from it. Even mid-level employees don't hesitate to stand up, even to a high-paying client or senior level leader, when demeaning or harassing behavior takes place.

Belonging and inclusion

When Abraham Maslow created his famous hierarchy of needs in 1954, he suggested that humans' most basic needs were physiology (for example, food and sleep) and safety. Belonging was the third need, followed by esteem and self-actualization. According to Maslow, those more basic needs had to be satisfied before people could truly focus on higher needs. Today, though, many thought leaders believe that a sense of belonging may well be the primary need of human beings. At the very least, the idea that human beings require connection to be healthy and whole seems undeniable.

In any organization, people need to feel a sense of inclusion and belonging to be their most authentic and productive selves. Even when tasks are repetitive or menial, a deep connection to the people on the team results in top quality work — and an environment that values and generates mental health.

Swift action and high performance

High-performing cultures are characterized by the ability to take swift action and achieve results. This kind of company culture isn't created overnight, and is only possible when all the other attributes on the right side of the Culture Spectrum I explain in the preceding sections are in place. Employees speak up; they trust their leaders and each other. Leaders respect their staff and make decisions on principle. Everyone in the organization is empowered to do what's right has a deep sense of connectedness and belonging. In this kind of company, swift change is possible because everyone is performing at the peak of their ability and able to work together at their highest capacity.

Exploring the Characteristics and Implications of Toxic Workplaces

The joy that comes from being a company that's on the right side of the Culture Spectrum (see the earlier section "Introducing the Culture Spectrum") isn't going to be an everyday occurrence, no matter how wonderful your company culture may be. You're going to have those moments when you wish the weekend would arrive, when colleagues disappoint you, and so on. That's normal (and, hopefully, infrequent).

But a *toxic* workplace is one in which most, if not all, of the characteristics on the left side of the Culture Spectrum exist every day along with a few other signs. Take a look at the following list and decide whether each statement is true (or usually true) for your organization:

>> **Communication**

❏ Most of my work assignments are vague or unclear.

❏ I consistently receive different messages than my colleagues.

❏ Communication at my company is often passive-aggressive, forcing me to read between the lines to establish the real meaning of what's being said.

❏ People, especially managers, listen to respond instead of listening to understand.

>> **Career opportunities**

❏ Promotions from within are rare in my company.

❏ I do not have access to professional development, either because of limited budget or time.

❏ Any conversations I have with my manager are focused on short-term actions or emergencies, not long-term growth or strategy.

❏ I've been doing the same thing for years and can't say I've learned much on the job.

❏ There's no clear path for me to grow at this organization.

>> **Leadership**

❏ When I look at the leaders of my company, I see no one who looks like me.

❏ I feel micromanaged and often receive communication from my manager after hours or on weekends.

❏ My manager rarely gives career guidance. When they do, it's usually about what has worked for them but is unlikely to work for me.

❏ I rarely receive positive reinforcement.

❏ Most of the feedback I get is negative but not solution-oriented (that is, what I'm doing is wrong, but I'm not sure how to fix it).

❏ My manager takes full credit for the work I've done.

❏ My manager takes no accountability for mistakes that are made on their team.

❏ My manager is moody, and determining when to bring issues to their attention can be difficult.

❏ My manager says inappropriate things that make me uncomfortable.

❏ My manager is harassing or abusive.

» **Peers and co-workers**

- ❑ My colleagues are largely unmotivated.

- ❑ I often take on more than my schedule will allow for fear that the work won't get done otherwise.

- ❑ Exclusive cliques exist within my team or company.

- ❑ Gossip is widespread within my team or company.

- ❑ My colleagues emulate the worst examples from leadership, with no accountability.

» **Work-life balance**

- ❑ I frequently receive communications from leaders and colleagues after hours or on the weekend.

- ❑ People rarely take vacations within my team or company.

- ❑ I do not take advantage of all the paid time off I'm allotted each year.

- ❑ When people do take time off, they're expected to monitor their email while they're gone.

- ❑ When people call in sick, they're questioned and doubted.

- ❑ People feel proud or are rewarded for working excessive hours or throughout the night.

WARNING

The implications of a toxic work environment are real and can have serious implications on your company's ability to infuse diversity, equity, and inclusion into the culture. They include, but aren't limited to, the following:

» **Recruitment:** Attracting top talent and even targeting underrepresented talent will be an uphill battle if your culture is known to be toxic. Workers today are doing their due diligence prior to applying for a position or accepting an offer at your company. They'll review your website and do an Internet search on your company to find out the good, bad, and ugly about working there. They'll reach out to current and former employees on social media to inquire about what working there is like and will ask probing questions during interviews to find out about your culture.

» **Disengagement:** Toxic work environments can provoke staff to disengage, usually as a coping mechanism to protect their own mental health from the stress and anxiety of working in a toxic space. Often, those who disengage from the work experience a form of validation from doing so ("my contributions weren't valuable anyway, and no one misses them"), which only serves to reinforce this behavior over time.

- » **Burnout:** When the clear majority of your staff members are disengaged, picking up the slack usually falls on a small number who refuse to disengage (usually through learned work ethic or a personality type that leans into hard work). As grateful as you may be for these people in the short-term, their contributions are often stifled by the eventual burnout they experience from shouldering too much responsibility. Symptoms of burnout can include depression, chronic headaches or other pain, self-doubt, and fatigue. Obviously, this model isn't sustainable for either the individuals or the organization.

- » **Turnover:** When people of high self-esteem encounter a toxic workplace, the most common (and probably the wisest) reaction is to look for another job where they can grow and thrive. Common estimates indicate that replacing an employee who leaves your organization can cost between one-half to two times that employee's annual salary. Of course, these costs are only the ones that can be calculated on paper. When turnover is high, you're likely losing your best, most talented staff, which compounds these costs in ways that may not show up on a spreadsheet. What you're left with are usually your lowest performers and many new staff members — several of whom may not still be here in a year's time.

- » **Business failure:** Looking at the preceding bullets, you can easily see that a common risk among so many unsustainable dynamics is that the business simply goes under, no longer able to keep its doors open. In fact, the very best that a truly toxic organization can hope for is a state of mediocrity, which usually results in a slow, arduous death rather than a quick, catastrophic one.

REMEMBER

If you fear that your company culture isn't just "less than ideal" but truly toxic, repairing it is not only important but also urgent, and you should address it as soon as possible.

Implementing a Sustainable Culture Transformation

When you know what kind of culture you have and an idea of what kind of culture you want, you can determine the specific steps you need to take to get there.

Setting the stage for change

In Chapter 7, I introduce you to one of the change models that I use in my culture transformation work, the Beckhard–Harris Change Model, or $D \times V \times F > R$. It means that for change to happen in an organization, the feeling of dissatisfaction with the status quo (D) multiplied by a clear vision for the future (V) multiplied by clear first steps that your organization will take (F) must be greater than the resistance to change (R).

REMEMBER

I don't want to get too bogged down in math, but note that the reason Beckhard and Harris wrote their model with multiplication signs is that if any of the first three values (dissatisfaction, vision, first steps) is equal to zero, then the total is zero and there will always be enough resistance to sink any change efforts you have. Therefore, all three are vitally important. You need to articulate a clear vision that inspires people to want to do the work. You need to tell them exactly what's expected of them now (first steps) to support that vision. You should communicate these points multiple times, through multiple channels. When you think everyone has received the message, you're probably about halfway there.

And you need to do what you can to make people less happy with the way things are right now (dissatisfaction), although that may seem counterintuitive. For some, this step can look like data (employee demographics, employee engagement scores, customer demographics), especially comparisons to your competitors who may be ahead of you. Others, who may not be aware that different experiences of the company culture exist, may need stories from those who have been made to feel excluded. Often, when I've led focus groups with people of color in an organization, I let them know that I may publish their words anonymously when delivering an assessment report to their leadership. Understanding that their organization isn't nearly as inclusive as they thought can be a very powerful experience for leaders.

At this stage, anything you can do to lower the resistance to change is also useful. Although the approach is somewhat risky, I've seen several organizations do this successfully by saving some room for a skeptic or two in the core strategic planning task force for DEI. When nearly everyone in the organization, even the late adopters of change, can see someone who looks like them leading the DEI effort, they're more likely to give it a chance. (This means including people from all levels of the organization as well, not just senior leaders.)

Because you know that there will be some resistance to change, consider what you can do to prepare and respond. Ask yourself:

>> Is there enough dissatisfaction with the status quo to move ahead?

>> Do you have a clear, consistent, and inspiring vision for the future to communicate?

>> Can you articulate some actionable first steps?

>> How will you manage resistance to change?

Mission, vision, and values

The next phase of communication in your change effort should focus on how your efforts to build a culture of inclusion, equity, and belonging are directly tied to your company's mission, vision, and values.

Consider these questions to get started:

>> What is your mission and vision, and what are your values?

>> If they currently exist, do they support your goals for inclusion, equity, and belonging?

>> What changes may be necessary before you begin your work?

REMEMBER

The mission statement outlines *how* you will get to where you want to be. The vision statement outlines *where* you want to be (a future state of being). The values are the core principles or fundamental beliefs that you operate under.

If this task is difficult, that itself is a valuable set of data; it may be an indication that your mission, vision, and values need an overhaul. In that case, this phase of your change effort is to introduce new language to describe what you do, where you're headed, and how you'll get there.

Policies and formal processes

Take a close look at your organization's policies and processes, specifically those that do not align with your (existing or new) mission, vision, and values, which I discuss in the preceding section. Data you get from an organizational assessment should be helpful in locating which formal ways of doing business conflict with the values of diversity and inclusion. In a strategy session with your core strategic planning task force, map out which changes will have high impact and which will be less impactful, as well as which are relatively easy to make and which will be more difficult.

TIP

If any are easy and high-impact, they should be where you start. You'll have to plan for changes that are difficult and high-impact. The best-case scenario for a culture change effort is to illustrate an impactful and relatively painless change at the very beginning, which helps build necessary coalitions for the more difficult change ahead.

You'll need to plan for changes that are difficult and high-impact. Ignore any changes that are difficult and low-impact for now; they're probably not worth your time.

A trusted partner (a consultant versed in DEI or a consulting firm that specializes in this work) can often be helpful at this stage. An external perspective can often see problematic policies or processes that people who are inside the system miss.

As you evaluate the policies and processes you currently have and determine which ones will need to be revised or created, here are a few questions to ask:

>> What policies and processes currently exist that clearly support your DEI goals?

>> Are any not in alignment?

>> Which of these policies and processes will be easy to change? Which will be difficult?

>> Which of these changes will have a high impact on your organization? Which will be less impactful?

>> Do you have a trusted partner who can guide you through this process?

Informal processes

Of course, not every business process is written down in a formal way. Often, team leaders have chosen a variety of ways to connect with their staff members, make team decisions, collaborate, assign tasks, and so on. Though they're informal, you also need to address these practices so they align with the organization's mission, vision, and values.

TIP

Often, the best way to change the informal processes of the team is to provide training specific to leaders and managers. Awakening your people-leaders to their implicit biases is often a good way to begin this process, followed by a workshop designed to investigate the organization's DEI goals and how their leadership styles and choices can either enable or hinder those goals. Leadership competencies that are aligned with the behaviors you seek can also be an important tool here.

The important thing is to allow leaders and managers to choose their own path within the parameters set forth related to DEI. Leaders can often unwittingly thwart a DEI change strategy, but they can also usually find a way to support those goals while also playing to their strengths as leaders.

As you consider what ways your team can support the DEI goals and what strengths and development areas they possess, also ask these questions:

>> What kind of talent management skills do you need to meet your DEI goals?

>> Do your leaders generally possess those skills?

>> What training or development would be useful in acquiring those skills?

>> How can you motivate managers to lead their teams in such a way that makes your DEI vision a reality?

Employee behavior

Because leaders have an outsized influence on their organization's culture, changing employee behavior may come somewhat naturally if your efforts to change leadership behaviors have been successful. Employees who want to succeed generally imitate their leaders to some degree, whether they know it or not. Still, this influence isn't effective on its own, and some effort to influence all staff behaviors is also necessary.

This work typically takes the form of rewards and accountability. In other words, you need to provide visible incentives for employees to change their behavior in a positive direction coupled with clear penalties for behavior that violates the company's values. Both are important, but rewards are usually more powerful in triggering a person's decision to change their behaviors. I've seen organizations institute DEI competencies that, when met or exceeded, can influence a greater bump in pay. In some organizations, employees know that taking a leadership role in an Employee Resource Group is a great way to facilitate a promotion to the next level in the organization. (To find out more about ERGs, refer to Chapter 14.)

I'm familiar with a large organization that throws a swanky dinner each year to acknowledge three individuals and two groups with an Annual Diversity Award, which is considered one of the most meaningful honors in that organization. Individuals who win the award sit with the CEO at dinner and later give remarks to a room full of senior leaders about their personal DEI journeys. To both the honorees and everyone who receives a copy of their remarks the next day in a organization-wide email, it becomes very clear how exemplifying the values of diversity and inclusion is a trendsetter for success!

Penalties, of course, can range from a conversation with a manager to disciplinary action to termination of employment, if the violations are significant enough. You need to form a written policy for these penalties, but you don't need to communicate them as broadly as the rewards. What's important is that you hew to them, without fail, even if the person who violates them is well-connected or brings in a lot of money. You may experience an initial setback financially by censuring or firing such an individual on the grounds of discrimination or harassment, but the message you're sending to your culture by doing so is invaluable. After the initial shock wears off, employees will clearly see what the organization's priorities are. Moving the company closer to the right side of the Culture Spectrum will result in long-term wins that dwarf your short-term losses.

It's important to ensure that your employees are rewarded and also held accountable for living the company's values. Here are a few questions you can ask as you evaluate both the rewards and the consequences:

>> What rewards currently exist for employees to behave in alignment with your organization's values?

>> Is it possible for an employee today to violate the company's values somehow and still be rewarded? How can you stop that from happening in the future?

>> What rewards can be created and introduced to drive behavior change among your staff?

>> What penalties exist to create accountability in this area? Which should be codified in your written policies?

Assessing progress and creating the next strategy

Diversity, equity, and inclusion work is a journey, not a destination. Therefore, it has no endpoint, no moment where you can emphatically state, "I've arrived!" and then stop thinking about the work. If you do, your organization (an open culture) will quickly slide backward to more closely resemble the society outside your office doors. You never reach the end of the road, but you can, and should, reach the end of a *change cycle*.

A change cycle can last anywhere between three and five years, with annual check-ins to measure progress. You should set goals for where your organization should be at the end of a change cycle and collect data (see the next section) at the beginning and end to measure progress.

Whether you've met your goals, fallen short, or wildly exceeded them, you should use this information to chart your next strategy. Given where you are at the end of your first change cycle, where do you want to be at the end of another three to five years? What's your organization ready for that you couldn't have introduced when your journey began?

Measuring the Impact of a Culture of Inclusion, Equity, and Belonging

Clients constantly ask me how to measure the impact of DEI efforts. What's being measured today has evolved since the 2010s, when it was focused mainly on compliance and not getting sued. Today, you can collect many kinds of data at the beginning and throughout your inclusion, equity, and belonging change journey so that you can compare where you along the way (milestones), on an annual basis, and at the end of each change cycle.

>> **Completion of concrete goals:** Sometimes, the answer is simply "yes" or "no." For instance, you may decide that one of your primary goals is to hire a Chief Diversity, Equity, and Inclusion Officer within your first change cycle. Perhaps you plan to integrate inclusive behaviors into your values or add them to your competency model for all staff during the first year, communicate them broadly during the second change cycle, and incorporate them into your performance assessment process by the third cycle.

>> **Staff inclusion and engagement scores:** If you don't already conduct an annual staff inclusion and engagement survey (as I describe in Chapter 6), the assessment phase of your DEI journey is a good time to start. Tracking your progress year over year, especially broken down by identity markers such as race/ethnicity, age, gender, tenure, and so on can give you an immediate sense of how your work is progressing.

TIP

However, consult with HR or your legal department to ensure that the demographic questions you ask are legal in whatever country or region you do business. In some places, asking whether a person has a disability is illegal, for example. Also, be as inclusive as you can when crafting categories for demographics to make room for people of all ethnicities, people who identify as gender non-binary, and so on.

>> **Retention and turnover:** As I note earlier in the chapter, exclusion and toxic work environments can lead to increased turnover, especially among underrepresented groups. Seeing your retention numbers increase and your turnover numbers decrease (again, also broken down by race and gender) gives you an excellent indicator of whether your change initiatives are working.

>> **Demographics:** Visibility does matter. Representation does matter. One of the key trends that leaders look for as an indicator of success is the organization's demographics. Look at who's employed in which positions at which levels and at what pay. Track who is leaving, who's being promoted, who is getting development opportunities, who has a mentor/coach/sponsor, how

performance ratings are being assigned, who's most and least engaged, what your supply chain looks like, and so on.

REMEMBER

These are important numbers to track, but you can't forget that positive demographic trends are a *lagging indicator* of success. In other words, you can be doing amazing work for a while before you see these numbers change significantly. And seeing less progress than you want isn't evidence that what you're doing isn't working. By all means, measure your demographic data, but don't act too hastily based on what you find.

>> **Anecdotal data:** Regardless of whether you began with a thorough cultural assessment of your organization (and I recommend you do), you can conduct focus groups and interviews with employees and key stakeholders at any time to hear stories about what working at your company is like. Feeding back this data anonymously to your senior leadership can have a profound impact on their commitment to this work.

>> **Customer/stakeholder demographics:** In addition to knowing who you employ, measuring your impact on an increasingly diverse marketplace may also be pertinent. Whether this population comes in the form of customers, patients, grantees, students, members, or businesses owners, measuring your increased reach as an organization is a powerful indicator of progress.

>> **Financial data:** Whether your goal is to make money or save it, a diverse organization with an inclusive culture typically recognizes some financial advantage. Many factors can contribute to increased profits or savings, but DEI initiatives are certainly one, and pair your progress in this regard to your bottom line can be very energizing. Another financial metric to track is the cost or the savings of lawsuits, settlements, reputational damage repair, and the associated legal fees spent year over year. If you implement DEI initiatives right, and you work to make your culture more inclusive, equitable, and respectful, you should see positive return to your bottom line.

5

The Part of Tens

Find answers to common misunderstandings about DEI.

Know what role boards play in supporting DEI.

Uncover pitfalls to avoid in leading diverse talent.

Chapter **19**

Ten Common Myths about Diversity and Inclusion

As you work to make your company more diverse, equitable, and inclusive; you're going to hear a lot of statements that just aren't true. Those who make these statements are usually well-meaning but ill-informed. Sometimes, however, they're deliberately trying to sabotage your work. In either case, you have an opportunity to correct the record. In this chapter, I debunk ten common myths about diversity and inclusion. Feel free to use these responses to educate others about DEI.

When We Check This Box, We Can Move on to Other Priorities

Diversity, equity, and inclusion work is a marathon, not a sprint. It's not about "checking a box," or completing a discrete series of tasks and calling it a day. It's not about hiring just enough folks who are considered "minorities" or putting the company through a single DEI training course and expecting the culture to change. DEI is about recognizing that talent comes in all shapes, sizes, colors, backgrounds, cultures, personalities, and the like. It's a change management process that requires time, effort, resources, support, and every staff person's commitment to fostering a culture where everyone is treated with respect, valued for their contributions, set up for success, and able to grow and thrive in their careers.

Isn't Focusing on Diversity Just Reverse Discrimination?

I like to think about DEI efforts as a pie that represents opportunities. There's enough pie for everyone, and as companies open new seats and expand the table, the pie gets bigger and is enough for everyone to get a slice. Focusing on diversity is necessary because many countries have laws against discriminating against a person based on their age, race, gender, religion, and so on. Underrepresented (diverse) talent brings all kinds of skills, experiences, ideas, and solutions that can benefit the company.

DEI means ensuring that those who've been historically marginalized or deprived of equal opportunities simply because of their identities should be given a fair and equitable chance to succeed. It does also mean looking within your organization's demographics and identifying where you have gaps — who you keep hiring and why, but more importantly, who you've consistently left out. In those cases, yes, you may need to target historically marginalized groups through programs and processes designed to create a level playing field and to ensure that they too can access career opportunities in your organization. That doesn't mean you're discriminating against historically dominant groups.

DEI Work Has No Place for Straight, White Men

The goal of DEI is to create teams, companies, and systems that work for everyone and that allow access to seats at the table where all voices can be heard. Of course straight, white men have a place in this work. That many may feel this way is understandable because they've been in positions of power and privilege for centuries, and this work means sharing some of that.

REMEMBER

I've found that straight, white men can make tremendous allies, great mentors, and effective spokespeople. Other times, I've found that they can be the biggest resisters. And if the resistance is happening inside the room, it's surely happening outside the room as well. Those who are allies, champions, and advocates can play a tremendous role in influencing the rest of their colleagues to be a part of the solution and not the problem and to recognize that DEI work is about everyone, including straight, white men.

"Diversity" Is Just Code for "Race

Diversity means all the ways individuals and groups differ from one another. It's a broad definition — so broad that it's hard to tackle all at once. Consequently, your work naturally addresses the needs of specific marginalized groups who have been/are impacted the most, and one of those groups will almost always be people of color.

However, I believe that DEI can take a "both-and" approach, meaning that as you address the ills and inequities experienced by people of color, you shouldn't ignore the needs of people with disabilities, people from the LGBTQ community, women, veterans, or other historically marginalized groups within your organization that can benefit from DEI work.

What We're Really After Is Diversity of Thought

Sometimes, to allay the fears of historically privileged people within an organization, DEI programs are presented as a search for diversity of thought rather than diversity of identity. Of course, if your organization was built so that only extroverts (for example) can get ahead, then solutions that give introverts access to success need to be created. But always, diversity of identity means diversity of experience. Women, people of color, LGBTQ people, and people with disabilities have different life experiences and different worldviews that may differ from those of the dominant group.

REMEMBER

You can't have true diversity of thought unless you have people who look, believe, think, communicate, and see the world differently.

I Support Diversity; I Just Don't Want to Lower Our Standards

Focusing on diversity doesn't mean lowering standards or selecting a less qualified person (which is what those who resist DEI efforts often assume). Sadly, many people who've uttered this statement or something like it think they've just said something sensible and wise. But think about it for just a moment. At the heart of this sentence is the belief that straight, able-bodied, white men are naturally smarter, more talented, more educated, and more capable of achieving results than anyone else. This belief indicates that as soon as you hire or promote someone outside this group, you run a significant risk of diminishing your team's intellect, talent, knowledge, and competence. There's no room for this kind of thinking in the workplace or in society.

If We Can Achieve Diversity, Inclusion Will Follow

You can have diversity and not have inclusion. And that's where too many organizations find themselves today. They've sought to achieve diversity goals by hiring a few underrepresented people and think that they can now expect to see inclusion. Not so.

The reason companies a century ago were so homogeneous is the same reason many people's social circles today aren't nearly as diverse as their workplaces. Homogeneity is closely linked with comfort. People who resemble each other — who are more alike than different — tend to get along. They naturally understand each other and can speak in shorthand and shared cultural references.

At work, of course, this uniformity is also linked with stagnation, groupthink, and the status quo. Organizations that want to thrive in an increasingly competitive, complex, and global landscape need to diversify. But more importantly, they need to cultivate a culture that requires all workers to respect and value differences, create a sense of inclusion and belonging, and ensure that all talent has equity and access to opportunities. Companies that don't do so run the risk of losing great talent, great ideas, great customers, and a lot of money.

All Bias Is Bad

A bias is just a decision you make, and not all decisions are bad. Bias is a natural human state. If you have a working human brain, you have the ability to make incredibly quick decisions based on patterns from your past and your current emotional state. You need bias to protect you from harm and stay safe, healthy, and alive.

But sometimes bias can result in the perpetuation of harmful stereotypes. Therefore, examining important decision for signs of bias is important. That examination doesn't necessarily mean that your gut responses are unfair or incorrect, only that you acknowledge the potential is there.

Succeeding as a DEI Practitioner Will Put Me out of a Job

When the DEI industry was young, this sentiment was popular among practitioners. The idea that we could build cultures so sustainable that our work would no longer be needed was aspirational at best.

Think about it: When a company has achieved consistent revenue growth and is experiencing long-term success, does the chief financial officer quit? When a company goes a few years with no safety incidents, does the head of safety step down? No. Likewise, today DEI work clearly can no longer have a timetable on it, no matter how much success the company has achieved in attracting, engaging, and retaining talent. Over time, evidence has proven the opposite; when you stop focusing on these important topics, you begin to move backward. This work is here to stay.

Is All This DEI Work Really Necessary When People Seem Happy Here?

If you haven't made a real effort to create a positive and inclusive workplace culture, your people likely aren't as happy as you think. When a powerful person is happy, they can easily believe that everyone is equally happy. And when those with less power have good reason to keep their less-than-happy experience a secret, the illusion of universal happiness is even stronger.

REMEMBER

Sometimes, when a DEI practitioner uncovers some pain in the organization, they're told that their work is "divisive" and just making everything worse. But the practitioner didn't create that pain; it was always there.

Chapter **20**

Ten Ways That Boards Can Influence DEI in the Organization

M ore than ever before, boards of directors are recognizing that DEI not only contributes to organizational performance but also promotes better decision making, prevents blind spots in board deliberation, and enables them to access more resources and reach a broader community. Boards play an integral role in leading their companies through business and social change in ways that promote sustainability, performance, and value.

High-performing boards operate to their fullest potential when they tap into a broad range of diversity by drawing from the expertise of people across race, ethnicity, sexual orientation, thinking, working, and other areas, such as professional experience. An exceptional board is a high-performing team with a shared purpose to drive the work of the organization forward toward an important vision. Fostering a space that values the experiences of a diverse group and applies them to the oversight of social impact organizations is important to addressing social challenges.

Here are ten steps boards can take to better influence and lead their companies strategically and systemically in their DEI initiatives.

Develop a DEI Statement and Center It in Your Business Strategy

Don't assume that everyone understands DEI or operates from the same point of view. Remember, diversity, equity, and inclusion are three separate concepts, yet they're often misinterpreted or used interchangeably. A DEI statement gets everyone on the same page. Make your DEI statement part of your governance structure (so you can make more-informed decisions and hold each other accountable) and a core ingredient in the design and execution of your business strategy.

TIP

Having a DEI statement not only expresses commitment but also serves a tool for the nominating committee as you consider and recruit new board members. Publish this statement on your website so that interested board prospects are clear about your commitment and where you stand.

Commit to Diversifying Your Board

Optics matter. Representation matters. When a potential board member doesn't see anyone else who looks like them, it communicates that their values and needs aren't important and that the organization isn't serious about DEI. If the board isn't both diverse and inclusive, it lacks credibility with management and likely with staff, customers, donors, partners, and other stakeholders as well. Diversifying your board should be an intentional and ongoing process. It should include recruiting for the attributes that you don't currently have (and will need in the future based on your organization's direction) and that are representative of the communities you serve and are located in.

Reassess your board's recruitment goals and selection criteria. Start by looking at the visible demographic makeup of your board (especially among racial and gender lines because they make up a significant portion of the workforce and are most underrepresented on today's corporate and nonprofit boards). Also expand your candidate pool to include *cognitive diversity* — different views and perspectives, experiences, and ways of working — as well as generational, personality, and communication style diversity and candidates who are outside your industry and sector. Some skills and experiences are transferable and can add tremendous value to any board. By assembling a board that reflects a broad cross-section of diverse perspectives and lived experiences, your company benefits from robust discussions, which lead to more innovative solutions that address complex problems facing the organization and its communities.

Cultivate a Culture of Inclusion on Your Board

Diversifying your board as I describe in the preceding section is critical, but you also need to focus on inclusion. *Inclusion* is about the culture: the ways you treat each other, the values you live by, and how you get things done. If the culture among your board members is one where trust is broken, conflicts and bickering are rampant, egos are inflated, and decisions are undermined, your board is toxic. This kind of culture doesn't serve the organization well in terms of strategy or productivity.

TIP

To create a culture of inclusion, board members need to develop and demonstrate inclusive behaviors. I recommend Deloitte's six C's of inclusive leadership for board members:

>> **Commitment:** Diversity and inclusion align with your personal values.

>> **Courage:** You're willing to speak up, challenge the status quo, and have the tough conversations.

>> **Cultural intelligence:** You're confident and effective in crosscultural interactions. You practice self-reflection and discovery to build honest and trustworthy relationships (cultural humility).

>> **Cognizance of bias:** You're mindful of personal and organizational blind spots and self-regulate to help ensure fairness.

>> **Collaboration:** You empower individuals and leverage the thinking of diverse groups.

>> **Curiosity:** You have an open mind and a desire to understand how others view and experience the world.

Establish Clear Board Roles and Responsibilities

Board members' role descriptions should outline expectations, responsibilities, fundraising requirements, and your organizational values. In your description, detail your organization's commitment to diversity, equity, and inclusion and what board members are expected to do in supporting those arenas.

Additionally, more boards have assumed the role and responsibility of aligning their strategies with Environmental, Social, and Governance issues such as climate change, social justice, employee diversity, corruption, human rights abuses, supplier diversity, and of course COVID-19. They are ensuring that ESG is built into the culture and business strategy of the company, and they are evaluating both the risks of the investments as well as opportunities that need to be developed.

Ensure Your Board Chair and CEO Are DEI Champions

Both the board chair and the CEO are internal and public facing positions that have lots of opportunities to speak on important issues that affect and involve the organization and its communities. Sometimes those issues are political and social and can get into DEI territory. They can be daunting to address given how sensitive and polarized they are in society, but these conversations are what the people these roles sign up for. You can't be about diversity if you don't talk about it.

For example, when the George Floyd murder occurred, board chairs and CEOs alike were thrust into the spotlight to speak on their companies' behalf about their stands on DEI. As more and more social and political issues work their way into the workplace and boardroom, these people should be prepared and willing to speak to them and take responsibility. Even when no cameras or media are around, the Board Chair and the CEO should be visible champions and spokespersons for the DEI strategy.

Provide Education on DEI-Related Topics

The world has become more diverse in every aspect and yet most corporate boards have abysmal representation of diversity. Education and training are first steps to ensuring that the board all speak the same language of DEI and can build new skills and competencies for working more effectively across differences. The following are examples of the types of training I'd recommend for board training:

>> Fundamentals of diversity, equity, and inclusion: terminology, the business case for your sector/industry, demographic shifts, regulations and laws that govern DEI, and the roles and responsibilities of board members

>> Implicit bias and its impact in decision making

>> Cultural competence and multicultural communications

>> Emotional intelligence

>> Group dynamics (including power dynamics)

>> Tactics for having impactful and courageous conversations (including taboo topics)

REMEMBER

Education and training should be ongoing and should resemble some of the education being offered to the organization's senior staff. It should also include the history of the organization and what may be the perceived or real issues related to inequities, discrimination, and/or lack of inclusion currently or previously (for example, racism, sexism, ageism, ableism, and so on).

Embrace an Equity Mindset

An *equity mindset* requires a board to be aware of systemic inequities and commit to promoting equity in what the organization does. Understanding how these inequities affect both the company's communities and society at large helps a board increase the organization's impact and contribution to the public.

To advance equity, the board must have an equity mindset in all its work. That includes allocating resources, implementing oversight to investigate issues that impact marginalized and underrepresented groups, and making sure the board itself is diverse as I explain earlier in the chapter.

Accept Responsibility

Boards play a critical role in creating an organization that prioritizes, supports, and invests in diversity, equity, and inclusion. The board sets the tone for the entire organization; whatever it makes a priority will trickle down to the rest of the organization. As board members, hold each other accountable for embracing and living the values of DEI, make DEI a frequent agenda item for board meetings, incorporate DEI into your governance structure (see the earlier section "Develop a DEI Statement and Center It in Your Business Strategy"), and hold the CEO/president accountable for making sure that DEI is implementing across the organization.

Get Comfortable Being Uncomfortable

This work is hard; it can be controversial, and it's definitely uncomfortable. But if you want to make substantial and lasting change in your organization, you have to commit to the process. And that means getting comfortable with being uncomfortable — having tough conversations, dealing with resistance, building new skills, and influencing others to change mindsets, attitudes, and behaviors. The payoffs of building a more diverse, equitable, and inclusive board can yield long-term benefits to the success of your organization, so you have to be willing to lean into the growing pains and challenges that come with change.

Measure Your Success

The age-old adage of "What gets measured gets managed" continues to confound many in the DEI space as diversity, equity, and inclusion gain momentum and commitment from boards of directors and the C-suite. Without clear and robust measures to track diversity and inclusion efforts and outcomes, people have a tendency to revert to habitual and ingrained thinking and behavior patterns. This backslide can severely hamper gains and accomplishments.

REMEMBER

Selecting meaningful diversity and inclusion metrics is an art rather than a science. You have to consider your business strategy and the DEI goals you've set forth as a board, which likely include the demographics of your board and how diversified you are (and not just in terms of race and gender). Additionally, you can include some of the following:

>> How open is dialogue among your members?

>> How well does the board get along?

>> How effectively do you manage conflict or disagreements?

>> How closely do you adhere to your guiding principles and values?

>> How strategic do you remain?

>> How productive are your meetings?

>> How effective have education and training programs been?

>> What's the sentiment of the staff and the general public about the board's effectiveness in its representation of the company?

Chapter **21**

Ten Things Underrepresented Talent Wish Leaders Knew

Building an organization where everyone across all dimensions of diversity feels included and can do their best work involves knowing what (and what not) to do and say. This chapter looks at ten of the most common pieces of feedback from diverse workers around the world — people who've been discriminated against, felt marginalized, and/or historically felt unheard, unvalued, or like they didn't belong. Sadly, these issues still occur today.

REMEMBER

If you show or have shown any of the behaviors in the following sections, you're not alone. What will separate you is your willingness to look at the people in your organization from a different lens and be open to feedback, change, and new ways of leading a diverse workforce. What do you need to change? What do you need to start doing, stop doing, or do less of? And what are you doing well that you can continue doing or do at a higher level?

Everyone Has Different Needs in the Workplace

Though individuals with shared diversity attributes may share the same ethnicity, culture, language, and certain values, they don't all have the same needs in the workplace. All workers come into an organization with a specific set of experiences, skills, knowledge, and abilities. Therefore, no one solution or way of doing things works for everyone. Here are a couple of examples:

>> An organization brought in outside coaches to help new managers from different cultures succeed as leaders. This move was a great way to recognize that people who weren't from the dominant culture (which in that organization was white and male) may have additional challenges in navigating the organization and being more assertive.

   However, one manager explained that he was a fifth-generation Chinese American, had a strong business and managerial background, and was an executive director at his last job. He said that he'd like to work with a coach but didn't have the same challenges or issues as other people in the coaching program, who were newer in leadership positions. He wanted coaching in more advanced areas. He stated, "I'm glad that the organization is making an effort to help new leaders or people moving into leadership who aren't from the prevailing dominant culture, but all of us aren't the same."

>> I was a single mom for 16 years of my career. I worked an 8 a.m. to 5 p.m. schedule (nine hours) each day for most of that career. When my daughter switched schools to one that didn't provide bus transportation home, my biggest need was flexibility in my work schedule to pick her up each day before the after-school program ended at 6 p.m. I was always willing and able to come back to the office after I got her home and settled with a babysitter. I was committed to working from home and on weekends to get the job done, and I was a consistent high performer.

   I worked for one leader who believed that you could only be productive when at the office. He didn't believe in working from home because he couldn't monitor whether you were actually working. So he gave me hard time for needing to leave to pick her up. Needless to say, he lost a high performer who got great results but didn't feel valued.

Representation Equals Diversity, Equity, *AND* Inclusion

In Chapter 1, I highlight the fact that diversity, equity, and inclusion are three distinct concepts; they aren't one and the same. I also stress that having a diverse workforce means many things: racial and gender demographics, yes, but also cognitive diversity, neurodiversity, diversity of skills, physical abilities, age, communication styles — the list continues. Sometimes when an organization has what you can call "visible diversity," leaders may feel that the work is complete, when in fact it has only just begun.

Employees in several organizations have expressed frustration with their leaders' complacency after the company establishes some visible diversity. One employee said that her manager kept pointing out the great job she did of hiring people from different backgrounds, abilities/disabilities, sexual orientations and so on as though that was enough. She was frustrated by her manager's lack of understanding that representation didn't equal equity and inclusion.

Other comments that reflect this kind of situation include the following:

> "I feel like we are just window dressing for the photo ops."

> "Why do they bother bringing us in if they're not going to use our talents?"

> "Diversity and inclusion don't stop when they hire people who are from different groups."

> "Do they even care whether I feel comfortable contributing or like I belong?"

REMEMBER

If you really believe that diversity is important for business, you have to go beyond representation and consider what you as a leader are doing to take diversity to the next level.

Here are some questions to consider:

>> What's the reason for increasing diversity in our organization?

>> What talents and skills aren't being utilized but need to be?

>> What's the organization doing to make people feel welcome and included?

>> What am I doing to make people from any and every group or dimension of difference feel welcome and included?

>> What more can we do?

Intent Doesn't Equal Impact

Here's a common occurrence: An employee tries to talk to their manager about offensive comments another employee made. The manager just brushes it off, saying the employee didn't mean anything and is a "good person" with good intentions. The offended employee feels dismissed and minimized, never shares anything else about inappropriate comments, loses trust in the manager, and exhibits lower morale and productivity. How many employees have these same experiences in your workplace?

REMEMBER

How the person making a comment means it isn't what matters; how that comment impacts the person hearing it is. You can consider intent in understanding the basis of an offensive comment or microaggression, but making a blanket statement and assuming that the offense was unintentional or that the person "didn't mean to be hurtful" doesn't rectify the situation. Too often these words become an excuse for continuing to be offensive and for excusing comments that are racist, sexist, homophobic, xenophobic, and so on.

Diversity, Equity, and Inclusion Are More Than Just "Race"

Diversity is the "who," equity is the "how," and inclusion is the "what." *Diversity* entails all of the beautiful attributes that humans may embody. Literally, it's all the ways in which they vary or are different — their uniqueness. *Equity* is the process by which you dismantle systemic discriminatory practices in society, the law, and the workplace so that all have a level playing field regardless of background, relationship, and status. Equity is the result of justice. *Inclusion*, then, is the outcome of diversity and equity work. An inclusive environment not only invites all to the table but also ensures adequate space at the table and that the voices at the table are valued and heard.

DEI includes sexual orientation, gender identity, ethnicity, and religion, among other dimensions. Focusing only on one area and one issue not only makes other underrepresented people feel excluded but also doesn't take into consideration that people are more than one identity. A Black employee said that she was glad that the organization was doing more to deal with racial inequity but felt that it was totally ignoring her needs as a person in a wheelchair. It was impacting her ability to get all her work done.

TIP

Consider the multiple identities everyone brings to the workplace and how those identities intersect. They create commonalities and opportunities for learning about differences.

Don't Tokenize Me Because I'm the Only One

REMEMBER

No "model minorities" speak for or represent an entire race or ethnicity. If you have only one or a few people from a specific diversity group, don't treat them like a token or put them on display by asking them to be in every public corporate photo or to serve on every diversity-related committee. This tokenism is alienating and acts as the opposite of inclusion.

Take, for example, a few statements about feeling tokenized from people in organizations where they're the "only one" from their group:

> "As the only Black person in my department, I'm often asked what other Black people think. I don't know; I only know what I think. I don't speak for other Black people."

> "As a Latinx person, I was asked to explain the impact of Cesar Chavez on 'my people.' I'm from Peru and would need to do my research like anyone else."

> "I'm the only Asian American person on my team. I was born in the United States, and my parents are from Viet Nam. Several people asked me what was happening in China with COVID-19. I read the papers like everyone else and have no inside information."

REMEMBER

Being an organization with a few "only ones" leaves a negative impression, as if the company doesn't value or prioritize diversity. If you're in an organization that has just a few "only ones," why do you think that is? What can you do specifically to help remedy this situation?

Do Your Own Work; Walk the Talk

As a leader in your organization, you must do your own work to discover your biases, mitigate those biases, and be a voice and proponent for diversity if you want to be an effective change agent. You must walk the talk by being an ally, advocate, mentor, and sponsor — a diversity champion. Don't just sponsor the

DEI program budget; actively participate. Share your own stories of your experience with learning about diversity. Actively participate in affinity group activities. Sponsor a corporate social responsibility (CSR) charity event. Establish a supplier diversity program.

One employee said, "It's good that my manager has everyone going to diversity training and learning about bias, but she has yet to attend. She talks about the importance of diversity and even hosts diversity related programs, but we have seen little change at the higher levels and our manager doesn't seem to be interested in looking at her own biases, of which she has many." Is this statement true of you, too? If so, you aren't walking the talk.

REMEMBER

You're most effective as an agent of change and leader of diversity and inclusion when you set the example and model the right behaviors. By being willing to look at your own personal history, identity, and relationship to diversity and inclusion, you develop a deeper understanding of how to be an inclusive leader.

Your employees will know, respect, and trust you more. They'll be not only more willing to share their concerns and issues with you but also more likely to provide ideas, suggestions, and feedback to help you and the organization be more successful.

Stop with the Overly Complimentary Language

Profusely complimenting underrepresented employees comes across as though you didn't expect the employee to be competent. Those backhanded compliments are actually microaggressions (which I cover in Chapter 7). You may think you're providing positive feedback, but what you're really doing is revealing your biases.

REMEMBER

For example, you don't need to describe every person of color as "amazing," "articulate," or "highly qualified." Using these descriptors indicates that you're surprised (or that you need to assure yourself or others) that someone from another culture can be successful, "despite" their background.

Consider the following examples:

> During a team meeting, a white woman said, "During the COVID-19 pandemic, I had the opportunity to work with some truly amazing Black women. I feel so fortunate."

When recommending a candidate, a white male recruiter declared, "You need to interview Enrique. He's so articulate and doesn't have an accent. You'd never know he's Latino."

A team leader who had just hired a woman who was blind remarked, "Marlena is so good at what she does; you'd think she was like everyone else. You'd never think of her as blind."

Don't Interpret Silence as Consent or Agreement

WARNING

Silence doesn't indicate consent or agreement. Here's what silence often does mean:

>> **An organization that doesn't value the voices of all of its members:** Consider your team. Do you have fully capable and talented employees who don't speak up in project meetings? Have you thought about why? Ask them.

>> **Fear:** Employees may be fearful of responding to questionable remarks from fellow employees and especially from senior leaders.

>> **Lack of interest:** Can you identify employees who just dial it in? Have you communicated with these employees about their perceived disinterest in work?

If you hear someone make an inappropriate comment about a particular group someone from that group doesn't say anything, don't assume they think it's okay.

For example, say an employee complains to a manager that another employee has made a joke about transgender people, and the manager replies, "Well, Tina is transgender, and she didn't complain, so it must be all right." The manager needs to understand that as the only transgender person in the room, Tina may have been afraid to speak up. She may have been afraid of being ostracized or attacked, or even of losing her job for saying something, especially when the manager took no action.

REMEMBER

This kind of situation is why allyship is so important. When you hear those jokes or comments, you need to speak up and be aware that the person being targeted may not feel safe.

Open communication is an aspect of an inclusive and high performing work environment; silence is not. When silence abounds, consider that your company may have a larger organizational concern.

Ask for My Perspective and Input Even Though I'm Different from You

Inclusive workplace environments value the input, expertise, and talent of *all* employees. *Affinity bias* is the tendency to rely on and give more weight to the opinions and input of people who are most like you. Unfortunately, this bias often applies to leaders in organizations and the people they bring into their inner circles.

At issue for people who are different from their managers is that after they get hired, they're ignored and feel invisible. At a tech diversity conference, a group of Black and brown computer engineers were talking about their experiences:

> "I was there for three months, and no one ever asked my opinion or ideas. I was completely underestimated."

> "I always saw people meeting with the manager, but no one ever invited me in."

> "I'd like just once to be asked for my perspective."

TIP

Be aware of whose opinion and feedback you solicit. Is everyone the same? You need to be intentional, even though seeking out the people on your team or in your organization from different genders, races, ethnicities, and so on and inviting their perspectives may be uncomfortable at first.

Your Staff Is Watching You

Not only are your staff members watching you and talking amongst themselves, they're also probably well versed in social media and will talk to the outside world. The flip side of the newfound employee respect I discuss in the earlier section "Do Your Own Work; Walk the Talk" is that people will talk about you negatively if you give lip service to DEI practices in your organization. You can't just spout slogans and take no action if you want their trust and respect.

Index

A

ability
  disabilities and, 20–21
  to mediate conflicts fairly, 53
ability to adapt, cultural competence and, 64, 66, 250–251
ableism, 23
acceptance mindset, in Developmental Continuum for Intercultural Sensitivity (DMIS), 260
accepting responsibility, 301
accountability, developing, 68–70
achievement *versus* ascription dimension, 257
acumen, globalization and, 33
ADA (Americans with Disabilities Act), 21
adaptation, as an attribute of cultural competence, 262
adaptation mindset, in Developmental Continuum for Intercultural Sensitivity (DMIS), 260
addressing unconscious bias, 168
advantaged, 28
advisory diversity, 211
affinity ("like-me") bias, 159, 225, 310
affinity clubs, 214
affinity groups, 214, 241
ageism
  defined, 23
  reducing bias against older workers, 144
agility, globalization and, 33
aging workforce. *See* generational diversity
AI (artificial intelligence), 43–44
Americans with Disabilities Act (ADA), 21
anchoring bias, 225
anecdotal data, measuring, 287
anti-bias training, 232
apologies, offering, 69–70
applicant tracking system (ATS), 137

applying
  core values, 53–55
  retention strategies, 160–161
Arbery, Ahmaud, 11
artificial intelligence (AI), 43–44
ascription dimension, achievement *versus,* 257
assimilation, 251
ATS (applicant tracking system), 137
attribution bias, 225
authenticity, exhibiting, 53–56
automation, 43–44
avoiding turnover, 86

B

balanced scorecard, 179–180
B-BBEE (Broad Based Black Economic Empowerment Amendment) Act, 195
Beckhard-Harris model of change, 109, 280–281
behavioral-based interviewing, 142
belonging
  about, 21
  cultivating, 171, 172–173
  in Culture Spectrum, 277
benchmarks, 99–100
benefits, as an attribute of employers of choice, 79
benign bias, 224
Bennett, Milton, 105, 258–260, 261
best practices, for supplier diversity programs, 196–198
Best Practices regression level, 100
BFOQs (bona fide occupational qualifications), 146–147
bias
  about, 221, 295
  affinity ("like-me"), 159, 225, 310

CDEIO (Chief Diversity, Equity, and Inclusion Officer)
about, 87–88
choosing, 90–92
positioning, 92–93
role of, 88
when to hire, 89–90
CEO, 300
change
commitment to, 70
communicating, 59–60
fear of, 110
setting stage for, 280–281
change cycle, 285, 286–287
Change Model, 57–58
Cheat Sheet (website), 5
Chief Diversity, Equity, and Inclusion Officer (CDEIO)
about, 87–88
choosing, 90–92
positioning, 92–93
role of, 88
when to hire, 89–90
Civil Union Act (South Africa, 2006), 14
classism, 23
coaching diverse talent, 151–153
coalition building, 58–59
Coca-Cola, 186, 193
code switching, 251–252
cognitive diversity, 298
cognizance of bias, inclusive leadership and, 242, 299
collaboration, inclusive leadership and, 242, 299
collaborative leadership, 156
commitments
to change, 70
communicating for DEI, 139
to diversifying board, 298
inclusive leadership and, 242, 299
keeping, 56
communication
as an attribute of employers of choice, 79
of changes, 59–60

commitment to DEI, 139
DEI and, 189–190
DEI plan across organization, 127–128
style differences in, 167
communitarianism dimension, individualism *versus*, 256
company culture, establishing, 264–270
compensation, measuring, 177
competence, cultural
about, 64–66, 247–248
assessing, 260–261
attributes of, 262
components of, 249–252
cultural humility, 252–253
cultural intelligence, 253–255
dimensions of culture, 255–258
mapping your cultural orientation, 258–260
competence bias, 227
competencies, of inclusive leaders, 241–243
complacency, in Culture Spectrum, 274–275
complimenting, 308–309
conducting
document reviews of policies, processes, and strategies, 100–104
employee focus groups, 106
leadership assessments, 104–105
staff inclusion and engagement survey, 105–106
confirmation bias, 225
conflict management, 61–62
consensus leadership, 156
consistency
bias and, 233
importance of, 68
Coqual, 81
core values. *See also* value
applying, 53–55
creating, 267–269
putting into action, 269–270
corporate social responsibility (CSR)
Chief Diversity, Equity, and Inclusion Officer (CDEIO) and, 93
DEI and, 190–192
cost, of turnovers, 86

D

dangerous bias, 224

data, reporting to key leaders, 182–183

Davis, Shirley (author), 5

decision-making
  effect of bias on, 227–229
  equity and, 63–64

deflection, 69

DEI (diversity, equity, and inclusion). *See also specific topics*
  about, 9–10
  benefits of, 75–86
  branding and, 185–189
  common organizational barriers to, 107–118
  communicating commitment to, 139
  communications and, 189–190
  corporate social responsibility (CSR) and, 190–192
  defined, 15–20
  embedding into mission, vision, and values, 120–122
  environmental social governance (ESG) and, 190–192
  history of diversity and inclusion in workplace, 12–15
  impact on organizational success, 76–78
  marketing and, 185–189
  messaging and, 189–190
  necessity of, 295–296
  Plans for, 122–127
  positioning as a strategic priority, 119–129
  reflection activity, 28–29
  re-shifting focus to, 10–12
  supplier diversity program and, 192–199
  terminology for, 20–28

DEI councils
  about, 201
  compared with Employee Resource Groups (ERGs), 202–205
  developing charters, 210–211
  establishing effective, 207–211
  recruiting and securing members for, 210

DEI disclosures, 179

DEI initiatives, Employee Resource Groups (ERGs) to support, 211–216

DEI Scorecard, developing, 179–181

DEI statement, 298

demographic trends
  about, 31–32
  digitization, 41–44
  globalization, 33–34
  increasing diversity, 34–38
  increasing flexibility, 39–41
  jobs experiencing greatest growth potential, 45–46
  measuring, 286–287
  skilled *vs.* unskilled workers, 44–45
  virtual work, 39–41
  workforce predictions, 32

denial mindset, in Developmental Continuum for Intercultural Sensitivity (DMIS), 259

Developmental Continuum for Intercultural Sensitivity (DMIS), 258–260

diffuse dimension, specific *versus*, 257

digitization
  about, 41
  artificial intelligence (AI), 43–44
  automation, 43–44
  COVID-19 pandemic and, 41–42

diplomacy, 62–63

disabilities, ability and, 20–21

disabled (differently-abled) workers, reducing bias against, 144–145

disadvantaged, 28

discrimination, reverse, 292

disengagement, toxic workplaces and, 279

diverse supplier, 192–193

diversity
  cognitive, 298
  compared with race, 293, 306–307
  defined, 15–16
  dimensions of, 16–17
  ethnic, 37–38
  executive, 211
  gender, 35–37
  generational, 34–35

employer of choice, becoming an, 78–79

empowerment, in Culture Spectrum, 276

enabling, in Culture Spectrum, 273–274

English Bill of Rights (1689), 13

environmental criteria, 191

environmental social governance (ESG), DEI and, 190–192

EQ (emotional quotient), 48–53

Equal Employment Opportunity Commission, 179

Equal Marriage Act (U.S., 2015), 14

equality, 17

equity
  compared with race, 306–307
  decision-making and, 63–64
  defined, 17–19

equity mindset, 301

ERGs (Employee Resource Groups)
  about, 201
  compared with DEI councils, 202–205
  establishing charters, 215–216
  importance of executive sponsors, 205–207
  launching, 214–215
  recruiting members/executive sponsors for, 215
  religious, 212
  remote work and, 41
  to support DEI initiatives, 211–216
  types of, 213–214

ESG (environmental social governance), DEI and, 190–192

establishing. See also building
  clear board roles and responsibilities, 299–300
  company culture, 264–270
  effective DEI councils, 207–211
  ERG charters, 215–216
  mission, 208–209
  roles and responsibilities, 209–210
  strategic areas of focus, 208–209
  vision, 208–209

ethnic diversity, 37–38

evaluating
  cultural competence, 260–261
  DEI leadership effectiveness, 48–70

  impact of culture of inclusion, equity, and belonging, 286–287
  performance, 157–160
  progress, 285
  success, 302
  success of supplier diversity programs, 198–199
  team needs, 153–157

exclusion, in Culture Spectrum, 274

excuses, in Culture Spectrum, 273–274

executive diversity, 211

Executive Order 11246 (1965), 13

executive sponsors
  importance of, 205–207
  recruiting for ERGs, 215

External Dimensions layer, 17

external direction dimension, internal direction *versus,* 258

F

failure, fear of, 111

Fair Work Act (Australia), 179

fairness, as an attribute of employers of choice, 79

faith, reducing bias against, 145

Fast Brain, 221–223

favoritism, 116–117, 173–174, 243

fear
  of change, 110
  in Culture Spectrum, 273
  DEI and, 24
  employee, 309
  of failure, 111
  of hardship, 111
  of moral judgment, 110–111
  overcoming, 110–111

feedback
  diplomacy and tact in, 63
  failing to provide, 174, 244
  measuring, 177–178
  negative, 118
  providing, 159–160

feelings of loss, 24

financial performance
  on balanced scorecard, 180
  driving, 237
  measuring, 287
flexibility
  increasing, 39–41
  teams and, 165
Floyd, George, 11–12, 14, 300
French Declaration on the Rights of Man and
    Citizen (1789), 13
Frito-Lay, 241

G

gay, 25
GDEIB (Global Diversity, Equity, and Inclusion
    Benchmarks), 20, 99–100, 180–181
GDS (Global Diversity Survey), 105, 261
gender diversity, 35–37
gender-coded words, 143
gender-neutral words, 143
General Motors, 194
generational differences, as key component of
    diversity, 16
generational diversity, 34–35
Global Diversity, Equity, and Inclusion Benchmarks
    (GDEIB), 20, 99–100, 180–181
Global Diversity Survey (GDS), 105, 261
globalization, 33–34
goals
  lack of, 173, 243
  measuring, 286
  setting, 209–210
Goleman, Daniel, 48
go-tos, 116–117
governance criteria, 191
growth potential, jobs experiencing greatest, 45

H

habits, 230
Hacking Diversity with Inclusive Decision Making
    study, 240
Hammer, Mitch, 105, 261
hardship, fear of, 111

health, enhancing for staff, 81–82
heterosexism, 23
hidden biases, 141–142
hidden figures, 114–117
Hidden Figures (film), 114
hierarchical leadership, 156
high performance, in Culture Spectrum, 277
hiring, for teams, 164–165
history, of diversity and inclusion in workplace,
    12–15
homophobia, 23
HRC (Human Rights Campaign), 25
HR/recruiting/selection/onboarding and retention,
    Chief Diversity, Equity, and Inclusion Officer
    (CDEIO) and, 93
Human Rights Campaign (HRC), 25
humility, as an attribute of cultural
    competence, 262

I

icons, explained, 4
identifying bias, 223–224
IDI (Intercultural Development Inventory),
    105, 261
illegal questions, avoiding, 146–147
impact, relationship with intent, 306
impairment, 20
implicit bias
  about, 22, 219–220
  addressing, 168
  bias, 221
  effect of bias on decision-making in workplace,
    227–229
  identifying bias, 223–224
  moving to inclusive leadership from,
    235–245
  origins of bias, 221–223
  reinforcing bias, 221–223
  reprogramming brain to make less biased
    decisions, 229–234
  types of bias, 224–227
  underrepresented talent and, 116
implicit person theory/personal growth
    mindset, 159

improving
  employee experience, 83
  employer brand, 237–238
inaction, in Culture Spectrum, 274–275
Inactive progression level, 100
inappropriate questions, avoiding, 146–147
inclusion
  compared with race, 306–307
  in Culture Spectrum, 277
  defined, 19
  history of in workplace, 12–15
  leveraging to drive innovation and creativity, 79–81
  measuring, 286
  myths about, 291–296
  relationship with diversity, 294
Inclusion Skills Measurement (ISM) Profile, 105, 261
inclusive leadership
  avoiding pitfalls of ineffective leadership, 243–244
  benefits of, 236–241
  competencies of, 241–243
  key traits of, 241–243
  moving from unconscious bias to, 235–245
  overlooked microbehaviors, 244–245
  six C's of, 299
inclusive marketing, 187–188
increasing
  employee engagement, 84–85, 238–239
  employee satisfaction, 239–240
  job satisfaction, 239–240
  team performance, 240
indigenous, 22
individualism versus communitarianism dimension, 256
industry standards, 99–100
inflexibility, 174, 243–244
informal processes, culture transformation and, 283–284
initialism, 24–25
innovation, leveraging inclusion to drive, 79–81
intent, relationship with impact, 306

intercultural competence, 261
Intercultural Development Inventory (IDI), 105, 261
interest, lack of, 309
internal direction versus external direction dimension, 258
internal perspective, on balanced scorecard, 180
Internal/Primary Dimensions layer, 16
Internet resources
  Cheat Sheet, 5
  Davis, Shirley (author), 5
  Human Rights Campaign (HRC), 25
  Society for Human Resource Management (SHRM), 99
interpersonal skills, 60
intersectionality, 23
interview panels, building diverse, 145–146
islamophobia, 23
ISM (Inclusion Skills Measurement) Profile, 105, 261
isms, 23–24
IT, Chief Diversity, Equity, and Inclusion Officer (CDEIO) and, 93

J

Jackson, Mary, 114
job descriptions, writing inclusive, 140–141
job satisfaction, increasing, 239–240
Johnson, Katherine, 114

K

Kahneman, Daniel, 221–223
know-it-all, 244
knowledge management
  as an attribute of cultural competence, 262
  globalization and, 33
Kotter, John
  Leading Change, 57–58

L

Larsen, Molly, 194
LBGTQ Enterprises, 193

minimization mindset, in Developmental Continuum for Intercultural Sensitivity (DMIS), 259

minimizing
bias in selection process, 141–145
employee complaints/lawsuits, 85

Minority-Owned Enterprises (MBEs), 193

mission
culture transformation and, 282
in DEI council charter, 211
embedding DEI into, 120–122
establishing, 208–209

mitigating bias, 229–232

moral judgment, fear of, 110–111

motivation (core values)
as a component of emotional intelligence, 48, 50–51
maintaining, 60

N

National Black Employees Caucus, 204

National Minority Supplier Development Council (NMSDC), 194

negative feedback, 118

negativity bias, 225

nepotism, 67

networking, building, 137–138

neurodiversity, 26

neutral *versus* emotional dimension, 256

Nike, 186

NMSDC (National Minority Supplier Development Council), 194

no-judgment zones, for meetings, 167–168

norms, 269

O

objectives, in DEI council charter, 211

office gossip, 67

office politics, 66–67

onboarding, 86

one-on-one conversations, 154

open culture, 266

open dialogue, in Culture Spectrum, 275–276

open door policy, in Culture Spectrum, 275–276

operational procedures, in DEI council charter, 211

opinions, avoiding presenting as facts, 57

opportunities, creating for team members, 166–167

oppressed, 28

Organizational Dimensions layer, 17

organizational success, impact of DEI on, 76–78

organizations, benefits of ERGs for, 213

overcoming fear, 110–111

ownership, taking, 68–69

P

participation
defined, 20–21
remote work and, 41

participatory leadership, 156

particularism dimension, universalism *versus*, 256

people of color, 22

PepsiCo, 241

performance, reviewing, 157–160

performance bias, 116, 225

personality, 17

Personality layer, 16

perspective-taking (empathy), 231–232

pessimism, as a resistance to change, 110

phobias, 23–24

Pierce, Chester M., 112

polarization mindset, in Developmental Continuum for Intercultural Sensitivity (DMIS), 259

policies
about, 269
conducting document reviews of policies, 100–104
culture transformation and, 282–283

politics, workplace, 66–67

positioning Chief Diversity, Equity, and Inclusion Officer (CDEIO), 92–93

Robison, John Elder, 26
roles and responsibilities, establishing, 209–210, 299–300
Rosener, Judy, 16–17

S

safe space, as an attribute of employers of choice, 79
safe-to-speak culture, 275
safety, enhancing for staff, 81–82
SBEs (Small-Business Enterprises), 193
SDGs (Sustainable Development Goals), 21
securing DEI council members, 210
selection process, minimizing bias in, 141–145
self-awareness
  as a component of cultural competence, 249–250
  as a component of emotional intelligence, 48, 49
  cultural competence and, 64, 65
self-regulation, as a component of emotional intelligence, 48, 49–50
senior executive, promoting DEI as a, 70–71
sequential time *versus* synchronic time dimension, 258
services, innovation in, 240–241
setting goals, 209–210
Seven Dimensions of Culture, 255–258
sex, 25
sexism, 23
Sharpeville Massacre (1960), 13
short-term goals, recruitment and, 134–135
SHRM (Society for Human Resource Management), 99
silence
  in Culture Spectrum, 272
  interpreting, 309–310
Singer, Judy, 26
skilled workers, 44–45
skillfulness, globalization and, 33
Slow Brain, 221–223
Small-Business Enterprises (SBEs), 193
social categorization, 142

social criteria, 191
social networks, 230–231
social skills, as a component of emotional intelligence, 49, 52–53
Society for Human Resource Management (SHRM), 99
sourcing bias, 230
Soweto Uprisings (1976), 14
specific *versus* diffuse dimension, 257
spirituality, reducing bias against, 145
sponsor, promoting DEI as a, 72–74
staff, trust and respect of, 310
staff inclusion and engagement survey, conducting, 105–106
standards, lowering, 294
stereotype threat bias, 226
stereotypes
  about, 26–27
  perpetuating, 112, 113–114
stereotypical bias, 224
Stonewall Riots (1969), 14
strategic areas of focus, establishing, 208–209
strategies
  clarity of, 59
  conducting document reviews of policies, 100–104
  creating, 285
  recruitment, 134–137
success, measuring, 302
Sue, Derald Wing, 112, 158
supervisor, promoting DEI as a, 71–72
supplier diversity
  DEI and, 192–199
  measuring, 178
suppliers, relationship-building with diverse, 195–196
Sustainable Development Goals (SDGs), 21
swift action, in Culture Spectrum, 277
sympathy, 51
synchronic time dimension, sequential time *versus,* 258
System One, 221–223
System Two, 221–223

T

tact, 62–63

talent

about, 133–134, 149–150

applying retention strategies, 160–161

assessing team's needs, 153–157

avoiding illegal and inappropriate questions, 146–147

building diverse interview panel, 145–146

building diverse pipelines, 137–139

coaching diverse, 151–153

developing diverse, 150–151

minimizing bias in selection process, 141–145

recruitment strategy, 134–137

remote work and development of, 41

reviewing performance with equitable and inclusive mindset, 157–160

underrepresented, 303–310

writing inclusive job descriptions, 140–141

Target, 193

task-oriented leadership, 156

Taylor, Breonna, 11

teams

about, 163

assessing needs of, 153–157

avoiding common pitfalls of, 173–174

building diverse, 164–166

cultivating trust and belonging, 171, 172–173

facilitating relationship-building, 171–172

increasing performance of, 240

inviting diversity of thought, 169–171

maximizing benefits of diverse, 166–168

remote work and building of, 41

technology, recruitment strategy and, 137

testing bias, 230

thought, diversity of, 169–171, 293

3M, 241

360-degree processes, 234

Tip icon, 4

tokenism, 307

tracking. *See* metrics

training, anti-bias, 232

traits, of inclusive leaders, 241–243

transformation, culture

about, 263–264

characteristics and implications of toxic workplaces, 277–280

culture spectrum, 270–277

establishing company culture, 264–270

implementing sustainable, 280–285

measuring impact of culture of inclusion, equity, and belonging, 286–287

transgender, 25

transparency, exhibiting, 53–56

transphobia, 23

trust

as an attribute of employers of choice, 79

building and maintaining, 56–57

cultivating, 171, 172–173

in Culture Spectrum, 276

for others, 57

Turnbull, Helen, 105, 261

turnover

avoiding, 86

measuring, 286

toxic workplaces and, 280

U

UDHR (Universal Declaration of Human Rights), 13

uncomfortable, being, 302

unconscious bias. *See* implicit bias

United Kingdom Race Relations Act (1965), 13

United States Civil Rights Act (1964), 13

United States Voting Rights Act (1965), 13

Universal Declaration of Human Rights (UDHR), 13

universalism *versus* particularism dimension, 256

unskilled workers, 44–45

UPS, 193

urgency, sense of, 58

urgency bias, 226

U.S. Constitution and Bill of Rights (1791), 13

About the Author

Dr. Shirley Davis is an accomplished corporate executive, global workforce expert, international speaker, certified leadership coach, and master of reinvention. She has consulted, coached, and presented to leaders at all levels, including boards of directors and C-suite executives. She has also worked in more than 30 countries around the world across all industries and sectors.

Dr. Davis is president and CEO of SDS Global Enterprises, Inc., a strategic development solutions firm that specializes in HR strategy development; talent management; organization transformation; diversity, equity, and inclusion; implicit bias; leadership excellence; and personal and professional reinvention.

Dr. Davis has over 30 years of business, leadership, and human resources experience and has worked at several Fortune 100 and Fortune 50 companies in various senior and executive leadership roles in sales, operations, banking, retail, manufacturing, utilities, and financial services. Her last role prior to launching SDS Global was as the global vice president of diversity & inclusion and workplace strategies for the world's largest HR association (SHRM). Prior to that, she was global head of diversity & inclusion at Constellation Energy (an Exelon Corporation).

She holds a bachelor's in Pre-Law; a master's in HR Management; and a PhD in Business and Organization Management, with a specialization in Leadership. She is certified as a senior HR professional through the Human Resources Certification Institute and the Society for Human Resource Management (SPHR and SHRM-SCP, respectively). Additionally, she is a certified speaking professional earned through the National Speaker's Association and a certified leadership coach.

She has been featured and quoted in/on NBC's *Today,* CNN.com. *Great Day Washington,* the *Wall Street Journal, Fast Company,* National Public Radio, Fox Television, *Black Enterprise* magazine, the *Washington Post,* and *HR Magazine.* She has been honored with numerous awards; in 2021, she was inducted into *Inclusion* magazine's Diversity & Inclusion Hall of Fame and nominated to Forbes/Know Your Value 50 Over 50 list. She's a former Miss District of Columbia, Mrs. Oklahoma, and Ms. Virginia, and in 2000 she was crowned Ms. America United States.

She is also the best-selling author of *Reinvent Yourself: Strategies for Achieving Success in Every Area of Your Life* (The Success Doctor, LLC) and *The Seat: How to Get Invited to the Table When You're Over- Performing but Undervalued.* In August 2021, she released *Living Beyond "What If?": Release the Limits and Realize Your Dreams* (Berrett-Koehler Publishers). Additionally, she is a featured LinkedIn Learning author of five popular leadership courses: *Inclusive Leadership, Leadership Foundations, Developing Accountability as a Leader, Building a Diverse Professional Network,* and *Making Your Seat at the Table Count.*

Dedication

This book is dedicated to all of my chief diversity, equity, and inclusion officer colleagues and my extensive network of DEI and HR friends, allies, advocates, freedom fighters, and peace seekers, who understand the sacrifice, courage, stamina, and strength that it takes to do this important work. Thank you for all that you do to make our world a more inclusive, welcoming, and safe place for *all* to live, work, and enjoy.

To the boards of directors, CEOs, and the many organizational leaders who *really* are committed to transforming your cultures through DEI, I applaud your efforts and encourage you to continue on the journey. Your organization's success depends on it.

And to my daughter — a millennial voice to her generation — who has grown up seeing me fight for equity, justice, and fair treatment and has come to appreciate why I do what I do. I love you and am so proud of the woman you are becoming.

And finally, this book is dedicated to the many leaders who simply don't understand why this work is so important and why their role is so critical. I appreciate that you decided to pick this book up to find out how you can become a part of the solution in making the world and your organizations a better place.

Author's Acknowledgments

This book was written based on my 30-plus years of experience as a human resources professional, a former chief diversity & inclusion officer, a corporate executive, and now the CEO of a global consulting firm. Along the journey I have led many teams, reported to many types of leaders, and worked in several kinds of cultures, all of which had varying degrees of dysfunction, toxicity, and lack of inclusion but all of which prepared me to write this book. Along the way I have built an extensive network of colleagues and friends that I've been able to tap into for resources, thought leadership, and partnership. That was the case when I was asked to pen this book. I knew that it would be a huge undertaking given my hectic schedule, so I tapped into my network and assembled a diverse group of talented and experienced thought leaders and practitioners who contributed additional perspectives, experiences, and tips. And because of them this body of work is even more comprehensive. Let me acknowledge and introduce them.

Eric C. Peterson, MSOD, is a recognized facilitator and educator in the diversity and inclusion space with over 20 years of experience in unconscious bias, diversity and inclusion, learning strategies, organization development, unconscious bias, allyship, the LGBTQ community, and whiteness as a social identity. He currently works with the Cook Ross team as senior consultant. Before he took this role, Eric was the manager for diversity and inclusion at the Society of Human Resource Management (SHRM). Prior to that, Eric was a member of the diversity team at Booz Allen Hamilton, where he managed diversity curriculum and worked extensively with the firm's employee resource groups. He has been a guest contributor for NBC Out and has been sourced as a DEI expert by CNN, National Public Radio, the *Washington Post*, the *Boston Globe*, the *Los Angeles Times*, and others.

Nicole D. Hawkins, PhD, is a two-time graduate of Ball State University, completing bachelor's and dual master's degrees in Communications and Organizational Development in the School of Communication, Information and Media. Dr. Hawkins earned a Doctor of Philosophy degree at the School of Business and Leadership at Regent University. She is also an alumnus of the Harvard University Kennedy School, where she completed the Executive Education Program in Adaptive Leadership Development. In addition to being both a professor and practitioner, Dr. Hawkins is currently a seminarian at Columbia Theological Seminary concentrating in Womanist Theology and Pastoral Care. She brings her 20-plus years of professional expertise to serve as a diversity, equity, and inclusion practitioner for human resources and faculty development at the University of Las Vegas, Nevada, and as a faculty member for Saint Leo University in the Donald R. Tapia College of Business Doctoral and Master of Business Administration programs.

Simma Lieberman is a diversity, inclusion, and culture change consultant, speaker, advisor, and facilitator. She has worked with several global organizations such as Applied Materials, Oracle, Genentech, Kaiser Permanente, UC Berkeley, Intel, McDonald's, and the U.S. Department of Transportation. She has written a number of articles that have been featured in the *Wall Street Journal*, the *New York Times*, *Fast Company*, *The Economist*, *Forbes*, *Black MBA*, *Human Resource Executive*, CNN, and National Public Radio.

Simma is the co-author of the books *Putting Diversity to Work* (Crisp Learning) and *The Diversity Calling, Building Diverse Communities One Story at a Time* (CreateSpace Independent Publishing Platform) and the author of *110 Ways to Champion Diversity and Build Inclusion* (CreateSpace Independent Publishing Platform). Additionally, she is the producer and host of the cross-race podcast *Everyday Conversations on Race for Everyday People*.

I can't thank the Wiley team enough, especially Tracy Boggier for seeking me out for this assignment and for the team you assembled to support me through this process (Vicki, Chrissy, Kristie, and Megan). You were all so patient, flexible, and supportive, and I appreciate you for trusting me to get this book written.

My team of rockstars at SDS Global Enterprises are engaged in some amazing and important DEI and culture transformation work, and I must acknowledge them for taking on extra assignments and putting in longer hours while I dedicated a lot of time to writing this book. In particular, Teresa, our head of business operations, kept things running like a well-oiled machine, and I am so grateful for her exceptional talent and service.

I thank God, my Creator, who has bestowed many gifts and blessings on me. I am so grateful that I wake up each day excited about living out my dreams, doing the work that I love, all while being in my happy place (by the ocean). I never dreamed that all of the experiences at work and in life (good, bad, and ugly) would be working together to prepare me to write *this* book at this time that will now be a road map and reference guide for leaders to use in creating more positive employee experiences at work.

And I thank God for my parents and three brothers, my bishop and church family, and my extended family and close friends who consistently support me, pray for me, and cheer me on. I am who I am because you have allowed me to walk in my truth, maximize the gifts within me, and be my authentic and unique self, unapologetically. Thank you for being on this journey with me.

Publisher's Acknowledgments

Senior Acquisitions Editor: Tracy Boggier

Project Manager and Development Editor:
Christina N. Guthrie

Managing Editor: Kristie Pyles

Copy Editor: Megan Knoll

Technical Editor: Wendy Lewis,
Wendy Lewis, LLC

Production Editor: Tamilmani Varadharaj

Cover Photos: © freshidea/Adobe

Take dummies with you everywhere you go!

Whether you are excited about e-books, want more from the web, must have your mobile apps, or are swept up in social media, dummies makes everything easier.

Find us online!

Leverage the power

Dummies is the global leader in the reference category and one of the most trusted and highly regarded brands in the world. No longer just focused on books, customers now have access to the dummies content they need in the format they want. Together we'll craft a solution that engages your customers, stands out from the competition, and helps you meet your goals.

Advertising & Sponsorships

Connect with an engaged audience on a powerful multimedia site, and position your message alongside expert how-to content. Dummies.com is a one-stop shop for free, online information and know-how curated by a team of experts.

- Targeted ads
- Video
- Email Marketing
- Microsites
- Sweepstakes sponsorship

20 **MILLION**
PAGE VIEWS
EVERY SINGLE MONTH

15
MILLION
UNIQUE
VISITORS PER MONTH

43%
OF ALL VISITORS
ACCESS THE SITE
VIA THEIR MOBILE DEVICES

700,000 NEWSLETTER
SUBSCRIPTIONS
TO THE INBOXES OF
300,000 UNIQUE INDIVIDUALS
EVERY WEEK

# of dummies

Custom Publishing

Reach a global audience in any language by creating a solution that will differentiate you from competitors, amplify your message, and encourage customers to make a buying decision.

- Apps
- Books
- eBooks
- Video
- Audio
- Webinars

Brand Licensing & Content

Leverage the strength of the world's most popular reference brand to reach new audiences and channels of distribution.

For more information, visit dummies.com/biz

PERSONAL ENRICHMENT

Staying Sharp
9781119187790
USA $26.00
CAN $31.99
UK £19.99

Facebook
Carolyn Abram
9781119179030
USA $21.99
CAN $25.99
UK £16.99

Guitar
Mark Phillips
Jon Chappell
9781119293354
USA $24.99
CAN $29.99
UK £17.99

Investing
Eric Tyson, MBA
9781119293347
USA $22.99
CAN $27.99
UK £16.99

Beekeeping
Howland Blackiston
9781119310068
USA $22.99
CAN $27.99
UK £16.99

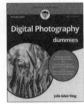
Digital Photography
Julie Adair King
9781119235606
USA $24.99
CAN $29.99
UK £17.99

Meditation
Stephan Bodian
9781119251163
USA $24.99
CAN $29.99
UK £17.99

Pregnancy
ALL-IN-ONE
9781119235491
USA $26.99
CAN $31.99
UK £19.99

Samsung Galaxy S7
Bill Hughes
9781119279952
USA $24.99
CAN $29.99
UK £17.99

iPhone
Edward C. Baig
Bob "Dr. Mac" LeVitus
9781119283133
USA $24.99
CAN $29.99
UK £17.99

Crocheting
Karen Manthey
Susan Brittain
9781119287117
USA $24.99
CAN $29.99
UK £16.99

Nutrition
Carol Ann Rinzler
9781119130246
USA $22.99
CAN $27.99
UK £16.99

PROFESSIONAL DEVELOPMENT

Windows 10
Andy Rathbone
9781119311041
USA $24.99
CAN $29.99
UK £17.99

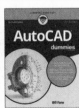
AutoCAD
Bill Fane
9781119255796
USA $39.99
CAN $47.99
UK £27.99

Excel 2016
Greg Harvey, PhD
9781119293439
USA $26.99
CAN $31.99
UK £19.99

QuickBooks 2017
Stephen L. Nelson, MBA, CPA, MS in Taxation
9781119281467
USA $26.99
CAN $31.99
UK £19.99

macOS Sierra
Bob "Dr. Mac" LeVitus
9781119280651
USA $29.99
CAN $35.99
UK £21.99

LinkedIn
Joel Elad, MBAs
9781119251132
USA $24.99
CAN $29.99
UK £17.99

Windows 10
ALL-IN-ONE
Woody Leonhard
9781119310563
USA $34.00
CAN $41.99
UK £24.99

SharePoint 2016
Rosemarie Withee
Ken Withee
9781119181705
USA $29.99
CAN $35.99
UK £21.99

Fundamental Analysis
Matt Krantz
9781119263593
USA $26.99
CAN $31.99
UK £19.99

Networking
Doug Lowe
9781119257769
USA $29.99
CAN $35.99
UK £21.99

Office 2016
Wallace Wang
9781119293477
USA $26.99
CAN $31.99
UK £19.99

Office 365
Rosemarie Withee
Ken Withee
Jennifer Reed
9781119265313
USA $24.99
CAN $29.99
UK £17.99

Salesforce.com
Liz Kao
Jon Paz
9781119239314
USA $29.99
CAN $35.99
UK £21.99

Coding
Nikhil Abraham
9781119293323
USA $29.99
CAN $35.99
UK £21.99

dummies®
A Wiley Brand

Learning Made Easy

ACADEMIC

Algebra I dummies
Mary Jane Sterling

9781119293576
USA $19.99
CAN $23.99
UK £15.99

Basic Math & Pre-Algebra dummies
Mark Zegarelli

9781119293637
USA $19.99
CAN $23.99
UK £15.99

Calculus dummies
Mark Ryan

9781119293491
USA $19.99
CAN $23.99
UK £15.99

Chemistry dummies
John T. Moore, EdD

9781119293460
USA $19.99
CAN $23.99
UK £15.99

Physics I dummies
Steven Holzner, PhD

9781119293590
USA $19.99
CAN $23.99
UK £15.99

1,001 Practice Questions SAT dummies
Ron Woldoff

9781119215844
USA $26.99
CAN $31.99
UK £19.99

Organic Chemistry I dummies
Arthur Winter

9781119293378
USA $22.99
CAN $27.99
UK £16.99

Statistics dummies
Deborah J. Rumsey, PhD

9781119293521
USA $19.99
CAN $23.99
UK £15.99

2016/2017 ASVAB dummies
Rod Powers

9781119239178
USA $18.99
CAN $22.99
UK £14.99

1,001 Practice Questions Praxis Core dummies
Carla Kirkland
Chan Cleveland

9781119263883
USA $26.99
CAN $31.99
UK £19.99

Available Everywhere Books Are Sold

Small books for big imaginations

9781119177173
USA $9.99
CAN $9.99
UK £8.99

9781119177272
USA $9.99
CAN $9.99
UK £8.99

9781119177241
USA $9.99
CAN $9.99
UK £8.99

9781119177210
USA $9.99
CAN $9.99
UK £8.99

9781119262657
USA $9.99
CAN $9.99
UK £6.99

9781119291336
USA $9.99
CAN $9.99
UK £6.99

9781119233527
USA $9.99
CAN $9.99
UK £6.99

9781119291220
USA $9.99
CAN $9.99
UK £6.99

9781119177302
USA $9.99
CAN $9.99
UK £8.99

Unleash Their Creativity

dummies.com

dummies
A Wiley Brand